SUBURBAN GANGS

THE AFFLUENT REBELS

SUBURBAN
GANGS

THE
AFFLUENT
REBELS

DAN KOREM

INTERNATIONAL FOCUS PRESS
Richardson, Texas

Published by
International Focus Press
P.O. Box 1587
Richardson, TX 75083

Copyright © 1994 by Dan Korem. All rights reserved under
International and Pan-American Copyright Conventions.
Published in the United States by International Focus Press. No
part of this publication may be reproduced in any form without
written permission from International Focus Press.

ISBN 0-9639103-1-0 (cloth)

Library of Congress Catalog Number: 94-96794

Printed in the United States of America

—For our Mrs. DeMoss,
Who loved our kids and put a joyful
melody in their hearts . . .

Contents

Section One

---◆---

THE REPORTS

CHAPTER 1

In My Own Backyard . . .

September 1993: Dinner conversation . . .

"They glared at me and started doing something strange with their hands. Making some kind of hand signals at me."

My wife thought it was a variation of the hook-em horns sign displayed by loyal University of Texas fans. After all, the event was ordinary enough. When backing the mini-van out of the garage earlier that afternoon, Sandy saw two teens wearing baggy pants coming down the alley. She thought their attire, though, was a bit out-of-place because it's blazing hot in Dallas in September.

Later the same day, just before dinner, my thirteen-year-old son, Erik, and I were in the backyard talking about his football season which was about to begin. He was excitedly telling me about starting at center, but as he spoke, I noticed a couple of teens like the ones Sandy later described. They were walking down the edge of our driveway, then disappeared around the side of our house.

"Erik, who are those guys? I've never seen them before."

"I don't know," he replied.

They looked suspicious. Their body language was covert, part slump, part swagger. They didn't really look at us; they peered. I suspected they were the same kids.

"Erik, stay here. I want to see what they're up to."

I rounded the corner of the house and saw two teens fidgeting with something on the bricked wall of our house.

"Hey guys. What's happening?" I asked casually.

"Nothing," the shorter fellow said, looking startled.

"We're just cutting through," he added, as they moved away from our house.

"What's your name?"

"Tony!"

"And what's your name?" I asked the bigger fellow.

He just glared back, hitching his thumbs in the waistband of his pants. He wore them low, just above his crotch—so low, in fact, that several inches of his boxer shorts were exposed. This is a trendy absurdity common to many rap music groups.

"What's your name?" I asked again.

The bigger, stronger youth, about five-foot ten-inches, seemed to bristle as he glared and arched his back.

"Hey. No big deal. I just want to know your name."

With a practiced swagger that started at his shoulders and moved to his hips, he suddenly started backing away. As he did, he fired off gang signs at me—those of the Crips, an inner-city gang. I couldn't believe it. This was the first time I had seen gang-signals used in *our* neighborhood. The big guy continued manipulating his hands, displaying a large number of gang signs as he backed off. He never took his eyes off me. My son cautiously peeked around the corner and saw the youths leave. He told me that the defiant youth was a boy I had coached on Erik's little league baseball team only four years ago. I didn't recognize him because he was now a foot taller. Fortunately, he wasn't a hardened gang member, only a "wanna-be" acting tough, inspired by other gangs that had formed in the neighborhood.

It wasn't the first I had seen gangs in the neighborhood, but it was the first time a youth blasted threatening gang signs at me on my own lawn. Gangs had quietly crept into our neighborhood four years before.

In 1989, a skinhead gang attempted to recruit youths at my daughter's *junior high school*. The gang was caught passing out literature to thirteen- and fourteen-year-olds that featured a graphic illustration of a skinhead driving a "white power" flagstaff through the chest of a man of ethnic descent. Members of that gang were later convicted of assault and murder.

Then, on November 1, 1992, three years later, when my daughter was a sophomore in high school, we had our first "drive-by" shooting. Seventeen-year-old Sean Cooper was murdered in the parking lot of Berkner High, a school noted for its academic excellence. My daughter's grades plummeted for several weeks.

As an investigative journalist, it's one thing to cover a threatening subject because it is an important story. It's another when it's being played out in your *own backyard*, neighborhood, or suburban community. When it affects and threatens *your* family . . .

CHAPTER 2.

A New Dilemma

For the first time in American history, youth gangs are forming in persistent numbers in *suburban* and middle- and upper-middle class communities. This new and dangerous trend is also growing in Europe. There have been isolated cases of affluent gangs in the past, but the current trend is unprecedented. The emergence of these gangs must be acknowledged, respected, understood, and successfully addressed. That is the purpose of this book.

In the mid-1980s I stated in lectures that gangs were likely to form in affluent communities, isolated from urban, inner-city communities. I believed that this was going to occur because I had observed that there was a predictable profile of the youth most likely to join a gang. As rising numbers of affluent youths fit that profile, I set out to find *preemptive* solutions that would target these youths *before* they became involved in a gang. I focused on preemptive solutions because I witnessed greater success convincing youths *not* to join gangs than trying to persuade youths to disengage from their gangs. Gang *intervention* efforts are noble and shouldn't be abandoned, but they usually only yield marginal success. Once most youths join a gang, it is extremely difficult to convince them to disengage. It's much easier thwarting an on-coming gang trend before it becomes chronic. (For a snapshot parallel, one just has to compare drug prevention versus drug rehabilitation programs. It's a lot easier convincing kids not to use hard drugs than rehabilitating an addict.) In respect to gang disengagement, however, I was able to identify eleven predictable reasons why youths will disengage from a gang—valuable information which can be used in intervention efforts.

Drawing upon a seven-year research base and travels in the US and ten foreign countries, I was able to identify the only gang prevention strategy that will arrest the formation of gangs. When this strategy was applied to over 400 severely at-risk Dallas inner-city youths, not one youth in six years (1986–92) joined a gang even though gangs were a constant nemesis in their crime-ridden neighborhoods. This strategy, which attacks what is called the Missing Protector Factor (chapter 7), is also the only strategy I have found that will work *long-term* and *broad-based* in virtually any cultural environment and will convince youths not to join a gang. (There are many other solutions, which shouldn't be scrapped, that will help *some* youths, but the strategy described in this text is the only one that will reach and help most youths in most cultural environments.)

It is my hope that this book will not only answer troubling questions about this new international affluent gang trend, but will also spur people to action, stimulating additional real-world solutions that will help youths resist the deadly lure of the gang.

THE THREAT OF THE GANG

I live in the Dallas metroplex: high-tech, diversified, multiracial, many affluent communities. In the affluent communities, people of numerous races and cultural backgrounds flourish together. It is a community representative of the rest of the US. We also have our inner-city gangs.

Gangs are terrifying. They haphazardly kill and maim without apparent provocation. There is a terrifying craziness about it. The motorcycle gang depicted in the famous fifties movie—*The Wild One*—is tame compared to today's gangs. Early Marlon Brando, who seemed so unpredictably dangerous in 1954, would be laughed at by contemporary gang members. Even though overall crime statistics are currently down when compared to the mid-1970s, juvenile crime is severely on the rise, and it engenders greater fear and sometimes terror because it's so senselessly random. No one feels safe. You dread reading the paper in the morning before your kids go to school.

In the Dallas-Ft. Worth Metroplex, during a *four-week* period in May of 1994, our headlines reported six senseless shootings and killings by youths from the "south" side of each town. The first was a baby in a crib that was shot by stray bullets on Saturday, May 14. The child, Erica Martinez, wasn't old enough to know what was happening. Fortunately, she lived.

The second shooting killed a young mother of two—ages 3 and 5—on Friday, May 20. Cheryl Smith, 26, was going through a drive-through line at McDonald's when she was shot point-blank in the head. Why? Gang members wanted her truck. Her last words before she was shot were words of praise for her five-year-old who had just received high marks on a standardized test.

The third shooting snuffed out the life of a nine-year-old boy named Cory Williams. Why? Cory, who was already saving money for college, was in the wrong place at the wrong time. He was eating an ice cream cone on his great-grandmother's front porch the day school let out for summer vacation. An *unaimed* bullet tore through the back of his head when his neighborhood was sprayed by gunfire. He died on Wednesday, May 25. Like they say, eyes cold as ice: "Life turns on a dime! Nothing personal!"

Then, on Sunday, May 29, honor student Eduardo Lopez was gunned down while working as a clerk at a South Fort Worth grocery store. He immigrated to America from Mexico, and his senior yearbook was filled with congratulations and messages of love. One of his teachers, Isabel Reid, said, "I can't believe it's happened to someone as fine as Eduardo. It makes me sad. He was someone who had a bright future. I remember he was kind, sensitive and cared about people, things, life."[1] Eduardo died on Memorial Day, when America was remembering the 50th anniversary of the D-Day invasion of Normandy. The sound of taps echoed across America, across Dallas, and from coast to coast it resonates in our uneasy sleep.

These are horrible tragedies. If you love kids and your family, you fear for them and grieve with those who suffer one of life's worst tragedies— the unexpected, untimely murder of a young person. It may be easy to shrug and shake your head when the murders occur hundreds of miles away or even in another city. But when they happen nearby, in your imme- diate vicinity, or *neighborhood*, you feel your stomach tighten as worry be- gins to form; and this worry will escalate into concern and a desire to do something.

MISTAKEN IMPRESSIONS

The term "inner-city gang" is frequently used by the American media. It is a ubiquitous fact of life, a menace chronicled daily in the press: images of crack houses, drive-by shootings, and mayors frantically convening task forces without success. To make matters worse, a few years ago news ac- counts began to filter across America. *Gangs were forming in affluent commu- nities.* The *New York Times* carried one of the first stories on April 10, 1990, "Not Just the Inner City: Well-to-Do Join Gangs." Some of the cities cited were Dallas, Seattle, Tucson, Portland, Phoenix, Chicago, Minneapolis, Omaha, and Honolulu. One youth boasted to the reporter, "This is the nine- ties, man. We're the type of people who don't take no for an answer. If your mom says no to a kid in the nineties, the kid's just going to laugh."[2]

Why did gangs appear in the suburbs? Many incorrectly assumed that inner-city gangs were seeking to expand their power base; that they wanted more turf and were recruiting youths from affluent communities. The real- ity was—affluent youths formed their *own* gangs in most cases without the help of inner-city gangs. I watched this trend happen firsthand in the neigh- borhoods surrounding mine. Something else far more primal was at work. The actual reason for the appearance of affluent gangs is detailed in chap- ter 6, "The Predictable Gang Profile," and chapter 7, "The Missing Protec- tor Factor."

Simultaneously, another false assumption accepted as fact was that economics was the primary factor that drives the rise of gangs in the inner- city. If this were true, why are gangs forming in affluent, American com- munities and even in Switzerland, a country virtually free of inner-cities?

Youths were seeking a payoff, but money wasn't the driving force. This popular misconception is addressed in chapter 9, "The PayOff: Three Cures Youths Seek."

It is easy to identify the epidemic of American inner-city gang-formation. It is institutionalized and has been persistent for decades. Affluent gangs, however, is a recent phenomenon in the youthful subculture. In addition to large metropolitan cities, many smaller cities and towns are being affected by this trend—once considered safe havens from the gang.

In March of 1994, I was asked to speak in several elementary, junior high, and high schools on the subject of gangs in the College Station-Bryan, Texas twin-city area, the home of Texas A&M and over 50,000 students. While it hadn't reached the chronic stage, gangs in affluent neighborhoods were already causing concern. One school asked me to speak to about two hundred kindergarten and first-grade students. I thought this was unwise because of their tender, impressionable age. I thought—It's unlikely that they were being affected by gangs! I asked to cancel this particular talk, but the teachers insisted and I quickly learned that my surmisal was erroneous. Approximately 15% of the youngsters knew of gang activity in their neighborhood. I carefully questioned the youngsters, parents, and teachers and discovered that their fears were not based on hearsay or on thirdhand television reports. It was based on their immediate, firsthand experiences. It was based on what they saw and heard in their neighborhoods.

Later that day, I spoke at the junior high where most youths knew about gang activity *firsthand*. I told them about my experience at the elementary school. I asked them if any of them had thought about gangs when *they* were in kindergarten. They unanimously shook their heads in disbelief— not because the notion was untrue, but because such a trend could have erupted so quickly in the short span of their own lives.

The kids at both the elementary and the junior high schools were riveted when I talked about gangs. Youths in well-to-do neighborhoods almost always listen intently when you talk about gangs—more intently than when the subject is about drug abuse. The reason is simple. Taking drugs requires the user's volition. You have to take drugs to harm you. It's a one-to-one dynamic. If you don't use drugs, you're safe. In other words, every individual has *control*. Gang-activity is another matter. You can't control gangs or their erratic, often lethal behavior. Gangs can harm and even kill you, even if you're trying to avoid them. Even when you're just an innocent bystander. Gangs are out of *your* control. In suburban youths' minds, gangs are a real threat because they are getting closer and more affluent and are now in their own neighborhoods.

POINT OF CONVERGENCE

The issue of affluent gangs has affected me professionally and personally.

Beginning in 1981, I investigated and covered a number of stories regarding criminally and socially dangerous aberrant groups and how they form. They ranged from followers of fraudulent psychics and cults to *how* faith healing groups formed. My research, which extended back to groups as early as the 1940s, proved invaluable when later trying to assess the new upscale gang phenomenon. These diverse groups often share many of the same characteristics, including, but not limited to: common background profile; power structures; manipulative techniques; expectations of those in each group; and why people will disengage from such groups. Often, I consulted noted experts such as Dr. Margaret Singer, an expert in sociopathic behavior, and Dr. Ray Hyman, an expert in the psychology of deception.

In the early 1980s, stories occasionally surfaced of groups of youths, not yet identified as gangs, but who manifested the same kinds of behaviors and criminal activity that are now commonly associated with youth gangs. Because of a number of sociological factors, I noted in several lectures during the mid-1980s that gangs would probably begin forming in affluent communities across America. Then in 1988, I began interviewing youths who would now be classified as affluent gang members, and documented their activities. Simultaneously, beginning in 1985 until 1992, I worked as one of several lay volunteers with over 400 inner-city youths, of whom over 30% had seen acts of violence, such as shootings and stabbings. During that period of time, *not one of the youths whom we tried to assist joined a gang*. While at the time we didn't think of our efforts as a gang *prevention* program, it turned out that way. The quality time spent with these youths became another invaluable source of information. I gained a unique perspective when trying to evaluate what would and wouldn't work when trying to convince youths that gangs were not the solution to their problems.

The affluent gang phenomenon then came to our neighborhood. Fortunately, the young man described in chapter 1 who fired off gang signs at me wasn't a hardened gang member. Defiant and angry about personal factors in his life, he adopted the gang façade as his way to rebel. Skinhead gang members, however, did try to recruit at our local junior high in 1989. Teachers at the school requested my assistance. When investigating this gang and its connection to another gang, reputed to be selling drugs, one youth threatened to kill me. It was a hard dose of reality for a suburbanite. Even though I had seen this new gang trend coming, it was still shocking when it arrived in our neighborhood. Then, three years later, in the fall of 1992, Sean Cooper (who was not a gang member) was gunned down by members of a local, delinquent gang.

This was personally threatening. I was living in a nice suburb where the average income is over $40,000 and most homes cost between $100,000 and $350,000. Experiencing firsthand the effects of this new affluent gang trend at first stunned me; then it spurred me into action. Coupled with my professional training, it provided the necessary impetus for this book.

The bad news is that this trend appears to be growing, not diminishing.

The good news is that affluent gangs are one of the few negative youth trends that is winnable and preventable. My conviction about this is based upon the following:

- Affluent gangs are not yet institutionalized.
- There is sufficient material and manpower resources available to take effective preventative action, if a community has the will to do so.
- My personal, firsthand experience helping youths from far more extreme conditions resist gang activity; and having firsthand experience helping youths from *affluent* communities resist and disengage from gang activity.

My optimism is tempered, however, by the fact that this trend is growing and growing fast. How long the window of opportunity will be open to attack this new youth problem successfully is uncertain. If communities and concerned persons fail to act and the trend proliferates, then we know the outcome. Look at the inner-city gangs and what they have done.

THE OBJECTIVE

The central objective of this book is to answer the following questions for those who desire to help youths, families, and communities affected by this new and growing trend.

- Why are gangs forming in *affluent* communities?
- Is there a *predictable profile* of a youth who joins an affluent gang?
- What are the "payoffs" these youths expect from gang activity?
- What are the *types* of gangs most commonly found?
- What are the inspiration points that influence gang formation and activity?
- Are there predictable reasons why a youth will disengage from an affluent gang?
- Are there effective strategies to help a youth disengage from an affluent gang?

• Is there an effective prevention strategy that will inhibit affluent gangs from becoming a chronic menace in a neighborhood?

Regarding the last two questions: As of this writing no program has
been found that will successfully and consistently cause youths to disengage from gangs *and* prevent gangs from forming, except unacceptable
authoritarian rule. This is based upon the opinions of numerous experts in
America and ten European countries I visited. Some programs have been
effective in small bites, aiding a few youths here and there. But none have
been effective over the long-haul.

Dr. Maria Kopp, a Hungarian sociologist and practicing psychiatrist at
Semmelweiss Medical University in Budapest, seems to have identified,
however, the one factor, above all others, that accelerates a youth's vulnerability to gang activity. Her 1992 study of over 21,000 people identified
what I have termed, the *Missing Protector Factor* (MPF), and it is explained
in chapter 7. I believe that addressing the MPF was the reason why we had
such remarkable success deterring Dallas youths from economically depressed areas from joining gangs. The strategy we used is detailed in chapter 20 with suggestions of how it can be implemented in *any* community—
affluent or needy.

Finally, it is not the purpose of this book to detail every specific shade
and variation of gang lingo, signs, dress, and activities. The youth culture,
driven by the current pop culture, changes faster than sociologists, cultural anthropologists, psychologists, and pundits can keep up with them.
Trying to create a catalog or definitive list that is current is futile. What
drives affluent gang activity, however, *has* been constant in the past and
appears likely to repeat itself in the future. The kinds of information provided in this book will give you immediate insights and discernment so
that effective action can be taken. When you reach the stage of needing
more specific information regarding a local gang, consult your local professionals who regularly monitor youth trends.

EUROPEAN FACTOR

It is not widely known in America that the affluent gang trend is also
present in Western and Eastern (Central) Europe. The youth subculture
now regularly cross-pollinates itself back and forth across the Atlantic. It's
a common phenomena since the mid-1960s for youths to mimic each other,
even though separated by cultures, languages, and physical distance. This
is particularly true for affluent youths who have the financial resources to
stay in touch with the latest trends, and keeping current with what's hot
and cool in the youth subculture movements in Europe. Many of the photographs in this book—particularly those of graffiti—look like they might
have been shot in American suburbs, reflecting this bi-directional cross-

pollination. (In fact, I have opted to include a significant number of these photographs so that the reader retains perspective, if but visually, that what drives youths internationally is universal. This, because of the inherent make-up of youths and in recent years because of the almost instantaneous exchange of subculture influences.) Not only do youths copy graffiti, music, and fashion trends, they also copy gang types and variants. For this reason, European gang activity must be a part of our discussion to predict more accurately why certain types of gangs form, what gang types and variants could appear in the future, and how to take effective action.

From 1992 to 1994 I visited England, Scotland, Germany, Holland, France, Austria, Poland, Hungary, Serbia, and Switzerland, chronicling gang activity and interviewing researchers, law enforcement officials, and teachers—anyone who had insight into this problem. The stories presented in this book demonstrate the predictability and universality of youth gang activity in diverse cultures—those governed by different political systems, in different phases of economic and social development. They will also help pinpoint universal ideas for addressing this new trend. Some of the ideas used in these countries to thwart each gang type and variant will be useful inspiration points for addressing current and new affluent gang trends as they appear in America and Europe. Of particular interest is a survey I was able to conduct of fifteen skinhead youths from several gangs in Budapest, Hungary that demonstrates the universality of the profile of a gang member.

Finally, respecting the inclination of friends from abroad, two conventions will be honored. The game of soccer in Europe is called "football." Except when it may cause confusion, soccer will be referred to as *football* in this book. To respect my Black friends from abroad, American Blacks are not called African-Americans. The reason for this is that most European Blacks prefer to be called "Black" rather than African-English or African-Germans. (For the sake of consistency and clarity, I have also capitalized the term "White.") I hope that my African-American friends and colleagues will accept this decision which acknowledges that we are brothers in a global village.

TECHNICAL DATA

The information in this book is based upon seven years of personal observation, along with interviews with scores of affected youths, parents, and professionals in the US and ten foreign countries. I also exhaustively reviewed the best available current literature and observed many cases over a period of several years. This gave me insight into the ebb and flow of affluent gangs. (Although this book represents the first comprehensive examination of the affluent gang, it cannot be considered definitive as the trend is continually changing. As with any "first" look at a trend, there is always the frustration that there aren't more studies to draw upon—in particular, the lack of quantitative studies identifying the familial factors of gang members. Perhaps this text may inspire such a study.)

Active and former gang members in America and Europe were interviewed. Information and perspective was sought from both active and inactive members because *active* members aren't always candid. Some are afraid of revealing something that might lead to somebody's arrest. Others resist *full disclosure*. They resist completely pulling the veil back and revealing everything going on in their minds or the specific activities of their gangs. Former gang members, however, are blunt and loquacious. They give details and are usually very helpful.

The reader will note that there are numerous photographs throughout the text that depict those elements of the youth subculture that have influenced affluent gangs in the US. Absent, however, are actual pictures of US gang members themselves who at the time of the photograph were currently engaged in gang activity. This decision was a deliberate one as the shocking visual of these youths often causes stereotypical impressions, inhibiting understanding. The stories throughout the text are sufficient to illustrate behaviors in these gangs and the thoughts of individual gang members. Also, as already noted, many of the photographs in this text were shot abroad, although they appear to be American graffiti. These European examples were included in order to help the reader recognize the universal nature of the gang phenomena and what influences youths as well as the fact that gangs can develop just as easily in Warsaw, Poland as a suburb of Atlanta, Georgia.

Following the convention adopted by most American newspapers, unless a youth specifically insisted that his/her actual name be used, pseudo-names are substituted. The exception are names of public record because of criminal convictions. This decision was made because most youths who join affluent gangs eventually disengage, and when they abandon their destructive bent, they eventually lead lawful, productive lives. Unwanted embarrassment and the stigma of gang involvement shouldn't be a permanent curse. (Also, in order to protect the welfare of one youth in one of the stories cited, one nonpivotal fact was changed. This device was only used once and does not affect the integrity of the story.)

Because this book revolves around youths, families, and neighborhoods, a narrative tone is used when describing specific cases. We don't want to lose perspective that what we are tackling is a family/neighborhood problem that has become international in scope. I ask that my colleagues, who are accustomed to a formal and perhaps academic tone, accept my populist and down-to-earth language. I want the message of this book to reach as many people as possible. I also hope that professionals who deal with these issues on a daily basis will be enlivened and motivated to work harder on the problems.

With respect to specific terms, the word "drugs" specifically refers to *illegal* drugs. Alcohol, a drug which is illegal in many states when taken by minors, is not part of the discussion except where explicitly stated. The reason is simple. Parents can legally purchase alcohol which can be illegally imbibed by a youth with or without a parent's permission. Cocaine, heroin, or PCP are another matter. Any purchase of these drugs is proscribed by law and these drugs are the ones sold by gangs, not beer or whiskey.

Unless otherwise specified, the word "gang" is always used to designate an *affluent* gang. The word "affluent" is specifically used to identify a gang in a middle- to upper-middle-class community within a city proper, town, or an outlying area such as a suburb. When necessary, inner-city gangs will be specifically identified. The reader is warned to keep this in mind because it is easy to mentally merge the discussion of affluent and inner-city gangs together.

At the end of appropriate chapters is included a section entitled "Personal Reflections." The gathering of stories and research extended over a period of several years and my personal reflective thoughts have been included in this separate section.

In order to provide updated information as it becomes available, two options will be employed. The first vehicle will be revised editions of this text. The second conveyance will be a semiannual mailing, described at the end of this text in the section "Other Materials."

Finally, if one must access specific information quickly in order to help a youth and cannot read this text chapter by chapter, then read the following chapters in the order suggested: 1) Chapter 3 will provide a feel for the kinds of gangs present. 2) Chapters 5-9 will furnish insight into what motivates youths in gangs. 3) Chapters 16-20 detail strategies for disengagement and prevention. 4) Finally, Chapter 4, "A Brief History of the Affluent Gang," includes a brief description of the three different gang types. Once the gang type has been identified that one needs to address, select the appropriate chapter in Section Three, "Gang Types and Their Activities," for more detailed information about a specific gang type and its variants. It is recommended, however, that one read Section Three in its entirety because a *cumulative* knowledge of the three gang types and related variants will greatly increase one's understanding of a specific gang operating in one's own neighborhood.

Now here are three stories of affluent suburban gangs. . . .

CHAPTER 3.

Real Tales from the Darkside

HEARTLAND GANG

The kid could have been anybody, but not long ago he felt like *nobody*—an outsider. He sounded like a lot of kids growing up in America's heartland. Where he lived was not quite Norman Rockwell's idealized, American town, but it certainly wasn't the urban, nightmarish underbelly often flashed across America's television screens during evening news broadcasts. But if you listened closely, you heard a dead edge to his voice: *"In my home I was a nobody. I hated it. When I was young, I was fat until the seventh grade, and kids bothered me because of my attention deficit disorder. I got in all kinds of fights with kids who were making fun of me."*

Residents of Minneapolis-St. Paul, the Twin Cities, use words like "nice" and "clean" when they affectionately refer to their city. Yet in this benign, seemingly innocent place, the nobody's path crossed the path of a nice, law-abiding, law-enforcing man. Jerry Haaf was a nice guy, who worked the streets. People didn't think that gangs would invade a smaller, more isolated metropolitan area like theirs. Big cities like Chicago, Dallas, Los Angeles, New York City, and Miami—yes! Minneapolis-St. Paul? No. Inner-city gang violence was commonplace in *other* places, but not in the Twin Cities, home of the 1991 World Series champs.

On September 24, 1992, officer Haaf met a nobody hell-bent on becoming a somebody—or at least he met the nobody's bullets. He was gunned down—shot in the back—while in a pizza shop in a run-down section of south Minneapolis.

The same night, another nobody was arrested. Andy Joseph Kriz, a suburban kid formerly of New Brighton, a suburb filled with $100,000-$250,000 homes, was taken into custody. As far as the police were concerned, he was somebody—somebody dangerous. He was the leader of the DFL (Down For Life) gang. He was ostensibly arrested for an unrelated shooting of several members of the Latin King gang in north Minneapolis. These shootings awakened people. They started talking about gangs, even in the suburbs.

Andy Kriz's parents divorced when he was young. Both remarried, but Andy never got along with his stepfather; and he never saw his real father on a regular basis until he was eighteen—the same year he started serving time at St. Cloud Penitentiary, a massive one-hundred-year-old, granite prison. Inmates called it the Greystone College—Gladiator School . . . a place you have to prove yourself.

Andy: *"Gangs were something I could relate to for once. When I was living in New Brighton, all these other kids had two parents . . . they cared what happened and could buy their kids stuff. I couldn't relate to any of them. I wanted power over the pain inside of me."*

In 1986, when twelve years old, he was with his father for the first time since he was three. That same year Andy started hanging out with the G.D.—Gangster Disciples, which were under the umbrella of the Folks nation of gangs. He visited his father in a deteriorating neighborhood in north Minneapolis. That's where he first became fascinated by the Vice Lords, the same gang that later shot and killed Officer Haaf.

"I was fascinated how nobody bothered them. They stuck together like a group [unlike his parents]. *They were like a family. But that's only a part of it. They had money. But it's an excuse. Your excuse is that you are hungry. But your greed grows, because greed always grows.*

"Gangs are so pretty at first, so shiny. But it just turns into hell. I remember how much fun I used to have gang-banging. You didn't live by any rules, whatsoever . . . but then it got bad. It wasn't fun anymore."

Andy was put in rehab for drug use when he was fourteen. The following year he joined the Gangster Disciples. *"The initiation lasted six minutes. Six guys beat you and you couldn't fall or say anything."*

Dealing drugs, breaking in and stealing from New Brighton homes, and ripping off were a part of the routine. By the time he was seventeen, Andy left the Disciples and formed his own gang, Down For Life—DFL. He recruited three youths he met in drug rehab and one from the neighborhood where his father lived. It was a racially mixed gang—White, Hispanic, and a Native American Indian. Each came from broken homes where the mother headed the household.

"Our sign was a four-pointed crown. Each point stood for pride, power, protection, and partnership. Joining our gang was a lifetime commitment."

By the summer of 1991, over twenty-five youths had been recruited. Andy could buy anything he wanted, eat out at restaurants, and regularly carried at least $500 in his pocket. Then the Latin Kings tried to invade his New Brighton turf. He moved again from New Brighton to the north end of Minneapolis, but DFL's turf was still New Brighton.

"I was walking up Tenth Avenue to Broadway going to Burger King. I had been drinking. A car stopped and four Latin Kings jumped out. We fought and they stabbed me in my arm, chest, and the back of my head. It took me a couple of

months to figure out that the house was at 18th and Taylor. So we drove by the house once and the second time we circled by, they all came out on the street. That's when I started shooting."

Andy pumped three rounds into the crowd from his 12-gauge shotgun. Three people received only minor wounds, but a fourth Latin King was sprayed in the face and chest. He later recovered.

"We then took off, rented the movie Lawnmower Man and watched it at the apartment of one of our girlfriends."

A short while later, the Minneapolis PD descended on the apartment, arresting everyone. Andy denied the shooting, but was convicted of the shooting and robbery. He was sentenced to six years.

Lt. Bob Jacobson, one of the officers who worked Andy's case and a youth gang specialist, said, "Andy's really a good kid. I think he's got better than a 50/50 chance of making it when he gets out."

Jacobson observed that virtually every youth involved in gang activity came from a broken home. When asked what he thought would be the most effective deterrent to gang activity, he said: *"Stabilizing the home. If that doesn't work, go to prison. It's about the only thing that will scare them."*

Andy agreed.

"Nothing would have worked for me to stop. There's nothing you could really do. I have a sister, right now, who joined the Latin Kings. I've tried talking her out of it. But she's just like I was."

Since he started serving his sentence in January of 1992, he has burned the bridges with his gang, earned his GED, and is now on the honor unit. Special privileges include: being out of his cell twelve hours a day, better food, and a separate store and weight room. And his attitude has changed.

"I'd rather be the geekiest person on the streets than the coolest sucker in prison. You can stay out of trouble when you don't feel you have to get respect— being a man shooting someone. My emotional mentality is only now just starting to grow because of what I did."

Andy wanted power over his pain from a lack of respect, but his prison caseworker, Doug Randall, says that the change in Andy seems genuine. Andy will have that to prove to himself when, at the age of twenty-two, he is released in 1996.

NO TEARS FOR THE SPIDER MAN

Warm, summer nights in the Dallas suburb of Plano, Texas, are meant for dreaming, especially if you're a fourteen-year-old girl, riding in a shiny, bright red, mint-condition '64 Mustang. She should have been able to lay back and swoon as the wind rushed through her long hair, but this girl wasn't dreaming , swooning, or smiling. She was riding through a gathering gloom, a passenger of someone who could have been the Spider Man.

Like the lyrics of Lullaby, a song she and her friends heard many times, the refrain snaked through her brain—

> *On Candy Stripe Legs the Spider Man*
> *Comes softly through the shadow of the evening sun.*
> *Steering past the windows as the blissfully dead,*
> *Looking for the victims shivering in bed.*
>
> *Searching out fear in the gathering gloom,*
> *And suddenly a movement in the corner of the room.*
> *And there's nothing I can do when I realize with fright,*
> *That the Spider Man is having me for dinner tonight.*
>
> *Quietly he laughs and shaking his head creeps closer now*
> *And closer to the foot of the bed.*
> *And softer than shadow and quicker than flies,*
> *His arms are all around me and his tongue in my eyes.*
>
> *Be still, be calm, be quiet now my precious boy*
> *Don't struggle like that or I will only love you more.*
> *For it's much too late to get away or turn on a light,*
> *For the Spider Man is having you for dinner tonight.*
>
> *And I feel like I've been eaten*
> *By a thousand million shivering furry holes,*
> *And I know that in the morning*
> *I will wake up in a shivering cold.*
> *And the Spider Man is always hungry.*[1]

Amy was feeling it was much too late—too late to get away or turn on a light, and she was shivering. Her terrible, untold secret made her feel even more terrible. She would remember her daddy's midnight visits just before falling asleep. He would touch her like the Spider Man, tongue in her eyes, alien, quicker than flies. He would trespass as a dark stranger, not as her daddy or deacon of the church, but as something worse—a dark, silent invader. And she wanted him to stop, to please stop, to disappear. But like the Spider Man, he never did. He was always hungry and he was always there.

One day I asked an abused youth drawn to these lyrics, "What do you think the song's about?"

"It's about nightmares," she said.

"But who's the Spider Man?"

"The Spider Man's the nightmare."

"I know, but doesn't it sound like incest?"

After a long, frightful pause, she added, "Yeah."

Amy's parents finally divorced when she was in the sixth grade, but that didn't stop her nightmares. Nothing did. She desperately wanted them to disappear and she didn't care what it would take or what she might need to do to rid them.

Jonathan was a recruiter for The Satanic Cult, a local gang of drug sellers. He too was fourteen years old, and he didn't know why Amy was withdrawn and frightened, but he knew one thing: Amy matched Terry's instructions: "Just find a girl at your school who looks shy and scared—who'd do anything to have a friend. Then ask her the four questions about drugs." Terry always used these four questions to recruit new sellers, who were then told to sell only to "long-hairs"—those with hair past their shoulders.

Jonathan saw Amy sitting alone at lunch. He recognized the opportunity, sidled alongside her, and softly asked, "What's your name?"

"Amy."

"Wanna do drugs?"

"I don't know. Maybe."

"What kind of drugs do you like?"

"I don't know," she answered, almost whispering.

"How about some coke?"

"I don't know."

Jonathan told Amy about his friend, Terry—the guy with the red Mustang, who had real powers. Amy's eyes widened. "Terry's got power over everything. Just name it! And he can teach you to have it."

"What kind of power?"

"Satan's power."

"What can it do?"

"Anything."

"What do I have to do?"

"Just try some coke a few times and sell a little to your friends."

Amy had never used or dealt drugs, but now she was thinking about her nightmares, her demons, the Spider Man. Maybe this power would work. So, she bought a few "nickel" bags (a five-dollar bag of cocaine packaged in cellophane). A few days later she was introduced to Terry, who picked her up after school. Amy climbed into the front seat of the red Mustang and then Terry blindfolded her and told her to keep her head down in her lap so she couldn't see anything. He didn't want her to know his destination—his apartment in Garland, a middle- to lower-middle-income suburb. Amy knew she ended up in Garland—only fifteen minutes away from Plano—because she lifted her head a couple of times and peeked under her blindfold.

Terry, a nineteen-year-old dropout, was five years older than Amy and in her nightmarish world, he had an edge. His red hair hung down the middle of his back and he had flashing, knowing blue eyes, an upside-down cross tattooed on his stomach and a swastika tattooed on his right thigh. He was a racist and later battered Amy for trying to recruit a black girl into his occultic gang. After grilling Amy, he asked her to submit to him sexually, testing her loyalty to the group. She agreed. *Perhaps this was the way to transmit to me some of his power,* she thought. They had sex in his small, sparsely furnished apartment. Amy was the second partner. "He always had two girls," she said. When they finished, Amy was blindfolded again and they drove to an isolated field in Plano. He forced her to kneel and when the blindfold was removed, she saw a crudely painted, red pentagram. It was several feet across and seemed to surround her. There was also a small, makeshift altar where a sacrifice would take place. This was the site of her secret induction, and she felt well-prepared. Her father taught her how to keep secrets and she kept them well.

At least a dozen young teens sat in a circle around the pentagram. (Terry liked young gang members because they were easy to control.) Because of their position in the gang's hierarchy, each one knew their role in Amy's "orientation."

The structure of The Satanic Cult from the top down was: Master, Slave, Orientor, Recruiter. Terry, who was only five-foot-one, was the Master. He liked to recruit kids from rich neighborhoods because their friends had enough money to buy drugs. The Slaves took orders from Terry and acted as runners. The Orientor, Jonathan, was in charge of induction rituals. Recruiters, like Amy, were at the bottom in the chain of command. They were lowly proles who sold drugs and recruited other kids to sell.

Kids recruited into the gang had to fit a specific profile. First, each recruit had to be new to the community. Students were sought who didn't have ties to anyone else in their school; that way the cult-like gang became their immediate circle of friends. Terry preferred fearful, reclusive, emotionally damaged kids. In 1989, Plano, population 150,000, was a good "technoburb" to hit. There were lots of kids from broken homes with "new money." Plenty of homes where kids came home to an unsupervised nest. (Although often touted as a premiere suburb in which to live, the seeds of discontent in some homes were observed as early as 1983 and 1984, when eight youths committed suicide, garnering national attention.)

Second, prospective recruits had to be blue-eyed with blonde, red, or black hair. Brown hair was forbidden. Amy had blonde hair and blue eyes; this satisfied Terry's tastes. And she was perfectly predisposed to be seduced by his empowerment scam. He knew they wouldn't receive powers, but they didn't. No matter, just as long as they sold drugs and he cashed in.

At the site there was the board and cinder-block altar, adorned with candles and a metal chalice. After ranting about how he *was* Satan, Terry savagely killed a cat, spilling its blood in the chalice. Amy drank some of the fresh blood and took drugs. While under the influence, she heard them chant in low voices, "We have the power to do anything," as they pledged allegiance to Satan.

Other induction rituals were held at a Motel 6 in Denton on a Saturday—the *sixth* day of the week, and in a room with a *six* in the room number (like 126). This formed the number 666—the mark of the Antichrist. During the next several months, the drugs and the gang made Amy feel important and affiliated with something that held the promise of power; however, none of it stopped or diminished her demonized nightmares. She still woke up, shivering cold. Terry couldn't kill the Spider Man. Terry's promise of power was a sham. When Amy entered a local drug treatment center, she asked her counselor to talk with someone about the terrors she experienced in the gang. But she was afraid of reprisals and harm from Terry when he realized that she entered rehab and was getting out of the gang.

In 1989, over a dozen such small, independent gangs had arisen in schools around the central and east Texas area with the name—The Satanic Cult. Amy's gang, was one of them. These drug-selling gangs helped set off a false panic that *adult* groups were after kids to be used as sacrifices. Two weeks after we talked about her gang, Amy moved to Alaska to live with a relative—far away from Terry's turf.

BURLY BOY IN JACKBOOTS

The boy-man was burly. His shaved head gave him the right, savage look; and he dressed in black. Macho boots, jeans, T-shirt, and heavy belt. His jacket of course was black leather. There were silver tips on his boots. He was dressed to march, swagger, menace, and to destroy. This was the uniform of the tribe, the skinhead colors.

"What the f— are you looking at?" he bellowed, standing erect, throwing his chair aside. The nattily dressed man looked askance, then moved away as quickly as possible to the remotest section of the atrium. Grabbing a fistful of fries, the boy-man flung them in the direction of the man's retreat.

Blaring, pulsating MTV music and video images filled the Burger King. Housed in a posh business complex, youths regularly dropped in for fast-food fixes. Management strategically constructed a separate, quiet atrium dining area away from the cash register lines. It was designed to attract a more genteel crowd—business and family types. It had the right look—subdued chrome, glass, and greenery providing an upscale environment to mollify the stress of everyday life.

The boy-man is Erik. He dressed to visually intimidate and attract attention. He used this as a device to lash out. Two months earlier, a bigger fellow with his own lashing out to vent, didn't like Erik's image and style. Without warning, he bashed against Erik's shaved skull, knocking him to the floor. It was a bad scene.

"He didn't know that I had any strength left," Erik later bragged. "After a couple of minutes, I reached into my pocket, grabbed my brass knuckles and *destroyed him*. He never got up."

Although Erik didn't maim or kill his attacker, he claimed to be a killer. No one knew if his stark and horrendous claim were true. It sounded authentic and everyone stayed away and gave him the benefit of the doubt.

This burly, six-foot two-inch figure seemed even more threatening in the sedate atrium. He should have been in the other room with the kids, but he chose the atrium to spew hate, shout vulgarities at men as they passed, and cheaply whistle at women. Eighteen-year-old Erik and his shorter partner were dyed-in-the-wool skinheads.

"When he was a younger boy, Erik's parents divorced and his father, a teacher, moved to Sweden. Erik wanted to be a pediatrician, but failed to enter the medical university. He was angry. . . .

He was angry about his absent, abandoning father. He was angry that he couldn't cultivate and keep friends; and he was angry that some Arab youths raped his girlfriend. This was a defining moment for Erik. The rest of his cumulative, simmering hate became sharply focused and he could express it with laser-like intensity as a hate-mongering, menacing, hell-on-wheels skinhead.

"I ordered my friends to kill him. They didn't do it, but he never came around again." Neither did his girlfriend, who was terrified of his rages.

No father. No girl. No future. Erik was a boy-man in pain, and he was poised to smash it into smithereens with his fists.

Dave watched Erik and saw flickers of the pain that nourished the hate. Possessing acute insight into counter-culture types, Dave heard in a university lecture earlier that year that it was the pain of broken homes that drives most skinheads.

The two skinheads trained their attention on him, mumbling derogatory remarks, laughing at Dave, the all-American guy and his bright red, white, and blue shirt.

Dave informally greeted Erik: "Hey, how ya' doing?"

The skin and his partner were stunned, then surprisingly they returned the greeting.

"Mind if I join you?" Dave asked casually. They waved him on.

Dave asked Erik where he came from and initiated some nonthreatening, small talk. Another adult passed and made the mistake of staring. Furious, Erik threw his chair aside, screaming, "What are you looking at? Am

I a show? Quit looking at me!" He grabbed his nunchaku, a martial arts weapon, and flashed them in the face of the man who only wanted to eat lunch in a quiet place. Then in an instant, he composed himself, sat down, and resumed our conversation.

"Do you enjoy being a skinhead?" Dave asked with brotherly directness.

"No. I don't know if any of my skinhead friends love me or not. I don't have any friends outside of skins."

"Skinheads are basically known because of their hate. Would you agree with that?"

"Yea."

"Who do you hate? Do you hate foreigners? Do you hate me?"

"No. I don't hate you."

"Do you hate Jews?"

"Yea, but I don't hate them as much as I hate Arabs. I hate Arabs. And I hate Chinese. And I hate Blacks. I guess I don't really hate Jews."

"Why hate Arabs?"

"Because an Arab raped my girlfriend."

As they continued to talk, Erik periodically shouted obscenities at those around him. Dave chastised him.

"I was amazed that Erik received me as a big brother," Dave later recalled. "When I directed my attention to him as a person, rather than a strange object, he responded."

Dave pressed him about his father.

As tears welled up, Erik said, "Last week my father embraced me. He was concerned about me being a skinhead. What will happen to me. He is concerned that I didn't get accepted into the university."

"Erik, it's so foolish to hate."

"I know. . . . It's eating me alive."

Dave had heard of skinheads in America, England, and Germany, but never expected to encounter a skinhead in Burger King in downtown Budapest, Hungary, in October of 1992. He had heard there was a profile of a youth who engages in skinhead activity, but never expected one to show teary-eyed emotion so quickly and openly.

Erik and his friend Gyula (pronounced du'la) were born in Budapest, the Paris of the East. They were like many of their counterparts in other affluent communities. Their expressions of hate were not learned at home. And like many skins in America, Erik, when pressed, admitted that he really didn't hate minorities which he impulsively had said earlier.

These stories, taken together, represent what is occurring in affluent communities in America and Europe. The kinds of gangs youths are joining are diverse, and which one is more popular at any given time can depend upon something as simple as which type of inspiring music is in vogue. Collectively, these stories illustrate what is going on in the minds of affluent gang youths and depict the three types of gangs—*delinquent, ideological,* and *occultic*—that have been present since the early 1980s.

Andy Kriz, inspired by inner-city counterparts, formed his own *delinquent gang.* Regarding the emergence of affluent gangs, his case is not typical one in that he was directly inspired by inner-city gangs. He stated, though, that he probably would have formed a gang when he was old enough even if he had never spent time around the Gangster Disciples, witnessed by the fact that he opted to form his own independent gang.

Most affluent gangs, like the *occultic* gang that snared Amy, have their own independent inspiration points, far way from urban areas. They don't form as a result of a spill-over from inner-city areas. Erik, the Hungarian youth who came from a well-to-do family, wasn't influenced by gangs from lower income areas. He derived his inspiration from the youth subculture—expressions of fashion and music—and formed the third type of gang addressed in this text, the *ideological* gang.

Until you have interviewed a number of these youths, it is difficult to imagine that there's a common, *predictable profile* of a youth who engages in these gangs, but there is. There are also predictable reasons why they will disengage. Before we examine these facets, let's take a brief look at the history of gangs in America.

THE SCOPE
OF THE PROBLEM

CHAPTER 4.

A Brief History
of the
Affluent Gang

The slang term "gang" has been fearfully and romantically used to indicate a group or band of persons bonded together because of common emotional and social needs, whose behavior is antisocial and criminal. Old West gangs such as the Dalton and James (Jesse James) gangs of the 1880s were romanticized in newspapers and pulp books, and this romanticism persists in today's cinema. During the Roaring Twenties, when the term "street-gang" became popular, gangs became highly organized and ruthlessly business-like, thriving on bootlegging, prostitution, extortion, and illegal gambling. Over a thousand of these gangs were summarized by researcher Frederick Thrasher in his classic book, *The Gang* (1936).

During the last twenty-five years, the word "gang" has been typically used in the American media to specify *inner-city gangs* primarily comprised of young men and women. (In the United States, "inner-city" refers to run-down or lower-income neighborhoods, whereas in Europe, it designates the section of town within the "ring" or highway that encircles the heart of a city—both business and residential. And it is not necessarily a lower-income area.) The images usually evoked by inner-city gangs are ethnic and racial bands or packs (even though there are White gangs as well) that flourish in economically depressed areas, where hope and opportunity are abjectly circumscribed. The self-perpetuating ferment in these places leads to moral decay, desperation, and dramatic lawlessness.

The current American psyche has been traumatized by soaring crime, random violence, daily murders, and the dark presence of youth gangs—not only in the inner cities, but in the usually calm rural and suburban areas. Americans are fearful. They have become defensive and wary. They invest in security systems, buy guns, and hire security people to patrol their streets. Some cities impose curfews, but the average citizen stays home, behind locked doors, at night; and they watch their backs. The 1994 Crime

Bill passed in Congress will put 100,000 new officers on the street, pump nearly $7 billion into prevention programs, and allow thirteen-year-olds charged with violent crimes—such as murder, armed robbery, and rape— to be treated as adults. In most metropolitan cities, killings and other violent crimes associated with these gangs occur daily and rising criminal violence among youths shows no sign of abating. While adult violent crime is down slightly—in New York City, for example, homicide was down approximately 15% and robbery and auto theft down 13% in the first nine months of 1994[1]—juvenile crime is escalating and even hardened homicide detectives are alarmed.

The reason for this fear is that violent crimes committed by youths are more unpredictable, victims are often randomly selected, and the assailants are increasingly younger. Innocent bystanders are also routinely killed or injured. The prevailing perception is painfully obvious: we aren't as safe as we were twenty years ago. The juvenile crime statistics show this to be true, and the increasing numbers of unpredictable violent crimes among youths exacerbate this fear. Slayings by teenagers, for example, rose 124 % from 1986 to 1991.[2] Minors killed over 3,400 people in the United States in 1992 and assaults with deadly weapons grew from 73,987 incidents in 1982 to 143,368 in 1992.[3] Contrary to the stereotypical opinion that most crimes are committed by ethnic groups, the breakdown is different: 49% of those arrested for violent crimes were *White* and 49% were Black in 1992. Only 13% of those arrested for violent crimes were females. The shocking and alarming figure is this: *30% of all youths arrested for violent crimes were under the age of 15.*[4] The 15-19-year-old age group commits 20.1% of all US crimes and is the largest group in the US. (Crime rates for all other age groups are as follows: 10-14, .04%; 20-24, 19.4%; 25-29, 16.2%; 30-34, 14.3%; 35-39, 10.1%; 40-44, 6.1%; 45-49, 3.2%; 50-65, 4.1%.[5]) Regarding murder, 57% were committed by Black youths, but White youths (56%) were more likely to be arrested for aggravated assault.[6] In 1992, seventeen-year-olds were almost *five times* as likely to be arrested for a homicide than a thirty-three-year-old adult.[7]

And there is only more bad news on the horizon.

Criminologists predict that because the number of youths under the age of 18 will increase from 60 to 70 million by the year 2005, *overall* crime rates are expected to rise as well as juvenile crime rates. James Alan Fox, dean of the College of Criminal Justice at Northeastern University, observed, "To prevent a blood bath in the year 2005, when we will have a flood of fifteen-year-olds, we have to do something today with the five-year-olds. But when push comes to shove, prevention programs often fall by the wayside in favor of increased incarceration."[8]

It should be noted that US crime rates have cycled through five- and ten-year cycles and some perspective is as follows:

Criminal justice experts say the reasons for the [recent] drop in [the overall] crime [rate] are many. Cocaine use has diminished in recent years. Local governments have imprisoned more criminals, and with longer sentences. More police officers have been put on street beats. Finally, and perhaps most important, the aging of the 76-million-strong post-World War II baby boom generation has made the population grayer.

[Regarding the national homicide rate], it soared from 4.8 to 9.8 per 100,000 in the 1960s and has hovered between 8 and 10.2 murders per 100,000 since 1970. . . . Criminologists attribute a dip in homicides from 1980 to 1985 to the fact that the number of baby boom youths between 17 and 24 peaked in 1980. Criminologists [had] predicted more than a decade-long decline in violent crime as the population aged; they just didn't count on the arrival of crack cocaine in 1985.[9]

Because a significant percentage of these crimes are committed around the periphery, if not directly by inner-city gangs, most of the public focus has rightfully been on inner-city gangs and associated violence. The infusion of crack cocaine and an almost unlimited supply of guns in the 1980s in the gang crime scene is believed to be one of the biggest contributing factors to the institutionalization of inner-city gangs and violent crimes associated with the drug trade. Some of the common characteristics observed in inner-city gang members and their neighborhoods are: absent fathers, depressed socioeconomic conditions, deteriorating schools, lack of recreational facilities and programs, absence of strong political and community leadership, and chronically high crime rates from theft, assault, and murder.

If it is still hard to imagine what could drive youths to commit vicious and senseless acts of violence and terror, this background profile of a female gang member who held her boyfriend's gang together while in jail will help.

The perception of what constitutes trouble depends on the magnitude of the dangers that are routinely survived. It's useful to look at violence from the other side, to suspend morality and, for a moment, fear. Imagine you are 15. Your stepfather has raped you, and the only thing keeping you from another year in foster care is your sinking mom. You have learned that the only way to keep your mother away from liquor is to beat her. It takes 20 minutes to subdue her. After you do this, you must calm your little sister. This private weekend life makes it easier to mug a stranger for money that you need, especially when a mugging lasts no more than two minutes. The money means you do not have to ask your overwhelmed mom, who hates you when she's sober. Or the money is for your mom or your little sister, people for whom you hold much shame, obligation and guilt.[10]

Fostered by this combined fear of violent youth crime and constant images of inner-city gangs on evening news reports, when gangs started to appear in affluent communities in the 1980s, many assumed that inner-city gangs were expanding their turf and recruiting more members. This is incorrect. The first gangs observed in affluent communities were either composed of White youths or youths hostile to ethnic groups.

APPEARANCE OF AFFLUENT GANGS

Since the early 1980s, essentially three types of gangs have been observed in affluent communities: delinquent, ideological, and occultic gangs. Each has one thing in common: the youths commit crimes in a *specific context*. A brief characterization of the context in which each gang type commits criminal acts is as follows:

- *Delinquent Gang:* Desire for profit and thuggery.
- *Ideological Gang:* Attachment to a specific ideology, which may or may not be political, such as skinhead gangs that target ethnic groups for assaults, justified by an ideology of "ethnic purity" or nationalism.
- *Occultic Gang:* Attachment to beliefs in occultic powers.

A more detailed explanation of the typology used for the three gang types is discussed in chapter 12 and a thorough examination of each gang type is found in chapters 12-15. The first affluent gang types to appear in the United States were the ideological and occultic gangs.

Beginning around 1983, *occultic* gangs were noticed on the West Coast and eventually became visible across the United States by the mid- to late-1980s. Gangs formed around the central theme of attaining occultic powers, which is why many were mistakenly labeled as cults. Their criminal activity was principally limited to small-time drug trafficking, although some violent crimes were committed. These gangs surfaced almost exclusively in affluent communities with few ethnic members.

Around the same time, *ideological* gangs—most notably skinhead gangs—also appeared. These gangs initially surfaced in middle-income neighborhoods and were aggressively anti-ethnic. Then in the late 1980s, youths from affluent communities started forming their own gangs as well as joining *existing* gangs. The criminal activity of these gangs involved physical assaults and even murder directed towards minority and ethnic groups, such as Blacks, Hispanics, and Jews. Some of these gangs also engaged in low-level drug trafficking. The assumption was that groups such as the Ku Klux Klan were solely responsible for spawning these gangs. Consequently they were not labeled gangs but subversive groups.

The emergence of the *delinquent* gangs as a trend didn't begin until the late 1980s and early 1990s. Isolated cases of delinquent gangs have always been present, but delinquent gangs as a *trend* is a recent development. The criminal activity of these gangs has run the gamut—assault, theft, burglary, and drug trafficking. This gang type will probably grow the fastest over the next ten years.

It is imperative to recognize that in the beginning youths from affluent communities chose to form their own gangs *separate and apart* from inner-city gangs. In most cases, these youths did not form gangs at the recruitment urgings of inner-city gangs. The spill-over effect of inner-city type gangs recruiting youths into their fold didn't become a significant factor in affluent communities until the early 1990s. The Andy Kriz case (chapter 3) is one such example. Typically, gangs that did form because of the direct influence of inner-city gangs became delinquent gangs and didn't attach themselves to a particular belief system or ideology like the occultic and ideological gangs. As of this writing, affluent gangs forming at the urgings of inner-city gangs doesn't represent the majority of affluent gangs. However, because of the large numbers of at-risk youths present in affluent communities and the increasing influence of inner-city gangs, this is a potential trend that warrants careful monitoring.

In the media an inaccurate characterization was often conveyed about the types of gangs that were forming in affluent communities. Gang members were usually characterized as those from *ethnic groups*. In the summer of 1993, the *New York Times* printed a front-page story on the spread of gangs to the suburbs, entitled, "Gang Membership Grows in Middle-Class Suburbs." Although the interior of the article recognized that "Gangs are attracting more teenagers from all backgrounds and socio-economic groups,"[11] the front-page picture used showed two *ethnic* youths. Pictures of White youths were noticeably absent. This kind of characterization in the media, often done to protect the local community's image or as a result of ignorance, fed the misplaced, popular belief that inner-city youths were the cause of *initial* affluent gang *formation*.

It is crucial to recognize that the affluent gang trend began and grew on its own—that affluent youths on their own (in most cases) formed their own gangs without direct external direction. Why? Because unless communities acknowledge the actual cause-and-effect relationship, effective action can be neutralized. When communities think that gangs are solely forming because of "outsiders," then valuable resources will be ineffectively appropriated and the problem will only grow and spread.

Another factor that contributed to the failure of recognizing these groups as gangs in affluent communities was due to "boosterism." City hall in many affected communities failed to acknowledge that they had a gang problem for fear of tarnishing its image and driving away business. A typical example was the suburb of Carrollton where I personally investigated several gangs around 1989 and 1990. City officials declined to acknowledge their own gang problem and initiate effective action. (As a counterpoint, neighboring Farmers Branch, a suburb with a similar community, recognized its gang problem and took action. They implemented a model for prevention that has attracted the attention of officials from cities across the US. How they approached this issue is addressed in chapter 19. It should also be noted that by 1992, Carrollton reversed its previous denial of its gang problem.) A police officer from another Dallas suburb during the same time period said, "You know there are gangs and I know that there are gangs. But the word from city hall is: 'We don't have a gang problem.'"

Vocal recognition of an affluent gang problem by a handful of local communities didn't begin until around 1990, but by 1992 many upscale communities were forced to acknowledge the growth of gangs. For example, in Tucson, Arizona, in the late 1980s the first recognition of gangs properly focused on inner-city gangs that were spreading to lower-income areas of Tucson. Gang members from other cities, such as Los Angeles, moved into Tucson. They were fleeing police crackdowns and were motivated by profits from the sale of "crack" cocaine. This began the public perception of gangs in the 1980s. But by 1990, local law enforcement acknowledged that gangs were now in *affluent* communities. This was puzzling to local officials because there wasn't a direct connection to the new inner-city gangs that moved to town.

In 1990, the *Arizona Daily Star* quoted several officials who noted the appearance of gangs in affluent parts of Tucson. Pat Carrillo, supervisor of juvenile intensive probation for Pima County Juvenile Court Center, said, "It's here now. . . . I've seen places where they let it go and let it go. . . . It's like doing nothing about cancer. Sure, it doesn't hurt now, but it will spread and eventually it will kill you."[12]

Sgt. Ron Zimmerling, then head of the ten-member, anti-gang unit for the Tucson Police Department, added that "our estimates are always low. There's so much intimidation in gangs that a lot of people don't report them."[13] Former Tucson police officer, Warren Allison, who worked for the Tucson Unified School District on a two-member anti-gang task force, observed that the gang phenomena was spreading to middle- and upper-middle class suburbs: "In Tucson, it used to be typical barrio gangs in certain neighborhoods [referring to Hispanic gangs]. But now it's spreading. I don't know why."[14] Mr. Allison's bewilderment was characteristic of many communities throughout America. Eventually by 1993, most communities that had gangs began openly discussing their dilemma. Even those that had formerly resisted began to take action. The problem couldn't be ignored.

The cause-and-effect relationship of why gangs are forming in affluent communities is presented in detail in chapters 5 through 11. For reference purposes, a condensation of a typical *flow of events* that lead up to gangs in affluent communities is as follows:

1. Chronic family breakdown in at least a segment of a community.
2. Severe expressions in the youth subculture is seen, evinced by their dress, hair styles, music, public behavior, graffiti, and so on.
3. Drug abuse, which includes alcohol, becomes chronically endemic.
4. Unexpected eruptions of violence.
5. The ferment now exists for the formation of gangs.

Naturally, not all communities will experience each of the above in the sequence presented before gangs appear, but most have.

HOW MANY GANGS?

A 1994 *New York Times/CBS News Poll* revealed that 18% of *White* youths stated that gangs were a problem in their school. The results of the seventy-three questions in the survey pointed towards the fact that most of the 1,055 youths were *not* from inner-city areas.

The number of gangs present in affluent communities, however, is uncertain. The trend is too new for law enforcement to have gathered abundant and reliable data. States don't require the mandatory reporting of gang activity by all communities. It has only been in the last couple of years that states, driven by public fears, have begun to collect reliable data on inner-city gangs. (Some states, for example, that have long been affected by chronic juvenile crime, are just now agreeing to share youth crime data with public schools so that they can more effectively be a part of the solution to reduce violent juvenile crime and gangs.)

Another reason for uncertainty is that the problem isn't nearly as chronic as it is in the inner-city. The wake-up call has been sounded. It's not perceived as sufficiently threatening to incite sophisticated, nationwide studies. Additionally, hard data is difficult to obtain because affluent youths don't usually brag about their gang membership. They don't want the police monitoring their activities, and they don't want to be hassled or arrested. This is very different from inner-city gangs where identification is part of their bravura code. In 1993, though, I noted that the number of youths who *had* indicated gang activity in their own neighborhood seemed to have markedly jumped.

Each summer from 1988 to 1993, I spoke to several thousand youths at sports camps on the subject of *deception* and how it appears in various social trends, such as gangs. These youths were predominantly from affluent families across America. At the end of these presentations, I asked: "How many of you know about gang activity in your *own* neighborhood?" The purpose of my question was to find out if the affluent gang trend was growing or if it was a *momentary* youth subculture phenomenon.

Up until 1992, only about 5%-10% indicated that they knew of such activity. The summer of 1993 was different. The needle jumped. The average response leaped to 40%-60%. Because of the extraordinary increase, I fine-tuned my question and asked, "Had you simply *heard* about gang activity from someone or through the media—you know, secondhand and thirdhand stuff? Or do you *actually know* people in gangs in your neighborhood?" The response was "personal contact." In October of 1993, I lectured at the FBI National Academy to over fifty law enforcement officers from across the US on the subject of gangs. When asked the same question, their response mirrored the student's response that summer. Like the students, the officers' perceptions were not based upon increased media coverage of this issue. They knew about it firsthand. The same percentage has continued to remain steadfast through 1994.

(Note: In 1993 and early 1994 I made a similar inquiry of college students in America at various universities, aged 18-21, during lecture presentations. Some of the campuses included: USC, University of Minnesota, Louisiana Tech, Penn State, and West Virginia University. Although my survey isn't strictly scientific, the sampling is compellingly empirical. Over 10,000 students indicated that only about 10-15% had come in contact with some kind of gang activity in their neighborhoods. However, a larger number, as high as 20%, indicated that they knew about gang activity in their neighborhood that began *after* they had started college. This suggested that the younger the youth, the more likely that he or she had come into contact with gang activity. This matches the typical age for gang involvement (12-17). Also, students polled in more stable communities with lower crime rates like Minneapolis, had predictably lower percentages than communities like Chicago or Los Angeles.)

There doesn't appear to be any particular reason why affluent gangs suddenly increased in numbers—seemingly overnight—other than it had been a growing trend that had finally reached a critical mass. As already noted, gangs such as skinhead and neo-Nazi types already existed and were now being recognized as gangs in local communities. This may have accounted for a sudden surge in law enforcement numbers.

A WORKING DEFINITION OF A GANG

I sought out numerous sociologists with expertise in gang research to obtain a workable definition of gangs. Malcolm Klein, Ph.D., director of the USC Social Science Research Institute, states: "A gang is a bunch of guys involved in delinquent and violent activity,"[15] His definition focuses solely on "street gangs" and excludes groups with a specific goal orientation such as biker and skinhead gangs. He writes in his book, *The American Street Gang* (to be published in 1995), that he finds it necessary to exclude almost as many different groups as he would include to avoid unwanted stereotyping.

Irving Spergel, Ph.D., a sociologist at the University of Chicago, when asked about the idea of affluent gangs, said, "It's almost a contradiction in terms," as his research has primarily dealt with inner-city gangs. About the possibility of affluent gangs, he characterized them as "a bunch of guys that get together and raise some hell. They're an odd-ball gang. Maybe they'll steal, but then they'll disappear."[16]

The *FBI Law Enforcement Bulletin* featured an article on gangs in which the authors, an officer with the Baltimore Police Department and a university professor, wrote: "A gang is a group of youths . . . banded together for antisocial and criminal activities."[17]

Developing a "scientific" definition for the term "gang" isn't practical because not all gangs are comprised solely of youths. Neither do all youths join gangs in order to commit crimes, nor do all gangs commit crimes of violence.

For the purposes of having a working definition for this book, I have modified the above definition to specify a *youth gang*. There is also a general consensus in America that the term *gangs* should specify that criminal activity is afoot, even if a specific youth doesn't have the intent of committing crimes. Groups of youths who adopt the gang façade—attire, hand signals, speech, etc.—but who don't commit crimes will not be labeled as a gang. To qualify as a gang, criminal activity must be a characteristic of the group. The crimes committed don't necessarily have to include more severe acts of violence, such as murder, but can simply be limited to assault—as in fist fights. In fact, some gangs may completely avoid violent crimes and simply buy and sell drugs. For these reasons, the definition of a *youth gang* is as follows:

> A group of youths who are banded together in a specific context and whose activities include, but are not limited to, criminal acts. Adults may or may not be a part of this group, but when there is adult involvement, they will only represent a small minority of the gang membership.

(The reason for the inclusion of the possibility of adult members is that young adults, under thirty years of age, are sometimes gang members.)

This modest refinement will help provide a specific context for the rest of this book, separating a youth gang from other terms that are part of professional and popular jargon—clubs, cults, social movement, mob, or even Mafia. Compare, for example, the definition of a youth gang to a working definition of a cult, whose application can be equally ambiguous:

> A cult is an isolated and/or anti-social group of persons who give their allegiance to a leader or leaders, whose purpose and/or goal it is to attain manipulative power through unquestioned loyalty to a system of beliefs.[18]

Cult is also a word that can be used quite broadly, and among sociologists is another word that has never been definitively defined with such specificity as to become standard. The definition included here was developed in order to provide a referential framework when comparing different groups. Gangs and cults can of course overlap each other. For example, in some youth gangs there might be a leader who seeks unquestioning allegiance to a belief system, but in many gangs this isn't present, such as the Andy Kriz case. In Kriz's gang, youths simply committed themselves to each other to profit from theft. There are cases, however, where a gang might also qualify as a cult, particularly in some occultic gangs in which youths give their allegiance to a particular belief system at the urgings of a manipulative leader, such as The Satanic Cult (chapter 3).

Popular expressions such as "hanging out," where youths simply gather together usually at a specified places, wouldn't qualify as a gang because crimes aren't typically committed. "Hanging out" is often a forerunner to the beginning of gangs, but by itself wouldn't constitute a gang.

THE DIFFERENCES BETWEEN INNER-CITY AND AFFLUENT GANGS

At the present, gang experts in America have focused their attentions on the inner-city gang problem, the affluent gang trend taking a back seat. One sociologist when asked for information about affluent gangs, expressed concern that attention shouldn't be diverted from inner-city gangs because this could lead to a reduction of resources and manpower to address this problem. This caution is well noted, but if the affluent gang problem isn't addressed now—especially in a preventative mode—the long-term effects could be disastrous.

Inner-city gangs have and will probably continue to dominate the public's attention for the next few years. The sheer volume of news coverage of inner-city gangs, however, has created inaccurate stereotypical impressions of affluent gangs. For this reason, it is important to clarify the significant differences between inner-city and affluent gangs. Each of the differences discussed should be preceded with the qualifying word "typically," because not every gang will follow every observed trend. The following explanations are only intended as guidelines and must be evaluated based upon individual cases.

Territorial—This is one of the most obvious differences between current inner-city and affluent gangs. Inner-city gangs are typically "turf" gangs. They mark out a specified territory as their own with graffiti and acts of intimidation and violence. Gang members know that to enter the territory of a rival gang is to take one's life in one's hands. Affluent gangs have rarely been seen to be territorial with an "own the neighborhood" mentality. The exception are some delinquent gangs that mark off territories where they can steal and sell illegal goods. Affluent youths have more money and are therefore more mobile. There isn't the need to feel that one has to stake out a territory; they like the idea of seeing new sights. Inner-city youths often don't have the same ability to be mobile, so there is a lot of currency attached to being the king of one's "hood." A large street gang with two or three hundred members taken as a whole, however, often does have mobility with increased illegal revenue, evinced by gangs spreading their crime networks to other cities. The average individual gang member, though, doesn't.

Institutionalized—Inner-city gangs are now entering the third and fourth generation of membership. It isn't uncommon for one's father, uncle, or cousin, or even grandfather to have been a member of the same gang. For this reason, inner-city gangs have well-developed infrastructures and are an intimate part of the substructure of economically depressed communities. Connections have been made and contacts networked that have endured for twenty and thirty years. Affluent gangs are a relatively new phenomenon and don't have these kinds of entrenched roots. Currently, they don't continue on in a community for more than a couple of years. Unlike inner-city youths, most affluent youths after a period of time lose interest and start thinking about getting a job or going to college. For this reason, affluent gang activity is a much easier problem to attack. Most of the youths in affluent gangs are separate and apart from the mainstream of the youth culture. They are more isolated and therefore easier to target for disengagement and preventative action. But unless affected communities act, individual acts of affluent gangs can be just as deadly as inner-city gangs. Bullets can kill just as easily when fired by a youth in a project as a bullet fired from a youth from a white-column home.

Ideology—Inner-city gangs typically don't have an ideological bent (some exceptions are noted in chapters 13 and 14). The turf and the trafficking of drugs are the key factors that bind inner-city gangs together, as well as social needs. Of the three affluent gang types, ideological and occultic gangs are more likely to attach themselves to an ideology. Most delinquent gangs, including those in affluent communities, usually don't form with an ideological bent.

Disengagement—Disengaging any kind of youth from a gang is difficult, but in the inner-city most professionals agree that once a youth is in a gang, it is a slim chance that he/she can be talked out of their gang. This isn't pessimism, this is just the reality of the problem. Many, including myself, are upbeat about preventative action that will keep youths out of inner-city gangs, but once a youth becomes involved, the hostile nature of many neighborhoods provides cover from attack. This doesn't excuse gang activity, but this fact has to be reckoned with before most youths will exit as most gangs have severe penalties for those who decide to disengage. For affluent gangs, the prognosis isn't as dismal. There aren't as many day-to-day pressures that would necessitate a youth remaining a part of a gang. Like inner-city gangs, however, it is easier to launch preventative measures that will work than to attempt to disengage a youth who is involved in a gang. Once a youth joins a gang, there is a strong bond that is often difficult to break.

Unpredictability—The random violence committed by inner-city gangs is one of the greatest threats they pose. You can't predict when or where they will strike next. What is predictable is that the allegiances are well staked out and easy to identify as they have persisted for years. Up until the present, affluent gangs haven't been as violent as inner-city gangs, but random acts of violence can appear just as easily as seen in cases cited later in this text. What is unsettling about affluent gangs is that money and increased educational know-how can combine together to create especially frightening terrorist types of gangs. The structure and nature of inner-city gangs hasn't changed much over the last ten years, except for the merchandise or drugs being sold. Affluent gangs, though, are more likely to change and develop rapidly, inspired by what is currently in vogue in the youth subculture. Secrecy is a big part of the affluent gang aura as well as a greater need to act out in new and creative ways, fueling their unpredictability.

Female Members—In inner-city gangs, female membership typically hovers around 10%[19] according to recent surveys, except for Hispanic gangs where "auxiliary" female counterparts are common. Affluent female gang membership is considerably lower. Precise numbers aren't available, but based upon firsthand inquiry into scores of gangs in the US and Europe, less than 5% is a reasonable estimate. Female crime as a whole has been persistently lower than male crime figures in the US and Europe. Logically, however, it is not uncommon for females to be found around the periphery of a gang dating gang members, although criminal participation is minimal except for the ingestion of drugs. (Because female affluent gang membership has not been a major factor in affluent gangs, discussion of females in gangs is limited in this text.)

Identity Factors—Identity factors refers to how a gang distinguishes itself from other groups of youths. Gangs usually rely upon things one can see or hear, with preference to what one can see. Turf, attire, initiations, lingo, hand signals (which operate like passwords) are some of the distinguishing devices used by gangs. This is true in inner-city and affluent gangs. Music fads, dress fashions, and visual media are quick inspiration points as they are easily conveyed to youths who look towards an idol to emulate. The key difference is that an affluent gang is more likely to rely upon non-visual or more subtle means of identification so as to remain invisible to adults. Affluent gang membership isn't yet something to be widely flaunted for fear of police monitoring. For some affluent gangs, such as an occultic gang, developing a concealed, secretive cover is part of the thrill. Being part of a group without even one's peers knowledge adds to the excitement.

EUROPEAN GANGS

As is true in the US, gangs are forming in affluent communities across all of Europe from England to Germany to Hungary to Switzerland to Poland to Holland. No country has been able to escape this new trend. The appearance of urban and affluent gangs has been rapid in some countries, while others are just now being affected. (Also in common with the US are the escalating violent juvenile crime rates in most of these countries. In England in 1994, for example, Scotland Yard broke with its long-standing tradition of unarmed British bobbies, and a few dozen specially trained officers in "armed response vehicles" started strapping on sidearms in hip holsters.)

In Hungary, after the fall of Communism and the authoritarian rule—albeit not as severe as in other countries such as Romania—gangs started to proliferate[20] according to Laszlo Czendes, an officer in Hungary's Department of Crime Prevention and one of Hungary's leading juvenile gang experts. He notes that crime overall from 1989 to 1990 increased 51.3% according to Ministry of the Interior studies. Regarding gang activity, Gypsy gangs were the first to begin to grow in numbers. (His comment is not a racial slur, but rather an observation similar to stating that inner-city gangs are typically ethnic in the US.) The hard authoritarian rule kept a lid on these types of gangs. This same observation has been made throughout Eastern (Central) Europe and the former Soviet Union—especially Russia. Czendes adds that most of these gangs weren't violent, just motivated by greed or survival. Currently, this trend is changing, though, and gang activity has been observed to be more violent. Additionally, affluent gangs have begun to appear with greater frequency. He attributes this to severely dysfunctional family factors that are further addressed in chapter 6.

Even in Switzerland, a country worlds apart from Hungary, gangs are forming in small but perceivable numbers in affluent communities for the first time. This is hard to believe. Switzerland was the first European country to embrace democracy, is virtually slum-free, has the highest standard of living in Western Europe, and has relatively few ethnic groups. The Swiss have traditionally felt safe in their country that maintained its neutrality during WW II.

During a 1994 lecture tour, I was asked to speak to a group of police officers in Zurich. My facilitator for the lecture drove me to a building in the equivalent of a downtown district in the US. His daughter, four, was in the back seat. He jumped out of the car, and started to escort me into the building. His daughter was still in the car. I said, "You forgot Sabrina."

"No, she'll be okay," he said confidently.

"You can't do this. Let's take her up. Someone could abduct her," I insisted.

"This is Switzerland. This is Zurich. Don't worry, my friend!"

"But what if a foreigner walks by who isn't Swiss? Aren't you afraid?"

"No. This is Switzerland," he said proudly and with authority.

This is how safe people have traditionally felt in Switzerland, but this is changing. Switzerland in 1968 did have social protests on campuses, but on a much lower scale than the US. (One of the worst took place in Lausanne. One result of these protests is that when the University of Lausanne was expanded, the campus was built on the outskirts of town with few dormitories. This forced students to live spread out across the city, thus making it more difficult for students to organize.) In 1992, during my first trip to Switzerland, I noted in my journal that gang activity was likely to surface soon. Grotesque volumes of graffiti, often a forerunner of gang activity, was evident throughout Zurich and Bern, and drug abuse had been a hardened trend among young people.

Although not chronic, skinhead gang activity had been present in Switzerland since the mid-1980s. The police officers to whom I presented my lecture in 1994 acknowledged that they were starting to see a marginal, but not chronic, increase of affluent gangs for the first time. The trend seems to be at about the same level seen in the US in the very early 1980s. There was unanimous agreement, though, that this new gang trend would probably continue to grow just as it has in every other European country.

The types of urban and affluent gangs found in Europe are far more diverse than in the US. Barbara Fatyga, a sociologist with the University of Warsaw and one of Europe's foremost gang experts, has charted numerous gangs that have formed in Poland. Many of these gangs have severe ideological bents like the skinhead groups in the US. She has documented, for example, ecological gangs that premeditate crimes such as assault. These aren't just social protests crying out against the pollution left by years of Communist rule that have threatened many of Poland's lush forests. She has observed that many of these ideological gangs commonly display street gang activity and violence similar to other nonideological gangs. And like other countries, many of these gangs are comprised of youths from families that are not financially destitute. This diversity of ideologies that Fatyga has found in Poland is common in all the Western European countries, and is explored in greater detail in chapter 14.

It has become increasingly important to maintain some global picture of the types and variants of gangs that are forming in Europe. Some, such as skinhead gangs, have already inspired American youths, and other types could appeal to educated affluent youths desiring to be "different." Emulating one's foreign youth counterparts to the puzzlement of adults is something that could have enormous appeal, and the nature of the youth subculture today makes it easy to transfer ideas back and forth across the Atlantic. For those who desire to take preventative measures in the US, keeping abreast of current European developments (or other affected areas of the world) is imperative as it can be a valuable source of information.

Finally, some might assume that youths in Europe join gangs for different reasons than youths in the US. This is a misconception. While the precise gang type and variant a youth joins will be influenced by the local culture, there is a predictable continuity of the profile of a youth who is likely to join a gang, what he/she expects from gang activity, and the reasons why a youth will disengage. In short, once one has spent time with youths of one type of gang in a country, one is likely to meet similar youths in another country. And after talking to a couple of dozen of these youths, the mysterious façade of gang activity easily peels away. Only the cryptic beliefs of a handful of gangs might pose a challenge.

RISE AND FALL OF CURRENT TRENDS

Gang activity in affluent US and European communities will continue to increase. This is almost a virtual certainty based upon current social conditions. Chapter 6 presents the predictable profile of a youth who is likely to join a gang, and there has been no change in the present social conditions that suggests that fewer youths will be at risk of gang involvement. Only more.

What is impossible to predict precisely is which gangs will and won't gain favor among affluent youths. My guess is that occultic gangs, which are currently not as popular as three or four years ago, could easily resurge in another few years—when another group of youths reaches the peak period for involvement, ages 12-17. For reasons explained in chapter 12, I think that delinquent gangs will become more popular and US expressions of European ideological gangs could become the most popular with those who possess the sharpest minds intellectually. But this is just speculation. What isn't speculation is that there is a definitive profile of a youth who is likely to join a gang and the numbers of these youths only appear to be rising.

CHAPTER 5.

Unholy Union

Summer nights in Arlington, Texas are sultry, but halcyon. The year is 1991. The place is the linking, upscale city between Dallas and Ft. Worth on Interstate 30. Dallas-Ft. Worth residents muse about ballgames at Arlington's Ranger Stadium and debate about Nolan Ryan, the ageless wonder. Would he throw another no-hitter. Next door to the stadium, thousands visit Six Flags Over Texas every night. Arlington seems like a nice place to live. It may not be America's heartland, but it's close enough.

Donald Thomas is a thirty-two-year-old Black man who lives here. His two buddies, Steve Sloan and Ed Richardson, who happen to be White, were relaxing on a flatbed truck after their shift at the Quality Beverage Company warehouse. They talked about the heat, their workday, and their regular weekend barbecue. Gazing at the clear, expansive, Texas sky, loaded with stars, Steve thought—I'm in heaven! It was a few hours before dawn. In such a spacious, tranquil place, your mind relaxes and freely expands to inhabit this heaven. Needless to say, he didn't see the car or the barrel of the shotgun protruding from its window.

They say you never hear the blast when you're hit.

Donald probably heard nothing. He never knew what hit him and blew his chest apart.

Steve heard and saw the blast. Though stunned, he sped after the vehicle, writing the license tag on the palm of his hand. Ed cradled a blood-spattered Donald. There was no solace except that they knew and cared for their friend.

The three youths who killed Donald Thomas—and were later sentenced for their crime—were from middle-and upper-middle class Dallas communities . . . all were fifteen years old and from broken homes. George "Trey" Roberts, who had long been estranged from his father, a Houston police officer, sported a tattoo on the inside of his lower lip that read "skinhead." Joshua Hendry snuck out of his house the night they shot Donald Thomas and pushed the car down the street so as not to awaken his mother. Christopher Brosky, who used to be a punker and sported a mohawk, was a founding member of Confederate White Vikings skinheads, which later merged with the neo-Nazi Confederate Hammerskins.[1]

It wasn't the first time that skinhead gangs—teenagers claiming to be neo-Nazis members of the Confederate Hammerskins—had terrorized the D-FW Metroplex. On March 2, 1990, in a US district court, five Confederate Hammerskins were convicted of: (1) the racial harassment of Dallas Blacks and Hispanics; (2) the desecration of Temple Shalom, a Reformed Jewish Synagogue, with Nazi graffiti, which emblazoned "Six million more!" and "This time we'll do it right!"; and (3) shooting out the temple's windows and doors with a .25 caliber semi-automatic pistol— just a few blocks from the residence of former Dallas Cowboy football star quarterback, Roger Staubach. Some who watched the evening news that night now felt a little safer—the ones who were the object of this neo-Nazi fury. The plans of the group to gas the synagogue through the air conditioning ducts[2] and other acts of terror had ended. The sentences, meted out by US District Judge Barefoot Sanders, were several years longer than recommended by federal guidelines and ranged from 4 1/2 to 9 1/2 years. Sanders called the five young men, Sean Christian Tarrant (20), Jon Lance Jordan (19), Christopher Greer (24), Daniel Alvis Wood (20)—each from Texas—and Michael Lewis Lawrence (21) of Tulsa, "a danger to the community." The US Justice Department, the FBI, the Dallas Police, and the Dallas district attorney's office had decreed a *force majeure* with this successful prosecution. According to James S. Turner, acting chief of the Justice Department's civil rights division, he hoped this case would "send a message" to other groups that hate crimes would be vigorously prosecuted by the federal government.[3]

Local police departments in the metroplex, however, acknowledged that the conviction didn't end this youth-hate movement. Just two days before the guilty verdict was handed down, another local skinhead group threatened to kill a Black woman. They broke her windshield, and spray painted, "Hitler is Lord" on her vehicle. Seven arrests followed: two were *juveniles.*

As if authorities needed a reminder, unrepentant Dallas skinhead, Daniel Wood, sliced the air with a Nazi salute, as he was escorted from the courtroom by US marshalls. His defiance triggered the memories of some viewers. They remembered another sinister gang comprised of other *teen* males, who associated with Dallas skinhead groups, including the Confederate Hammerskins.

Ben and his two friends, Cindy and Laurie, lived in Carrollton, a north Dallas suburb in 1987. They had three things in common besides all being twelve years old—their parents were divorced and they weren't handling it very well. Each had also been violently invaded by a group of older teens who were members of gangs.

Cindy started drinking when she was eight, right after the divorce—

the primal rip. "My dad was rich and he left me," she says. "I hated him, and so I drank to hurt him and kill what I felt." Cindy's first "killing."

"When they divorced, we stopped going to family parties, and I started to lose friends. I was angry and lonely, so I made others."

Laurie also started drinking at eight and was one of those new friends. She introduced Cindy to the "escape route." Actually it was Laurie's older sister who poured Cindy's first drink. It was the older kids, brothers and sisters of her new friends, that opened the door to the alcohol and drugs. Cindy didn't like the taste or losing control, but she embraced anything that released her from the hell at home. Her family was ostensibly a church-going family, but now it was splintered and nothing more than a broken promise. Kids don't like it when parents break their promises.

The newly banded friends knew drinking was wrong, and they never intended to do drugs. Then they met Ben. When he was ten, Ben met an older kid, Mark, hanging out at Prestonwood, a posh mall fifteen minutes from his house. Mark invited Ben to a party. Ben was scared about sneaking out at 1:00 A.M., but Mark told him it would be worth it. At the "party" he gagged on his first drag of "pot," taken on a dare. Laurie and Cindy and a number of their other friends soon followed, encouraged by Laurie's sister. There were no complicated schemes, just reacting and hiding from their pain. Inept sex followed a few times for the three, always with older teens, the new role models. "For me it was just technical," says Cindy. "It was the holding I liked."

On the weekends during that fall, their parents dropped them off at another suburban mall, Furneaux Creek Mall, where they hung out with over a hundred other youths. Drugs and drinking were plentiful. "We're just going to the movies," they told their folks, who never suspected anything. One mother didn't care, and the other two mothers had self-imposed blinders to shield them from accepting that their divorce had devastated their child. That's when the sinister ones, the boys with the shaved heads and "hawks" (a spiked shaft half-moon of hair) in their later teens, started hanging out with the younger kids. Mark, Richie, and "Hog" had formed their own occultic gang of sorts. They were the ones who stroked the younger kids' egos. Hog publicly declared at school that he worshipped Satan and often called on the Prince of Darkness. Everyone, even the teachers kept their distance from him or created it when it wasn't there. Only a few students knew that Richie was a *skinhead* who ran with another gang, and that Mark *wanted to be* but was rejected by the Confederate Hammerskins because he was part Black—the product, he said, of a rape.

The cops finally clamped down on the drunk and stoned teens who were accosting suburbanites at Furneaux Creek Mall. A memo sent home from the local schools cautioned parents about dropping their kids off at the mall, but not before Mark, Richie, and Hog, who participated in low-level drug dealing and assaults reeled in Ben.

Mark liked Ben, and Ben wanted supernatural powers.

Cindy told Ben about Diana, a teen friend, "I adored . . . who was a good witch." (Some initiates believe that evil witches cast evil spells for harm—black magic; while good witches beckon the spirits for good purposes—white magic.)

"One day, I asked her about her spells after I saw her cast a spell on a boy she had just broken up with. Five minutes later, there he was banging on her window asking for her," Cindy said. She was convinced that her friend had summoned up supernatural forces. She told Ben and his curiosity was piqued.

Ben believed that Mark and his friends held the key to obtaining these "powers." So for a few months he helped Mark with his "pick-ups": kids on Saturday nights who were looking for some drugs and fun, waiting under the overpass at Frankford Road and Interstate 35. There Mark, or one of the trio, scooped them up. Then Mark and his entourage drove their pickups to Lewisville, twenty minutes up the interstate, to a secluded wooded area about fifteen minutes from the Hampton Inn Motel to "party."

A day before Christmas Eve, the trio invited Ben to go to a *special* party— an initiation rite. "This is a place we haven't taken anyone to, dude," Mark told him. "Just be prepared."

Ben kept his mouth shut. He didn't tell anyone. Not even Cindy or Laurie knew about it until it was over.

They drove for a while and made a lot of turns to confuse Ben, who was blindfolded with Mark's bandanna. When the blindfold was removed, the only discernible landmark was a railroad trestle. Ben jolted. There - hunched down before a large table-like rock was a black-robed old man, his wrists tied behind his back. His deep blood-shot eyes jagged back and - forth between Hog's crazed eyes, which looked down on him, and the machete that lightly swung like a pendulum, clenched in Hog's right fist. Cracks of light from a thick red candle placed between Hog's feet, snapped by an occasional breeze, illumined the horror in the old man's face. His long gray hair, a shadowy silver, was unkempt but glistened.

Mark shook his fist at the old man and declared, "All right, dudes. It's time to party. *Worship* and party."

Ben's perceptions were earlier dulled by the "primo" he smoked—a marijuana joint with cocaine. From the periphery of the dark, about ten obscure figures, some who were local skins, appeared. Among them Ben made out two girls who steered their eyes downward; they shook while they tripped on Purple Haze, the acid of the seventies, now making a comeback. With anticipation, the group pressed closer to the makeshift altar.

With a sudden thrust, Mark extracted from his black leather jacket, dotted with small metal spikes, a dark-feathered pigeon. In one well chor-eographed move, he pressed it to the stone and the downward sweep of Hog's machete severed its head.

With two fingers, Mark, that night's priest of horror, moved the small flowing stream around the stone to form a crude melon-sized pentagram, symbolized by an upside-down star inside a circle, the alleged apex of Satan's power. Mark's pentagram, if drawn on a sheet of construction paper in green, could have easily been mistaken for a child's finger painting.

Then suddenly, steel again clanged hard on the rock and sparks flew where the old man was bowed over. Hog screamed deep at the pit of hell, and the ball of glistening gray hair rolled—the old man's head. Clutching his temples, Ben screamed, "Oh, God! Oh, God," while other youths from his neighborhood were safely gathered with their families singing Christmas carols.

Stripping away the gruesome veneer of the gang, a careful examination of this case revealed that the "killing" of the old man was a staged trick, which Mark had presented a couple of years before at a local haunted house fund-raiser. His enactment was so realistic, it was removed. On another occasion, Cindy said that other teens associated with the gang showed her a body bag with an old man who had been bludgeoned to death. What convinced her that it was a real body was the fact that one of her friends had actually been shot just a few months before while hanging with the same group. By carefully questioning the affected youths, local teachers, law enforcement officers and parents, much of the mystery was solved regarding this small gang's activities.

One of the youths drawn to this group was Trey Roberts, then thirteen years old. He was one of the skinheads sentenced in the slaying of Donald Thomas. He also lived near Ben's neighborhood.

What remained a mystery for a while longer, however, was the question: Why did an occultic gang and youths from a racist gang gather together? What does chopping up animals and pledging allegiance to the Prince of Darkness have to do with clubbing Blacks and racial hatred? The youths in the occultic gang weren't racist. Why would they hang out with youths who were. Another question: The skinhead and occultic gang youths were from completely different parts of town. Where did they meet? How did they meet? Was there a common identity that united them together? The answers to these questions are found in the next chapter, "The Predictable Gang Profile," and in chapter 11, "Youth Subculture ≤ Gangs—Similar Inspiration Points in the US and Europe."

CHAPTER 6.

The Predictable Gang Profile

A powerful strategic advantage could be gained if it were possible to predict the likely profile of a gang member. If one knew which youths were likely to be at risk of gang involvement, then preventative measures could be initiated to prevent these youths from ever joining a gang. Additionally, intervention methods could be sharpened to disengage youths from gangs.

In this chapter and the next this profile is identified. In chapter 20 is presented the only strategy that I have found in the US or Europe that successfully prevents gangs from forming, and this strategy directly keys off this profile.

In the past, profiling gang activity has principally focused on socio-economic factors. This focus took root because gangs were first observed in the US in economically depressed communities. The assumption was that economic factors were the principal culprits that drove gang formation. The appearance, however, of affluent gangs forces a reexamination of this assumption. As noted in chapter 7, economic hardship is typically not a factor when gangs *first* appear in a neighborhood, although it is a driving force in the *institutionalization* of gangs.

Reflecting on the three cases from the previous chapter, at first blush it appears that the Dallas youths from the occultic and skinhead gangs had nothing in common. They lived in affluent *and* lower-income sections of Dallas. They attended *different* schools. Some were straight "A" students and others were struggling to stay in school. Some were creative, exhibiting genius; others showed little imagination. Each gang preferred different types of music and dressed differently. Typically, students who don't have common origins or mutual interests aren't attracted to each another, especially in group settings. Who could have predicted that these two extreme gangs would come together?

The reason these two gangs were attracted to each other, however, was because they *did* have something in common—something so primal that it overcame all barriers. What was it?

The answer . . .

Every youth in each of the gangs came from a broken, unstable, or severely dysfunctional home. For each youth, one of the following factors was present in their families:

- Divorce
- Separation
- Physical abuse
- Sexual abuse
- One of their parents was severely dysfunctional—alcoholism, bulimia, etc.

Each youth shared a similar, primal pain that acted as a powerful, identifying magnet, negating their many differences. Coupled with this, many of these youths became more rebellious due to a lack of parental restraint and discipline, enabling them to stay out into the early morning hours where they could meet with their gangs. Once I identified what these Dallas youths had in common, the reason why these completely diverse gangs were drawn to each other was no longer mysterious. It wasn't difficult to imagine why youths from completely different backgrounds and with wholly different ideological agendas would be attracted to one another. (Throughout the rest of the book, the term "at-risk youth" will be used to specify a youth with one or more of the above family characteristics).

OBVIOUS BUT NOT ADDRESSED

When typical suburban parents are asked why gangs are forming in their neighborhoods, they usually are at a loss for answers. Affluent gang activity comes as a complete surprise. But when given time to reflect on the profile identified in this chapter, the response is usually, "Well, that makes sense."

Sociologists, social workers, and juvenile officers have long known the connection between broken/severely ruptured homes and the catalyst it provides for gang formation. (Regarding the federal and state prison populations taken as a whole, typically over 75% of the inmates in any given facility come from broken homes.) Yet, as noted by Malcolm Klein, USC Social Science Research Institute, no comprehensive studies have been made regarding this profile.[1] Most research in the US and Europe has centered on socioeconomic factors rather than family conditions. I believe that this is one of the primary reasons that no effective strategy for gang prevention has emerged apart from the one presented in chapter 20.

Since 1987, virtually every youth involved in gang activity whom I interviewed in the US and ten European countries has fit this profile. Also, every social worker, law enforcement officer, teacher, and juvenile judge has said, *"That's about right,"* when asked if this profile fits those youths in gangs with whom they interact. This doesn't mean that a youth who *doesn't* fit the profile can't be recruited into a gang, but when it occurs, it is an extremely rare phenomenon. (One such example is provided in the next chapter.)

In the mid-1980s I stated in lectures that gangs would probably become a presence in affluent communities because of the dramatic increase of youths with this profile. As more youths were thrown into this pool, I believed that more youths at the extreme edges would act out radically and join gangs.

Rebellion of some form is common for most youths once they reach puberty. Some test their parent's curfew while others sneak their first beer. By the early 1990s, though, many youths with a rebellious streak who fit the profile didn't just go out and get drunk or bloody someone's nose after a football game. Neither did they just hang out with a local clique and identify themselves as a "hard core" or a "goat-roper." These youths didn't choose to rebel as former generations of American youths. They formed gangs, and their actions were more extreme. Criminal activity was not just a few sporadic acts, but rather a persistent trait of these groups. For these youths, deteriorating family conditions acted as a magnifier of their rebellious tendencies. Gangs became the surrogate family in which to commit their crimes.

The fact that these youths typically have severe family troubles doesn't excuse or justify their criminal behavior. They must be held accountable when they break the law. Neither should their background profile be construed as blaming specific families for their child's criminal acts. More youths who fit this profile resist gang involvement and criminal acts than those who choose to rebel by joining a gang. In most cases, committing crimes is a matter of choice.

In addition to the family profile of a gang member, other youth subculture factors such as the glorification of violence in media and music adds to the problem. These issues are addressed in chapter 11. But one thing is clear. If one beams harmful media messages to youths from stable, healthy homes, some may become more violent, but they don't join gangs. Gangs provide a warped alternative to a broken/ruptured home. That's why identifying the correct profile of a gang member is so important. With this information we can better identify who is likely to be at risk of gang involvement and implement target-oriented preventative measures, develop reliable strategies for disengaging a youth from a gang, and when necessary, law enforcement and state juvenile justice systems can more effectively enforce the law and protect a community from the threats posed by gangs.

PROFILING—A USEFUL TOOL

When dealing with any type of chronic criminal behavior, it is important to understand what makes someone tick. How and why they operate.

This is especially true of the current and increasingly unpredictable nature of juvenile crime. Regarding juvenile gangs, it is crucial to identify the individual traits or background factors that are the most likely to inflame a youth's desire to join and remain in a gang.

If we could predict the *psychological* profile of a youth who is likely to become involved in gang activity, this would obviously be useful. But there isn't one consistent personality type(s) that is drawn to gangs. Some youths possess leadership traits, while others possess conformist traits. Gangs are like any group: We can predict that the leader will usually possess strong "tell" traits (actions that are confident, strong, directive), but youths on a debate or sports team might also possess the same trait. About the only trait that you can predict about youths when they are together in a group is that some of their collective actions will tend to be *unpredictable*. In short, we can predict unpredictability.

A specific youth, for example, might have strong conformist traits manifesting themselves in predictable actions, but when he joins a gang, his actions and those of his gang will tend to be unpredictable. This trait of gang behavior especially alarms police officers. They can't predict what these youths will do next. Gangs often act impulsively, inspired by the rapidly changing pop culture or what they are feeling at the moment. Only local intelligence gathering will yield increased accuracy when predicting a gang's *specific* activity. Unpredictability and spontaneity are of course common for most teenagers and not just for those at risk for becoming involved in gang activity. The difference is that unpredictable gang activity poses a threat while the unpredictability of teens in general doesn't.

The only profile that is common for virtually all gang members cross-culturally—inner-city and affluent—*is the family background of a youth*. In the US and Europe, it is a rare exception when a youth from a stable home joins an affluent or inner-city gang. And by stable home, we are talking about homes where the following is present:

- Love freely shared and expressed between parents and with their children.
- Open lines of communication.
- Consistent nurturing of the youth's whole psyche, such as regular reading to a child when he/she is young, maintaining discipline, and spending quality and quantity time with him/her. In short, there exists a reciprocal bond between the parents and their child that entails the development of a whole person, sustained by conscious effort and abundant affection.

To repeat, this is not to suggest that youths who fit the profile described in this chapter are doomed to be gang members. Of those who fit this profile, more resist than join gangs. The gang phenomenon, though, has been a part of life in increasing numbers in most inner-city communities for decades. As recognized by most ethnic civic leaders, if the deterioration of the family can breed gangs in the inner-city, why not in *affluent communities* as well?

This is precisely why I predicted in the mid-1980s that gangs would form in the suburbs. Beginning in the 1960s, the numbers of youths from unstable homes in all socioeconomic sectors of America skyrocketed. Why wouldn't a percentage of youths in affluent communities act out their rebellion in the same way as their inner-city counterparts?

Let us now take a brief look at each of the five characteristics of the gang profile and how they can contribute to gang formation.

THE DIVORCE/SEPARATION FACTOR

One of the most important social stories during the last half of this century is the current, runaway divorce rate. It began in the middle 1960s in America and other Western countries. Of the five family characteristics, divorce is the easiest to track and quantify because couples must file legal documents, which are easily surveyed.

Today, 49.2% of all children in the US—32.3 *million*—do not live with both of their biological parents.[2] "It tells us that the glass is half empty, confirming the popular suspicion that America is going to hell in a handbasket," said Rutgers professor of political science, Ross Baker.[3]

In 1940 the population of the US was about 132 million. That year there were 1.6 million marriages and only .26 million divorces and annulments.[4] The marriage to divorce ratio was 12 marriages to only 1.9 divorces or about one divorce for every six couples that entered into marriage for every 1,000 people.[5]

In 1989, the American population was about 248 million. The divorce rate mushroomed to an estimated 1.1 million divorces versus only 2.4 million marriages. This amounted to 9.6 marriages and 4.7 divorces for every 1,000 people.[6] *That's almost one divorce for every two couples who entered into marriage.* The divorce rate peaked in 1981 at 5.2 divorces per 1000 people, but still remains unacceptably high.[7]

The divorce rate has had a catastrophic effect on whether youths live with both parents or not. In 1970, 66% of all children lived with both biological parents—popularly dubbed the nuclear family.[8] By 1980, the rate plummeted to 57%. By 1991, it was only 50.2%.[9]

For years, many in the various counseling disciplines downplayed the severe emotional damage experienced by youths from divorced families. That perspective has rapidly eroded as hard data comes in. Dr. Judith Wallerstein's ten-year study of sixty divorced families confirmed and quantified what many suspected: Divorce can be devastating to young lives and its effects stretch long into adulthood. She wrote:

> We were able to see clearly that we weren't dealing simply with the routine angst of young people going through transition but rather that, for most of them, divorce was the single most important cause of enduring pain and anomie in their lives.[10]

In another study, one woman who was interviewed said:

> You accept as an article of faith that your parents will stay together until they die . . . and then they pull the rug out from under you and you want to scream out and ask, "How can you break the very rules you yourselves wrote?"[11]

Most youths in gangs whom I have interviewed identified divorce and separation as the *deepest source* of their anger. One doesn't have to be a trained professional to conclude that broken homes can produce broken youths. The home is the place where we are supposed to develop our strongest, deepest bonds of love, trust, and respect. When Mom and Dad say, "I do," then turn around later and say, "We don't," a youth's psyche and spirit are often agonizingly shredded.

During and after the crucible of divorce and separation, it is not uncommon for youths to change dramatically. This can result in an icy, uncaring attitude, followed by withdrawal. For some youths, having to choose which parent to live with is a hellish experience. Others experience the misplaced guilt that they caused the divorce.

One teenage gang member started secretly drinking when she was eight because she thought it would hurt her father. Adults may deem her actions illogical because her father never knew that she was trying to hurt him. But her age and naiveté, coupled with her pain and anger, blinded her ability to reason lucidly. When I asked her about this, she said, "I was too young to realize that I was only hurting myself."

Another teenage youth told me that the reason he joined a gang was because his parents beat him. When further pressed, however, he conceded that his parents never *physically* beat him. The "beating" was the emotional and mental flogging meted out by his parents' actions, especially their divorce.

It is important to note that I never encountered a youth, nurtured in a loving and stable home, who joined a gang for the sole reason that his parent(s) *died*. Death is inevitable and if it happens without blameworthy circumstances, is eventually accepted by most youths. Therefore, death, no matter how tragic (except for suicide), does not usually have the same effect on a youth as willful acts of divorce. Divorce is replete with aspects of blame. When parents say, "I can't (or don't) want to live with you anymore," it represents a *human choice*. Death is inexorable; divorce or separation, is a decision that puts other loved ones—namely children—in harm's way.

Although divorce and separation are key factors found in the majority of youths who engage in gangs, they aren't the only factors that sow seeds of discontent. Any of the other factors can produce the same effect.

THE ABUSE FACTOR: PHYSICAL, SEXUAL, AND EXTREME VERBAL

Except for *sexual* abuse, physical (or extreme verbal) abuse are not usually the sole factor for gang-engagement. When the family is whole, there is a greater resiliency in many youths to rebound and cope. When divorce or separation becomes a factor, the risk factor for the youths I interviewed escalated significantly. Because of the large number of youths I have interviewed over the years in several countries and cultures, it's difficult *not* to arrive at this intuitive conclusion. This is *not* meant to encourage spouses to remain in abusive, life-threatening situations. But *occasional* physical or verbal abuse that isn't life-threatening doesn't seem to initiate gang activity. This, of course, is not to suggest that even chronic verbal abuse cannot adversely affect a youth for years. But the subject of this book is affluent gangs, and it is not common for youths to join gangs unless there is something more severe than occasional physical or verbal abuse.

As a sole factor that propelled a youth into a gang, sustained, regular physical abuse, especially *repeated* physical abuse was more commonly the dominant factor. Sexual abuse was observed in occultic gangs as a dominant factor for engagement and involvement—the expectation being that one would receive power over one's aggressor.

SEVERELY DYSFUNCTIONAL PARENT

A family may appear to be mentally healthy to an outsider, but if even one parent is *severely* dysfunctional and a youth takes the *brunt* of that dysfunction—it can be the activating mechanism that initiates gang involvement.

A noted psychologist defined *dysfunction* as: persons who function at less than an optimum level in view of their age, education, social class, and training related to their total social, behavioral and emotional well-being.[12] Other psychologists define dysfunction as representing *a state when emotional and relational boundaries are not respected in a relationship*. In a family, this can translate into family members subjugating their needs to the dysfunctional one. For example, empathy and respect are replaced by indifference and nonacceptance.

Interviews with youths, however, reveal that youths from dysfunctional but *not severely* dysfunctional homes don't join gangs. Some examples of severe dysfunctions are *addiction, bulimia, schizophrenia, and anorexia*. Additionally, with the exception of one case, I have never observed a youth who joined a gang who had a sibling with a severe dysfunction but *neither* parent could be classified as severely dysfunctional. (This exception is noted in the next chapter.) It is only when the parent is severely dysfunctional that it seems to trigger the desire in some youths to join a gang.

However, a severely dysfunctional parent can evoke a reaction in a youth, even if the youth isn't aware of the parent's dysfunction. One youth, for example, who had contemplated joining a gang, grew up in a family in which love was openly expressed and shared among most family members. Beneath the surface, though, he became the brunt of his mother's unintentional rejection. Her closet-bulimia, triggered by childhood sexual abuse, had translated itself into an unstated rejection of her son. The youth, who loved his mother, knew the alienation existed. He secretly grieved over it, and sought ways to rationalize her passive rejection. When he reached the age of sixteen, having failed to understand his mother's problem and how it affected him, he became briefly involved in a gang; it was a distraction, a diversion. He disengaged from the gang when, through counseling, he made the connection that the gang was a negative, destructive, nonproductive way of dealing with his mother's severe dysfunction and how it affected him.

HUNGARIAN SURVEY AFFIRMS
UNIVERSALITY OF PROFILE
America and Hungary: Different Cultures, Similar Youth Trends

America and Hungary are culturally quite different. While Americans were blithely and innocently watching Jackie Gleason's "The Honeymooners" and Ed Sullivan's variety show in 1956, the Hungarian revolt against the Soviet block was brutally repressed. Geographically, we have the Grand Canyon; they have the majestic Danube. We eat lots of fast-food; they eat Hungarian goulash, laden with paprika. We watch football; they play soccer. They lived under Communism until the mid-1980s, whereas we were governed by a democratic republic. Yet, both countries, beginning in the early 1980s, experienced increased gang activity in inner-city and affluent communities. America and Hungary also have a chronically high incidence of teen suicide and divorce rates per capita.

What most Americans don't know about Hungary is that it has the highest teenage suicide rate in the world. In 1988, a staggering 16% of all Hungarian youths attempted suicide and one-fourth required medical attention. This figure, however, is believed to be much higher because many suicide attempts are not reported by doctors.[13] (The adult population has been similarly affected in the southeastern sector of Hungary, where 70 out of every 1,000 adult males have attempted suicide. The elderly consume weedkiller to commit suicide, which is attributed to the fact that so many live on isolated farms.)

In the US that same year, *8.3%* of American youths said they had attempted to commit suicide. Additionally, 27.3% of all American students (grades 9-12) said that they had seriously contemplated suicide; 16.3% said they had made a *specific plan*; and 2% reported that their attempt resulted in injury that required medical attention.[14] This was a fourfold increase since 1950, when the American family was relatively stable.

Regarding divorce rates, America and Hungary are also similar. Both countries are experiencing approximately one divorce for every two couples who enter into marriage.

The recent increase in gang activity is new to Hungary as it is in many communities in the US. Laszlo Czendes, an officer in Hungary's Department of Crime Prevention and one of Hungary's leading juvenile gang experts, says that until the mid-1980s most youth gangs were driven by greed and survival (such as Gypsy gangs), not by violence. Since then, however, aberrant groups and gangs, such as occultic and skinhead gangs, have begun to form for the first time. He attributed this to the deterioration of Hungarian families, reflecting his professional counterparts in America. (He also noted that the number of gangs increased because the tight controls of the previous Communist regime have been relaxed or removed, providing youths with greater freedom to assemble. For example, in the fall of 1992, skinhead youths protested near Parliament during the celebration of the 1956 revolution against the Soviets.[15])

Recognizing these similarities, it seemed that it would be immensely helpful to discern if the *same root-factors* were operative in each country. For this reason, I spent a significant amount of time in 1992–94 in Budapest, a city of over two million—just to see if such factors existed. What I discovered mirrored my findings in the US. Particularly enlightening was a survey I conducted of Budapest skinhead gang members from different gangs. Their profile affirmed the American profile of a gang member.

Hungarian Profile

Before I left on a 1992 European lecture tour, I sent faxes to social scientists and law-enforcement officers, seeking their assistance in obtaining the above-mentioned survey. Each responding fax wished me luck with my venture, but couldn't offer any assistance.

Getting in close range to these kinds of secretive and unpredictable youths, whose groups are constantly mutating, is difficult and can be dangerous—let alone getting straight, candid answers to survey questions. So when I failed to obtain the survey, I wasn't surprised. Still, I was disappointed because such a survey might confirm the profile I had developed in the mid-1980s.

Dr. Maria Kopp, head of the Department of Psychiatry at Budapest's Semmelweis Medical University, is one of Hungary's foremost social scientists. She not only conducts extensive research, but she is also a practicing psychiatrist, permitting her direct and regular contact with the kinds of people she surveys. I asked her if she knew of any European studies identifying the family profile of skinheads. She said, "No, but such a study would be extremely helpful."[16]

The next year, in February 1993, I presented a lecture to a group of high school teachers in Budapest, affectionately called the "Paris of the East." I made known my desire to make contact with a skinhead group. One teacher said she might be able to help because she had reliable contacts with skinheads from various gangs. When I left Budapest two days later, her requests were rebuffed. A few days later, much to my surprise, I received a small, soft-green, plain-paper notebook. On its cover was neatly written: *Hungarian Skinheads*. It contained answers to my questions . . . with some careful prodding, she had succeeded.

Surprisingly, fifteen Budapest skinheads from several, different gangs agreed to be surveyed with the condition that only their first names be used. What wasn't surprising was that thirteen of the fifteen *matched* the US gang profile.

The questions the fourteen males and one female answered were:

1. Name
2. Age
3. Number and ages of siblings
4. Age span of those in your skin group?
5. Number of members in your group?
6. Attire common in your group?
7. What is the status of your family?
8. Why did you join your group?
9. Do you know anyone who left your group and why?
10. What else are you interested in?

Here is a summation of their candid responses, which often mirror the kinds of responses received from American youths engaged in similarly destructive gangs.

- **Number /Ages of Siblings**—One-third had none. The rest had 1-6, ages 2-21.
- **Ages of Gang Members**—13-21. One was 27.
- **Number of Members in Each Gang**—8-10. Two had larger numbers of 25 and 32.

- **Attire**—Black leather jackets, chains, buzz hair cuts. The attire, accouterments, style, and attitude seem cross culturally homogeneous. Most Amercan skinheads at that time dressed similarly.
- **Family Status**
  —Divorced parents: 8
  —Parents separated: 2
  —Live with abusive alcoholic uncle who beats him (parents dead): 1
  —Physically abusive or severely dysfunctional parents (such as alcoholism): 2
  —Only two of the fifteen described their family life as "ordinary."
- **Why They Joined the Gang**
  —Hatred of Gypsies and "foreigners": 7
  —Hates Jews, Gypsies, and Blacks: 1
  —Wants to form Nazi party: 1
  —Idolizes Hitler: 1.
  —Wants to be a "faithful soldier of the German Empire": 1
  —Patriotic feelings: 1
  —Wants to fight for something good: 1
  —Thinks skins are "good people" and "doing it right": 1
  —The only girl surveyed responded that her reason for joining was because her boyfriend persuaded her to join.
- **Who Left the Gang and Why**—The most common reason that gang members left their gangs, as noted by seven of the youths, was that their friends got married. In a sense, a legitimate family replaced the illegitimate. Four of the youths stated that they didn't know anyone who left their group. The other responses ranged from "he didn't take the group seriously" to "three left when they were 24-25."
- **Other Interests**—Three youths said they "liked to talk about anything," reminiscent of Marlon Brando's line in the fifties film, *The Wild One*. An old man asked, "What are you rebelling against?" Brando shrugged and mumbled, "Whadda yuh got?" The following responses tally more than 15 because some of the youths had more than one interest.
  —Girls: 2
  —Films: 1
  —When the Nazis were in power: 2
  —Cars: 2
  —Death: 1
  —Likes to torture people or talk about doing the same: 1
  —Future: 2 (the only female respondent in the survey gave this as her sole answer)
  —Nothing: 1
  —War: 1
  —Weapons: 1

—Sex: 1
—No response: 2 (one didn't respond and another said, "I don't like to discuss or have an interest in anything")

Further Evidence from Poland and England

A week after the survey was completed, I interviewed one of Warsaw's first skinheads (circa 1983), Kuba Belok, now a twenty-seven-year-old statistician. Kuba came from a divorced home and each member of his gang was also from broken or severely dysfunctional homes. His story is recounted in chapter 10. Additionally, University of Warsaw sociologist, Barbara Fatyga, interviewed over 50 different skinheads during the early 1990s with the same profile observations.[17]

While in England in January 1994, I inquired about gang activity. Those most talked about were football (soccer) gangs, which are discussed in detail in chapters 8 and 14. I inquired of the leading social scientists in Great Britain, but they didn't know of any studies that sought to identify the family background of those in football gangs. As in the US, most of the academic discussions focused on *socioeconomic* factors. University of Aberdeen sociologist, Richard Giulianotti, an expert on football hooliganism, said that he wouldn't be surprised, however, if the same profile applied to many, if not the majority, of the teenage football hooligans.[18] I was fortunate, however, through the efforts of Tony Henry, a school teacher and now a student at the University of Greenwich, to locate and interview a former gang member, Ivan Rock. Ivan said that the fellows he ran with also came from broken homes. His story is recounted in chapter 8.

While none of these interviews or modest surveys by themselves can be considered scientific, when coupled with the observations offered by professionals who work with youths, it's difficult not to come to the conclusion that the profile identified here is not a universal one for youth gang involvement. Even in India, one nurse who frequently interacted with youths noted that over 75% of the youths in gangs came from broken homes. Again, although anecdotal, the same consistent profile is observed.

To summarize, virtually every youth whom I have interviewed over a period of seven years and the observations of social workers, juvenile officers, sociologists, etc. in ten countries point to the same profile.

PERSONAL REFLECTIONS

When I first started investigating affluent youth gangs, I didn't have a clue why they were forming. In fact, I had never formed an opinion about why inner-city gangs were growing. I assumed, due to media reports, that economically depressed living conditions breeds gangs. This opinion changed, though, when I actually interviewed affluent gang members and noted the same common profile. I then contacted experts who had worked with inner-city gangs for their input. I thought perhaps my observations were unique. They weren't. Most who had dealt with inner-city gangs said the family background of a typical inner-city gang member was common knowledge.

When there is severe trouble at home, common sense dictates that youths are more likely to experience depression, become more rebellious, or hang out with the wrong crowd. A parent's worst nightmare. While not all youths necessarily react in this manner, it's predictable that if the number of youths from severely ruptured/broken homes increases, so too will youths who will be adversely affected. Needs such as love, trust, nurturing, guidance, security can all be undermined and even drive kids who don't have a severe rebellious streak to acts of rebellion and even gangs.

(In fact, it is extremely common for corrupt power figures such as cult figures—David Koresh and Charles Manson—and dictators—Hitler and Saddam Hussein—to possess the same profile. Even a majority of fraudulent faith healers, for example, possess this same predictable profile [this observation is based upon my research of such individuals extending back to the mid-1930s]. For some people, a severe upbringing exaggerates what might be considered lesser forms of illicit behavior, such as lying, thuggery, and thievery. For these individuals, a severe family upbringing magnifies their behavior, deviant need for control, etc.)

Those who are confronted with gangs for the first time often ask: "Why are gangs *here*?" The progression of gang formation and growth as it affects at-risk youths usually follows something like this: When there are just a few at-risk youths in a community, like in the 1950s and early 1960s, some will rebel but without much cohesion as they feel isolated. Increase the number of at-risk youths and you'll start to see "rebellion" in a "pack" context. Allow a sustained at-risk environment for a prolonged period of time and rebellion takes specific shape and context, which can result in gangs. When gang activity is unaddressed and grows in proportion to chronic numbers of at-risk youths, then gangs become institutionalized—membership is passed down father to son. This results in greed-driven structures (rather than just an outlet for rebellion). Gangs are now immeasurably difficult to dismantle. When institutionalization continues, the stage is set for the desire to manifestly control, which naturally reflects itself in the desire to affect political institutions to further gang agendas.

In order to prevent gangs from forming in an environment in which nearly 50% of the youths in America could be classified as at-risk, gang prevention strategies must directly address the predictable profile for youths involved in gangs.

A word of caution, though . . .

Most youths who match the profile never join a gang, commit crimes, or display violent behavior. A difficult upbringing isn't necessarily synonymous with destructive behavior. Criminal behavior can't be excused with "my parent made me do it" defense. A parent(s) may share responsibility for the *magnification* of rebellion in a youth's life, but the parent is *not* responsible for the rebellion itself. It is the youth who decides to rebel and not the parent. Acknowledging a youth's family background cannot be used as an excuse to commit crimes. Many youths experience family hardships and use their tragedies as motivation never to repeat their parents' failures and/or sins. One obvious explanation for this is simply a function of character. One youth chooses to endure one's inequities within the bounds of the community; others don't. Another reason might be attributed to one's tolerance of pain and how one handles fear.

Still, when initiating prevention, intervention, and even sentencing strategies (when a youth has committed a crime), if one doesn't take into consideration the gang member profile, such strategies are likely to fail. Youths who commit crimes in a gang context do so, in part, because they want to belong to someone or something. It's a need and desire all youths have. Yes, a rebellious youth can commit crimes even if he/she grows up in a stable home. But most youths don't join a gang unless the primal needs that a family is supposed to provide are ruptured.

Regarding the profile of a gang member, another question should be raised: *Is there another factor that, when added to the family profile, might accelerate a youth's desire to join a gang?*

The answer is "Yes," and this factor was identified in a definitive survey conducted by Dr. Maria Kopp—the subject of the next chapter.

CHAPTER 7.

The Missing Protector Factor

Some rebellious youths who fit the profile detailed in the last chapter join gangs while others don't. For the majority of those youths who do join a gang, there appears to be one other factor that, when added to the family profile, prompts gang engagement. Over 75% of the gang members I have interviewed stated that this factor was operative in their lives. Conversely, I observed as a lay volunteer that directly addressing this factor in the lives of over 400 Dallas County inner-city youths provided a vaccine against gang enticements over a period of six years.

What is this factor that seems to tilt the balance in at-risk youths towards gang involvement? It is called the Missing Protector Factor. It was first identified by Dr. Maria Kopp and sociologist Arpad Skrabski in a definitive study of 21,000 Hungarians (1,635 were ages 16–20, representing 0.2% of that age group) in 1988 and later published in their book, *The Hungarian Mind* (1992).

MISSING PROTECTOR FACTOR IDENTIFIED

Against the backdrop of the world's highest suicide rate for teenagers, Kopp and Skrabski sought to uncover the primal factors that increase a youth's risk of committing suicide or pursuing other destructive behaviors, such as drug use, gangs, criminal acts, etc. Kopp reports in their book, and in subsequent interviews I had with her in 1992–94, that the most compelling factor that increases a youth's risk factor for the above is: *When a youth cannot count on an immediate family member during a crisis.*

This means that when a youth is faced with a crisis, a family member is unable or unwilling to act as a protector—or there are no family members present, due to abandonment, foster care, etc.

For practical purposes I have dubbed this the Missing Protector Factor (MPF).

According to their survey, Kopp states that the MPF can also become operative if a youth cannot call upon *any* adult or mature sibling when faced with a crisis. The effect of this factor was almost as important as the effect of the lack of family support. She offered this opinion based upon her hands-on clinical work as a psychiatrist who regularly sees a broad cross-section of patients.

Kopp says that when the MPF is operative, a youth's fears and anxieties can be gravely magnified, which, in turn, forces some youths to seek escape, solace, or relief elsewhere. She observes that this can lead to hostility and apathy (an absence of future life goals) which often spawns harmful behaviors, including gang involvement. Kopp's and Skrabski's research reveals that the MPF is more likely to appear in homes that are broken and unstable than those that are whole and stable. Kopp states: "If the parents live together, neurotic and depressive symptoms are less likely than in those families that are separated or divorced."[1] She also states that the MPF can appear in homes that are severely dysfunctional, but have not experienced divorce or separation.

Specifically, the Kopp and Skrabski survey revealed, as detailed in *The Hungarian Mind*:

- Of the 1,555 youths (ages 16-20) surveyed, 22% expressed that they couldn't count on an immediate family member or extended relative or friend in a crisis. This virtually coincided with the same 21% who experienced some form of depression, neurosis, expressing itself through "suicide, drug use, gang and cultic involvement, criminal acts. . . ."[2]

- Youths who can count on a parent during a crisis are more likely to have future life goals, complain less of anxiety and melancholy, are less likely to attempt suicide and have less hostility to the environment, consume significantly less alcohol and commit fewer crimes.[3]

- After the age of 20, a youth does not seem to be as vulnerable to the MPF, probably because a youth becomes more independent.[4]

- "Frequency of criminal convictions for a youth is almost solely tied to the [family protector factor]."[5]

- A person from a home that has experienced divorce or depression is *twice* as likely to be at risk of some form of depression as those who are from a home that has not experienced divorce and where a husband and wife live together.[6]

- Poor financial conditions by themselves do *not* typically cause clinical neurosis or depression.[7] (During a February 1993 interview, Kopp expressed that this is also her experience with those who engage in gang activity).

- Youths perceive the following individuals to provide the most to the least amount of influence as a "protector" in a crisis: 1. Immediate family 2. Extended relatives 3. Friends.[8] (This seems to negate the popular notion that "peer pressure" is a more powerful input in a youth's life than family and parallels a 1994 survey in which only 10% of American youths said that they were under "a lot of peer pressure,"

23% said "some," 41% said "not much," and 26% said "not at all."[9]

Regarding depression, the Kopp and Skrabski study revealed that families that experience mild dysfunctions, but which are intact, are less likely to spawn depression. The total number of individuals from intact homes who experienced some form of depression was only 5.5% of the population, while those from broken homes were almost *three times* more likely to experience depression. The statistical breakdown of those who experienced depression in the Hungarian population was as follows:

- Married and spouses living together 5.5%
- Divorced but spouses live together because of financial
  considerations 13.5%
- Divorced and spouses not living together 14.6%
- Separated and not living together 16.8%

THE MISSING PROTECTOR FACTOR AS A CATALYST

Gang leaders often play off the MPF, voicing a common theme to potential recruits: "Don't worry. We'll take care of you. We understand you. We'll be your family." Gangs in America and abroad capitalize on and exploit this anxiety, of which Kopp writes:

> Arousing anxiety is one of the most important instruments of tyranny. Arousing anxiety is a weapon used not only by dictatorial societies, but also by the dictators of the family, school, workplace or organization. The essence of anxiety is the inability to actively control situations perceived as threatening—the experience of this lack of control and the inability to avert the impending threat causes this (arousal of anxiety).[10]

My personal observation is that at-risk youths who have the predictable family background *and* for whom the MPF is operative are those most likely to be snared by gang enticements promising resolution for their anxieties and fears. For example, a youth who is from a divorced home, but who can depend on a parent, sibling, or outside adult for help in a crisis, is less vulnerable to gang activity than a youth from a similar home environment but who has *no one to turn to*. As already noted, approximately 75% of the gang youths I have interviewed responded that they have no protector at all. (This observation should be qualified by acknowledging that potential "protectors" might assist if called upon, but separation by physical distance and other strategic problems could inhibit a youth from seeking their help. In other cases, an adult may simply have never let a youth know that he/she would be such a protector, thus it doesn't even occur to a youth to ask for assistance.)

The concept of the MPF squares with the fact that divorce and separation are the primary factors that gang youths share as a family-factor. Obviously, if one parent is absent from the home, there is a greater chance that a youth won't have an immediate family member to turn to in a crisis. Additionally, if a family member is severely dysfunctional or a youth is being abused, but the family is still together, there is a greater chance that a youth will have a parent or responsible sibling to turn to for help.

A 1994 Louis Harris Poll co-sponsored by MetLife and the US Chamber of Comerce Center for Workforce Preparation, even noted a correlation between youths who have been victims of violence and parental input in their lives. The survey, which interviewed over 1,000 parents and 2,500 students in grades three through twelve, noted: "those who have been victims of violence are more likely to believe their parents cannot help them (29%), that adults do not understand their problems (47%), that they will get into trouble (22%), and that their parents are not interested or are too busy to help them (17%)." Clearly, for nearly 50% of these youths, the MPF appears to have been operative in their lives.

To summarize, when the MPF is layered onto any of the factors in the family profile of a gang member—divorce, separation, abuse, or severely dysfunctional parent—escalation of a youth's vulnerability to gang activity significantly increases.

SOLELY THE MISSING PROTECTOR FACTOR?

With the rising number of at-risk youths and gangs, a reasonable question is: Are we likely to see increased incidents of at-risk youths encouraging youths from *stable* homes to join gangs?

To date, this hasn't been a commonly observed phenomenon. It is likely, however, that the Missing Protector Factor operating alone could be present in a youth's life who joins a gang. Consider the following example.

In 1994 in Boca Raton, Florida, Detective Ebeneezer Palkai observed an unsettling trend. A small but identifiable number of youths from intact families living in $250,000 homes were joining gangs.

"None of these kids were from broken homes or where there was abuse," Palkai stated.

"But both parents were working trying to keep up with the Joneses and the kids were out running loose."[11]

When asked why he believed these youths would join a gang, he stated: "We have middle-school kids—six, seventh, and eighth grade—being bused fifteen miles to other neighborhoods to go to school." He noted that affluent youths were being bused to communities that had gangs and some gang youths were being bused to areas that hadn't previously had gangs.

This combination had frightened youths who didn't feel they could go to the principal or school security officer when they needed protection from being beat up by gang members.

These youths had told Palkai: "What am going to do when I'm on the bus ten, fifteen, twenty minutes and I'm being pounded? No one is going to protect me."

Palkai adds: "And when they get off at some bus stops, [these kids] got other gangs pounding on them. And so they think, 'Enough of this bull, I'm going to protect myself. I'm going to join a gang. Dad's working. Mom's working. There isn't anybody to protect me. No one.'"

Fortunately, the scenario that Detective Polkai observed is not common in the US. Youths from homes in which none of the at-risk factors are operative typically don't join gangs. In Boca Raton, however, these youths did share the Missing Protector Factor. When faced with an external threat they didn't feel there was someone to call upon for protection. For these affluent youths, both parents were working—not to survive, but rather to increase their stature. Divorce, separation, abuse, or severe clinical dysfunctions weren't present in these families, rather the absence of parental care that said: I will be there for you regardless of whatever it takes. In affluent communities, this is one potential trend that should be watched closely.

THE ECONOMIC FACTOR: IS IT A FACTOR?

When considering the protection of a youth, economics naturally comes to mind. Regarding the *initial formation and appearance* of inner-city gangs, many have assumed that economic deprivation was the key factor. This has been a serious misconception. Economic deprivation is not a dominant factor when gangs *initially* appear and form in a community.

In the inner-city, depressed economic conditions produces fewer employment opportunities, substandard education, deficient youth facilities, and so on. Because of the obviously depressed conditions in which most of these youths live, it has been a common mistake to assume that money will fix the problem. The conventional wisdom on the subject has been: youths act a certain way primarily because of their economically depressed conditions. The Kopp and Skrabski survey, however, demonstrated that depressed economic conditions by themselves do not increase a youth's risk factor. This is also my experience having worked directly with many inner-city youths.

Economic conditions no doubt make a bad situation worse. Some youths want to exit a gang, but can't because leaving would bring them harm. A manifest solution is for a family to move to another neighborhood, but most are unable to do this because they lack funds. For other youths who lack education, the gang gives them their only source of revenue, albeit it's illegitimate income.

Simply put, though, most youths I have worked with can deal with holes in their tennis shoes, cold nights, and slim diets, but harmful fears dominate many when there is no one to nurture and protect them.

What brings the family factor into even sharper focus is that gangs are forming for the first time in American communities that *do have* economic stability. Youths in affluent communities joining gangs attend good schools and have access to all kinds of youth facilities and school activities. When there are economic pressures on a stable home—or any other kind of adversity for that matter—families are often brought closer together as they struggle against their dilemma. This deepens the bonds of the family. This was common during the Great Depression and even during the recent recession in the mid-1980s.

For affluent youths who match the predictable profile and are inclined towards gang activity, money may slightly *slow* the growth of gangs in a community, allowing youths to buy more distractions—everything from movies to drugs. But financial means in affluent communities can actually fuel gang activity, providing the means to buy more drugs, exotic gang raiment, and CD's of music groups and concert tickets that reflect what they think and feel. Money can also provide more mobility so that youths are freer to recruit youths from *outside* their neighborhood and meet in isolated locations far away from their own "hood." An example is the convergence of the skinhead and occultic gangs in North Dallas, noted in chapter 5. It is unlikely that these youths, who lived as far as twenty miles apart and met at a music concert, would have met had they not had the money and means to buy tickets and travel to the same concert.

Economic deprivation, however, does play a significant role in the *institutionalization* of gangs. That is, once gangs have rooted themselves in a community, the lure of easy money and the desire of an established gang to spread out to new territories becomes a driving force. Unchecked greed gives rise to organizations that keep gangs structurally potent. Allegiances are set up to protect financial interests, ushering in infrastructures to support illegal activities. As noted in the Chicago example cited in chapter 4, the Gangster Disciples have sought to develop a political base from which they can influence city officials.

It is vitally important for affluent communities to recognize the distinction between what initially causes gangs to form and what causes them to become an institutionalized, structural force. Currently, gangs are not the menacing over-powering force they are in inner-city communities. Preventative strategies can be implemented that will derail gang growth, but only if the primal factors are addressed. Effective use of funds and resources can help, but my experience is that nothing is more powerful than addressing the MPF in a youth's life.

THE MISSING PROTECTOR FACTOR AND GANG PREVENTION

Gang activity is unique in that crimes are committed in a *group* context. It is different in its form and substance from youths who choose to commit crimes solo. Youths in gangs have a powerful desire to belong to a supportive group. For many, crimes committed are just a part of the package and not a central focus.

There doesn't seem to be a sure-fire method for predicting exactly when gangs will appear in a given neighborhood. The consistent factor, though, is when there has been a critical mass of family deterioration for a period of several years. In countries that have been governed by totalitarian regimes, their repressive nature often inhibits any type of groups from forming, including gangs. Thus, the appearance of gangs may be forestalled, or limited.

The only strategy that I have found that will deter most at-risk youths from joining gangs in an open and free society is to address directly the MPF. That is, identifying protectors for these youths at an early age, before they reach puberty, and sustained monitoring until they finish high school. I believe that the reason 400 Dallas inner-city youths whom I worked with resisted gang activity was because we let them know that whenever and wherever they needed help, we would be there for them. They could call us anytime, night or day. It wasn't a "mentoring" program because we didn't have enough manpower to give each youth *individual* guidance on a regular basis—although this would have been preferable as one could aid youths in their development beyond just providing a safety net of protection. We found it more difficult recruiting mentors versus *protectors* because mentoring requires a greater investment of a volunteer's time in order to guide a youth in all areas of their life.

These youths did, however, trust that we would be there for them if they had to face a crisis, thus neutralizing a gang's exploitation of the MPF. Of all the ideas presented in this text, the strategy for addressing the MPF in chapter 20 is the most important for those affected by gangs to consider and implement. As already stated, it is the only strategy/program that I have encountered anywhere in the US and Europe that will work long-term and broad-based in any community—affluent or urban.

———◆———

We've examined the root source of the affluent gang problem: ruptured home lives and the MPF. Now let's examine in chapters 8 and 9 what youths expect to get from a gang once they join. What they want is not what most people think. . . .

CHAPTER 8.

Ivan Rock: Football Hooligan

Gooooooners! Gooooooners! Gooooooners!
—The chant of an English Arsenal football hooligan.

While the match ensues on the pitch—the green turf—and players battle to kick the ball into the opposing goal, football hooligans have their own match or battle in the stands. They call it "taking the end." Football hooligans—gangs of youths and adults that follow soccer clubs—infiltrate the area just behind the opposing team's goal—the terraces, where people stand and don't sit in assigned seats. The hard-core fans and opposing team's hooligans are usually there or in the middle.

With stealth, they push and elbow their way through to occupy enemy territory. They don't wear their team's colors, which they usually wear and cherish. Only the dads and sons do that. Once ensconced, a loud, booming chorus of voices cries out their chant . . . *"Gooooooners! If we, get beat, we're ripping out your seats!"* When violence doesn't erupt, "taking the end" amounts to territorial invasion without violence; a mild parallel to an inner-city turf war. If their club loses and they are in the mood, they will indeed smash seats and throw them onto the pitch. This is "life" for a football hooligan.

In America, soccer is considered a *nonviolent* sport—fast, wide-open, and pastoral. Most families are initially exposed to soccer through organized, suburban leagues for elementary school children. Few moms and dads are concerned for the safety of their children, and certainly not for the safety of the spectators. Americans are never frisked by police before entering a stadium to watch a professional *soccer* match. That's why it seems odd that gangs in Europe would form around such a nonviolent sport, especially when it's compared to bone-crushing football and hockey.

In Europe, football (as soccer is properly called) is a *passionate* sport. Part of the lore of English football of centuries past was the sight of hundreds of people in a town kicking a ball a mile or more through streets into a neighboring town's goal. Football hooligan gangs are a recent development in this century where youths and young adults—some may be as old as thirty-five—attach themselves to a football club and commit weekly mayhem. Sometimes it's just a shoving match with rival hooligan gangs supporting their teams. Other times, people, including innocent bystanders, are severely injured, maimed, or killed. One British club (Manchester United) resorted to banning its own fans from attending a match in 1984 held in Turin for the Cup-Winners Cup.

Hooligan gangs usually restrict their criminal activity to assaults—they bloody someone's nose or break a bottle over someone's head. But they also touched off terrifying *mob riots* that resulted in scores of injured and killed per incident. In England, it's common for families to choose to attend rugby matches, a far more violent sport, because it's a safer option for the fans. Football hooligans never do this. The most common type of European gang member never attends rugby matches. Only football. (An expression often used in Britain is: Football is a gentleman's sport played by hooligans and rugby is a hooligan's sport played by gentlemen.)

Football hooligan gangs are heterogeneous. You will discover a mix of working class, affluent youths, young adults, and older members who are white-collared professionals. For the gang, their *team* is treated like the neighborhood street of inner-city gangs. The team becomes their turf. When their club travels to another city, the hooligans travel with them to protect their turf. Many travel by train for each away game and rioting often breaks out in "grands" (English term for train station). When I was in Poland, Switzerland, and England, I witnessed several times the menacing presence of these gangs. Each time it was a Saturday and the locales of each melee were different. Sometimes it occurred in a train station. Other times, it happened in a trolley car or a charming platz. Bill Buford, who spent considerable time among hooligan gangs, wrote: "It was one of the things you put up with: that every Saturday young males trashed your trains, broke the windows of your pubs, destroyed your cars, wreaked havoc on your town centers."[1]

The menace posed by football hooligans can be seen throughout Europe, and it's also the kind of gang that could easily develop in affluent, American communities because it involves rallying around a weekly contest where someone wins and loses. It's cut and dried, clear-cut, without ambiguity. You win or lose and your gang responds accordingly. It's instantaneously reactionary with *immediate gratification*. If you win, you taunt the opposition's gang and try to instigate a fight. If you lose, you actively look for a fight to vent your anger.

I'm not suggesting that soccer gangs specifically will develop in America, but something like it could, particularly when disaffected, affluent youths have money to burn.

Although the following story takes place across the sea, it captures the heart of what drives youths who are in affluent gangs better than anything

I've encountered in the past six years.

Ivan Rock will pull at your heart. He is without guile, and his story will cause you to remember someone in your own neighborhood.

"Hooligan" is a peculiar word to Americans. We think of the old Soviet regime labeling political dissidents as "hooligans," an archaic label for troublemakers. In Europe, hooligan is rarely regarded as being archaic. It's a term both feared and loved. (The word *hooligan* was derived from a "noticeably antisocial Irish family [the Patrick Houlihan family] in nineteenth-century east London."[2])

Ivan was a football hooligan who followed Arsenal, an English club nicknamed the Gunners. The Arsenal hooligans called themselves the Gooners—another English slang term for "a hired thug." Always the underdog, Ivan's family attached themselves to Arsenal because they were the closest club. The Rock family lived in Stevenage, a London "overspill" twenty-five miles north of London. It's a working class, nonslum community where the government in the fifties and sixties offered people a job and a house if they moved out from London.

For Ivan, football was not just an outlet. It was life itself.

"I went to my first Arsenal game when I was five, and I started playing organized football when I was seven."

"What was your most memorable experience as a young player?"

"I love scoring goals. I was a center forward. A striker. Every goal I scored was a good moment for me. When you go to battle, and you battle hard, and you win, and you score the winning goal, that was good for me. Once, I scored the winning goal at the end of a match. The feeling was one of passion."

"What was life like at home?"

"My parents split when I was six. My mother walked out because of abuse, so we [sister and a brother] *were taken to a refuge* [home for battered wives]. *There were six families there. Then we moved to another home where there was just one family. My best mate also came from a broken home, Ian. He's an alcoholic who also used to run with the Gooners."*

"What was the greatest pain you felt as a kid?" Ivan, now twenty-five and a university student at Greenwich University in London, looked off into space. There was nothing to distract him in his campus apartment. He felt safe here. Arms folded, a gritty lump formed in his throat. . . .

"When I was five, my father had a fight with my mother. He had her down on the floor. She cried for me to go get the neighbors. Every time I'd start to get up, my dad yelled at me: 'Sit right back down. Don't you move.'

"I couldn't distinguish between what was right and wrong.

"What your parents do is always supposed to be right, when you're that age. So you think your mom needs help, but when your dad is threatening you as well, you don't. That memory still haunts me and is one that I'd like to put right with him."

Ivan went to school until he was sixteen, then he apprenticed as a precision engineer at British Aerospace. (Many young people finish Senior School, ages 12-16, and then pursue a technical or trade career. This often encompasses on-the-job training as well as additional education, which Ivan later pursued at the University of Greenwich, where he was interviewed in 1994.)

Life before Greenwich was Arsenal for Ivan. He buried himself in the team, the first and only club his father took him to see. From the time he was ten until he was twenty-one, there was only one club, one life.

"I became a regular when I was ten. It was just a passion. I made money running milk and newspaper routes and I went to every home game. When I was thirteen, I traveled by train to every away game. Every week, I spent all I'd earn— over 2,000 pounds a year [three thousand dollars US].

"Your whole week would be geared up to going out to seeing Arsenal. It became rather like a religion. And anyone who said anything about Arsenal, it was against what I believed in and therefore it annoyed me."

"But why become so immersed in Arsenal? Why not something else?" The sturdy, well-built former hooligan with tragic roots, responded with conviction.

"Arsenal was the only thing that was permanent for me. I could go to Arsenal every week and stand in the same place, amongst the same people every week. We even had friends from Essex who stood next to us every week. Do the same things every week. Ate the same foods. We used to go to a chip shop just outside the grounds and we could ask for our 'usual.' We wouldn't see this bloke for two weeks because we'd be home and then away. But we could ask for our 'usual' and he knew what we wanted. It was the same turf and the same rules. Arsenal was stability.

"That was why if people started to take a dig at Arsenal, they were taking a dig at me. I took it personally. And as I got a bit bigger, I found I could change how people spoke about the club," he recalled with a charming wink of a smile.

Although Ivan wasn't the most violent of hooligans, he did enjoy a good fight with opposing hooligans.

"Did you ever carry feelings about your home with you to the grounds?"

"I never thought about my home when we went to see Arsenal. Arsenal was good. It was a good feeling. You didn't think about s— like that. You think about the good things. You're going to have a drink. Sit with all the people that you like. It was good. There was no revenge in it.

"If I was going to fight with somebody else, it wasn't a revenge attack against them or my dad. I just hated fans who supported other teams because they were against Arsenal, which was everything that I believed in. And what I believed in was Arsenal and their cause. They're the team to win. So if we lost, it ruined my week until the opposing team lost. To see goals scored against us gave you aggressive rushes because they were going against you.

"*People in football are blind to another teams' abilities. They only talk about their own team. You never watch what the opposition is doing. Only your own plays. If the other team attacks you, you don't watch the attackers, you just keep watching to make sure you can see the goal. There is a real bias. You make sure your players aren't illegally infringed upon. You don't care about watching what happens to the other team. Rugby fans aren't like that. They appreciate other team's abilities.*"

"Were you part of the inner-core of the Gooners?"

"*I wasn't a gang boss, top leaguer, top man, or a top boy. I just ran with them. When I was thirteen, I was too little to fight. But I knew the faces and who to watch for. I'd be out on the fringes. There are a lot of people right along the out-skirts. As soon as the going gets tough, it looks a bit heavy, you're on your toes and you're off and on your way. Just running along got your adrenaline going. It made you feel that you were safe, but at the same time you knew that you were in a dangerous situation. Not only did you have to watch out for the fans, but you had the police as well to avoid. It's like a dangerous game of run-out or tag. It was a game. But you didn't run away or you'd be laughed at as a joke and be disregarded the next week.*"

"You never fled another gang?"

"*Well, yea, a couple of times when I was young. My first game away was Arsenal versus Brighton. I ducked off into a sweet shop when the going got tough! It was the nearest thing that was open at the time! Another time Gavin . . . we called him the 'statistician' because he knew all the crap facts, useless information, but he was a good boy who was an engineer at British Aerospace as well . . . we got jumped by some West Ham fans. The fight lasted uniil we could run to a church until we could be picked up.*"

"How did you know where to meet or what to do when you took an end?"

"*Leaflets were passed out days in advance for a major operation, otherwise it was just word of mouth. Sometimes we met at a pub. Once, a couple of hundred of us crowded into Millwall's* [another team] *pub, and the police locked us in there to stop the trouble!*

"*For most of us football hooligans, there is more threatening behavior and body language than actual fighting. A lot of 'eye to eye' stuff. By the time you get near, the police are there and they have dispersed everyone. There've been times when I've actually been thankful to see the police!*"

———————◆———————

May 26, 1989—one of the greatest moments in all of sports history. The perpetual underdog, Arsenal, pitted against Liverpool for the First Division Championship. Liverpool had dominated the League for fifteen years and this was the English equivalent of the Super Bowl. This match was the equivalent in Britain of combining Babe Ruth's 60-homer season, Michael Jordan's "unconscious" shooting during the 1993 Bulls "three-peat," and Cowboy quarterback Roger Staubach throwing his "hail Mary" pass to Drew Pearson all rolled into one frenzied moment. The last time Arsenal beat Liverpool in Liverpool was in 1974, when Ivan was only three.

"In all the years I had been going, I had only seen Arsenal score just once against Liverpool. We didn't have a prayer. I was trying to sell my ticket, but no one would buy it. That's how worthless the ticket was that day. I've got friends who didn't go to that game and still have the ticket. It was on a Friday night, which meant you had to take off from work and waste a Friday night going out. There was no question that Liverpool was going to win."

Ivan sat directly behind Arsenal's goal. Millions of television viewers across England saw him—a bright splash of yellow, waving his red Arsenal scarf. He wore his "colors" that day because he wasn't trying to "take an end." Arsenal had to win the match by two goals, an almost impossible feat in a game where only two to four goals are generally scored by *both* teams *combined* in a game. American football scores often have scores of more than thirty-five points. In English football, 2-1 is a typical score. To win by two goals against the League's most formidable opponent on their own home turf was as likely to happen as "a trip to Mars in a row boat."

As the match unfolded, Arsenal made its legion of fans delirious with hope. They were keeping Liverpool scoreless. Remember, football is a passionate sport. Because there are few scores during a game, the crowd is incredibly tense. When a goal is scored, unlike basketball or football, the emotional release is explosive, almost ecstatic. Imagine that scoring one basket counted for *fifty* points. Then one can get an idea of the tension that builds in a soccer match as teams jostle and spar across the pitch. The game itself is all-at-once and vitally dynamic. There's always something happening, unlike the linear game of baseball where the pace is slow and pastoral, and where ten minutes can be chewed up changing pitchers.

Entering the final minute of play, Arsenal was ahead 1-0. Then . . . on the last kick of the game, in the last minute of the game . . . Arsenal buried the ball in Liverpool's net and scored.

"There were tears everywhere and things just went mad!" Ivan gushed, remembering, smiling.

The Arsenal-Liverpool game is often relived as one of the greatest moments in sports history. English writer, Nick Hornby, wrote: "I ran straight out of the door to the off-license on Blackstock Road; I had my arms outstretched, like a little boy playing aeroplanes, and as I flew down the street, old ladies came to the door and applauded my progress. . . ."[3]

It meant something different for Ivan. Arsenal's victory contributed to his withdrawal from football hooliganism.

"I went to the opening game the next season and it was just rubbish. It had no

meaning because we had achieved the ultimate. The game just paled in such insignificance, and then fighting broke out in the next game. I was twenty-one and I thought, 'This was crazy. I'm going to get hurt.'

"I had the same feelings to stand up and fight for Arsenal, but the game was irrelevant. I did care how Arsenal got on, but I didn't have the same kind of passionate feeling. But I was still against everyone who was against Arsenal. My feelings weren't so much for the love of Arsenal as the hatred of everyone who was against Arsenal. I lost the love and just hated everyone else. I was fighting for the wrong reason.

"Looking back, I can see why I gave up running with the Gooners. First, Arsenal had achieved everything and anything else paled. Second, I started playing football, which helped me disassociate myself. I was spotted by Stevenage Borough, a semi-pro team, and I played for them on Saturdays when I was twenty-one. I didn't have time to go to see Arsenal. And third, it was getting to a stage where it was getting dangerous, legally dangerous. It was more likely that I might be arrested. I didn't want to get myself into a lot of trouble and ruin my future. When I was younger, we were running around. We knew we weren't going to get arrested because we weren't causing any trouble, we were just running around. Now that I was older, it was different."

"What would you do to encourage a teenager today to stay away from football gangs?"

"I'd tell him not to do it and to be careful and stay out of trouble. Fighting is a pointless exercise. If you carry on, you're going to get hurt."

"Would that have worked with you?"

"No!" he said with a boastful laugh and a wide, boyish grin..

"I was blind to it. There is nothing that would have dissuaded me. You must have something else to rally behind." [4]

In current law-enforcement lingo, Ivan was a "wanna-be" football hooligan. He wanted to be part of the action. He would willingly risk a fistfight or two, but he didn't want to be isolated where he could be maimed or worse.

For Ivan, the Gooners was a mask for the pain he carried inside. Literally, his Arsenal kit—a jersey and pants with a price tag of up to ninety pounds ($150)—made him feel special. The Gooners was also his distraction from his pain: Preparing for each week's row with the opposition was diversionary. Matches took his mind away from his circumstances and gave him something to anticipate and fantasize about. The Gooners was also his power device over his pain: He gained esteem—albeit illegitimate—from his peers for his decision to face the unruly mob. He could defiantly stand up and take his chances. He could bury the childhood memory. Sitting where his father told him to sit, immobile and afraid, while he watched his mother being beaten.

There is another quality of the whole hooligan ritual: It's a symbolic home, a substitute affiliation that fills a familial void. It was Ivan's surrogate family.

After returning home from a trip, we don't say, "I'm family." We say, "I'm home," because we are returning to a place that is safe, secure, and where love is unconditionally expressed. The "bloke" who served Ivan his "usual" chip dinner was like a family member who remembers your favorite pie, movie, or favorite sweater. He was a guy who cared enough to remember, because Ivan was important. The entire Gooner persona and its environs was home to Ivan. It was more than recognition. Being a Gooner was a tacit bond, a psychic state where affection and being with those who cared about you seemed to exist; and this for Ivan, like all youths, is something desperately sought and needed.

Kids want to feel safe, even though they desire independence. And they want excitement—to be at the epicenter of what's hot and happening. Being a football hooligan created for Ivan the illusion that he had all these things. But, alas, there was a dark side. What looks like wild, crazy, full-tilt fun can be *fatal*. Ivan knows and understand this now. That's why he abandoned the "life" and forsook hooliganism. On April 15, 1989—just six weeks

8.1. University of Greenwich, London, England, 1994. Ivan Rock, former football hooligan displaying his Arsenal regalia, including flag, scarf, jerseys and posters. Photo by Dan Korem.

before Arsenal upset Liverpool—more than ninety Liverpool fans *died* in a thrashing riot in Sheffield when Liverpool played Nottingham Forest. It sent a nation into deep contemplation. It was a heartrending reality-check. The riot made Britain reexamine a problem that had been callously building. The British magazine *The Economist*, that week wrote: "Britain's football grounds now resemble maximum-security prisons, but only the feebleness of the regulations has allowed the clubs to go on pretending that crowd safety is compatible with prison architecture."

Thankfully, Ivan Rock was spared a tragic fate. He escaped his football hooligan days with a few good stories and a healthy sense of what's real and important. Today, he is finishing his engineering studies at the University of Greenwich in London, and *plays* in an organized football league on the weekends.

CHAPTER 9.

The Payoff: Three Cures
Youths Seek

I van Rock wanted to escape from painful memories and he also wanted excitement. Nobody can blame him for that. We can easily see how Arsenal provided excitement, but what did the Gooners *specifically* do for his pain? The focus of this chapter is to identify explicitly what youths expect gangs to do for their raging turmoil. This is invaluable information when attempting to disengage a youth from a gang or when discouraging a youth from joining a gang. To begin, let's look at some parallel examples from the early 1980s.

A MARCH OF EMPTY FACES

Time: 1983. A T-shirted teen with torn jeans pockets trailed behind his parents as they shopped in the Olla Podrida, an upscale arts and crafts mall in affluent north Dallas. It was an odd match: casually attired, comfortable, down-home suburban parents with a despondent-looking youth in tow. There was an implicit "story" in his body language and the way his shoulders slumped and his vacant eyes looked at nothing in particular. His left ear glinted. With closer scrutiny, anyone could see ten, small safety pins impaled along the outside rim of his ear. These pins stood out against his shaved scalp (except for a center strip—a jet-black Mohawk, explosively teased upright.) His parents moved along comfortably, oblivious to the third-party casualty that trudged behind. They were a surreal trio.

When the youth was out of earshot of his parents, a stranger approached and diplomatically asked the boy, pointing at his pins, *"Please don't take offense, but tell me what these mean."*

The fifteen-year-old lifted his eyes and considered the question. He knew it was straightforward and aimed at something *meaningful to him.* *"They say that I am in pain,"* he replied. He wasn't referring to the momentary pain he felt when his ear was pierced ten times, but to his internal, roiling anguish. It was deep and constant, a migraine of the soul.

He replied to my question in the spring of 1983, the same year President Reagan labeled the Soviet Union "an evil empire"; Polish Solidarity union leader, Lech Walesa, received the Nobel Peace Prize; the US Marine barracks in Lebanon were bombed, killing 241 American soldiers; and astronaut Sally Ride became the first American woman in space. The youth with a migraine of the soul seemed oblivious to such a changing world around him, and his short, plaintive reply resonated in my consciousness. It seemed a consonant, repetitious cry of youths across the land—a rarely uttered, pitiful, mournful statement of being. And it was my first experience with what would become a torrent of dramatic cries by youths, each a slight variation of *"I am in pain."*

A few months later at a computer store, I asked the owner, *"How are things going?"* No small talk followed. Instead she confessed that her daughter was wearing black dresses and wildly spiked her hair, dying it purple.

"Do you get much time with her?" I asked.

"Are you kidding? I don't know where she's coming from. I can't wait to get to work and put in a twelve-hour day. It's the only peace I have."

That same year on the evening news, a Briton in his late teens was asked why he liked punk music, a violent forerunner of heavy metal music.

"We have lost our hope," he said, his eyes looking like the teen in the mall.

From Moscow in 1987, *New York Times* foreign correspondent Bill Keller observed the same expression of youthful despair. During the maturation of *glasnost* to *perastroika*, Mikhail Gorbachev's first-wave initiative to create a new Soviet society with stronger ties to the West, Keller wrote:

> On the stage of the Maxim Gorky House of Culture, beneath a red banner urging all good citizens of the Soviet Union to "fulfill the decisions of the 27th Party Congress," Anatoly Krupnov, the lead singer of Black Obelisk, is howling out the lyrics to "Disease." Bare-chested except for a guitar and chain, he struts through a cloud of artificial smoke. Below him, crowding the stage, ecstatic teenagers punch the air. Gloved fists and spiked haircuts twitch in the strobe lights as Krupnov bellows:
>
> *People are burning, their souls on fire!*
> *A march of empty faces.*[1]

Not all youths express themselves or identify with this fatalistic corner of the youth culture, but many do. Their numbers are growing, and many of these burnt-out youths are filling counseling clinics across America. Since the mid-1960s, disenfranchised youths have used drugs, alcohol, and other devices such as image-rich violent music to deal with their internal anxieties, fears, and insecurities. Then in the early eighties gangs in affluent communities was added to the list.

A well-intentioned, but incorrect misconception is that the sole *foundational* reason that youths join a gang is that they want a family. Gang members often state this and so do those who work with gangs: street ministries, juvenile officers, and teachers. In fact, this was my assumption for about a year. It seems to make sense: youths from wrecked homes want a family. They want something to replace what they don't have. This is only part of the story because there is something even more primal that youths seek from gangs. Even more basic than a family.

What most of these youths are consciously or unconsciously seeking is a release from pain—pain inflicted from an unstable home. And specifically, they hope that a gang will provide one of the three antidotes to their pain:

- Mask for their pain
- Distraction from their pain
- Empowering device over their pain

When youths say they join gangs because they want a family, what is meant is often not the same as what is heard by adults. Yes, many want a surrogate family. But more importantly, they want release from their internal angst brought on by a ruptured home. They want permanence, not the anxiety of not knowing who will take care of them. They want to know that they are important to others, not the isolation brought on when families explode apart. Yes, they want a family, but it is more than just a desire to belong to a group.

If there was no distress involved with the shattering of a home, it is unlikely that most youths would join a gang. Andy Kriz, in chapter 3, wanted self-respect and a sense of self-esteem that failed to be nurtured in his home. He wanted power over his pain. This doesn't excuse his crimes, but it does cut closer to what he was after: a release from pain inflicted by a lack of self-esteem. Added to this, he piled on greed, thinking that if he had more material possessions than his peers—clothes, stereo, able to eat out any time he wanted—he would be something in his and everyone else's eyes. If he had grown up in a stable home with typical nurturing, love, discipline, etc. he could still have chosen to be greedy, but he probably wouldn't have chosen to express that greed in a gang. Rather he might have expressed his selfishness in the same way that other youths do: lack of sharing, taking something that wasn't his, etc. An unstable family, though, is just the magnifying catalyst needed for some youths to express their selfishness and greed by committing crimes in a gang context.

Identifying that youths want release from pain is one of the most important ingredients in preventing gang involvement, helping a youth disengage, and rehabilitating those who commit crimes to become law-abiding and productive citizens. Why is it important to recognize that it is pain that is driving most of these youths? Because when developing an antidote for the affluent gang problem, the antidote must address the core factors that are driving the problem.

When helping youths resist gang activity, those who intervene must drive home the point that the pain antidote that youths hope to get from a gang is a lie. It doesn't work. Yet, pain is one of the most powerful forces that urge a youth to buy into a lie. Pain is an even *greater* motivating force than greed. Greed is when we want to *get* something for nothing. Pain is when we want to get *rid of* something. Buying into the lie can't be excused, but it must be acknowledged and reckoned with.

The three ways that youths, like Ivan Rock, typically try to deflect their misery is by using the gang as a *mask* for their pain, a *distraction* away from their pain, and an *empowering device* over their pain. In all three cases, youths eventually find out that the gang is a lying antidote and one that cannot be trusted, but not until the damage is done to themselves and others. In chapter 17, we will examine the eleven predictable reasons why youths disengage from a gang by utilizing the knowledge that there are three predictable payoffs—antidotes—that they are seeking. Chapter 18 reviews how to use this information in order to disengage a youth from a gang. This information can also be used by youths themselves to discourage their at-risk friends from joining a gang. For now, let's examine the three antidotes youths seek.

THE MASK DEVICE

With a mask, we can do two things:
- We can pretend we are something that we aren't.
- We can hide from others those things we don't want them to see.

Masks can be used positively and negatively.

After surgery, medication is used to mask discomfort. After a stressful week, some people like to get dressed up and go out as a way to ease the pressures of the week. At costume parties, masks are a way to have fun and forget the cares of the day. Superman's ridiculous disguise of glasses to appear to be Clark Kent and the Lone Ranger and his mask were both fanciful escapes for television viewers in the fifties.

A negative example of a mask is an insecure person's consumption of alcohol to present an illusory front that he is the life of the party. Another example is the consumption of steroids to exaggerate one's actual physique.

Cultures isolated from each other all over the world have developed facial and other types of masks since the beginning of history. In the story of Adam and Eve in the Garden of Eden, fig leaves were used as a mask to hide nakedness. Masks are a common device used to hide behind something when we are afraid or feel threatened or inadequate.

For some youths, gangs are the destructive mask that promises relief from excruciating anxieties. The masking device is typically made up of the visual persona of a gang and gang activity.

Here is a partial pictorial inventory of the visuals currently in vogue and often associated with a gang's masking device:

- **Hair**—shaved scalps and spiked styles in a myriad of colors (though a youth can also adopt an average style)
- **Caps**—professional sports teams
- **Unique Attire**—black leather jackets, jackets of professional sports teams, Doc Marten boots (big, black, and clunky)
- **Vehicles**—to be a member of one skinhead gang you had to ride a red moped
- **Tattoos**—These can vary from icons that represent the gang to symbols that become a part of the gang persona, such as swastikas, occultic symbols, etc.
- **Bizarre jewelry**—from skulls to crystals to a specially designed insignia
- **Hand signals**—communicate everything from a gang's name to specific words
- **Language**—secret passwords, etc.

For gang members these visuals provide a visible mask behind which they can hide, cultivating a false sense of belonging and security. If Dad is abusing you—verbally or physically—in the gang you can pretend you're tougher. If you're feeling afraid because no one's home, the gang provides the façade—the illusion—that you're safe. The gang as a mask provides a false sense of self-esteem. At meetings, there is a twisted sense of order, knowing to whom you belong. On the streets, gang members bust heads, showing people how tough they are. Acts of gang intimidation, coupled with the physical appearance of a gang member, make people fear you; you think you are something.

It must be reemphasized that youths don't typically realize at a conscious level that they are seeking power over their pain, anxieties, and fears. Teenagers are not usually in touch with these kinds of abstract thoughts. For that matter, neither are many adults. Andy Kriz thought his gang's activity was fun, acting as a numbing device for what was really raging inside. Only when the gang activity turned deadly and he was incarcerated did he realize that the gang only worsened and didn't improve his condition.

To help youths who are at-risk of involvement or who are already enlisted, the mask must be stripped away and revealed for what it is: a lie. A mask doesn't ultimately fix the home, their fear of the streets, or their lack of self-esteem. Creatively, it must be demonstrated that the mask of a gang is a glorified con game that doesn't work: it's for people who want to bow down to a lie—who have a craving for deception.

If a youth is in a gang for the mask antidote, then those who are trying to reach that youth must attack the problem from *that youth's perceived antidote*. That is, focus on strategies that provide that youth with constructive activities that amplify self-worth, discipline bad behavior, and communicate insight that will give him the opportunity to develop a sense of accomplishment, self-discipline, etc. He must be instructed to love transparency in a person and hate concealing deceit. To help make the connection in a youth's mind, point out examples of other harmful masks that are not gang related but which he/she can realize are only for those who love a lie. Drinking, drugs, a person who puts on false airs trying to impress others are some of these.

In a word, help a youth by exposing the mask for what it is; direct a youth to replace it with acts of character that won't be afraid to face whatever life dishes out; and instill in the youth a sense of self-worth nurtured from those same acts of character.

THE DISTRACTION DEVICE

In day-to-day life, distractions take our mind off our personal woes: music can soothe; books transport us to another time, land, or circumstance; coming to someone's aid takes our mind off our own problems; attending a play, movie, or ballgame, lightens the day's load. Some distractions relieve small pains, like daily stress from the office. Other, more intense distractions, like a good hard run, help us to relieve the stress of a toe-to-toe argument.

Many youths join gangs as a distraction from the turmoil they feel inside. Attendance at gang meetings, practicing gang hand signs, "hanging out" with gang members, taking drugs and alcohol, chasing girls, and committing crimes can all be a part of the distraction package. In short, the gang distracts the mind from personal misery, acting as an escape. The gang as a distraction device fills the void of idle time, lack of hobbies, interests, goals, focus, and direction. The distracting activities of the gang provide youths with a device to avoid being in touch with what is really going on inside of themselves. It's kind of like youths who turn up the volume on their stereo to drown out their problems; while others watch TV nonstop for hours.

Unless there is something to *replace* the gang's distraction device, disengagement from a gang is difficult. No one wants to live with internal torment. Youths need things to engage their energetic days positively. To combat the distraction device, hobbies, a job, time expended doing homework, or involvement in a youth church group can all be effective ways to positively neutralize the distraction device.

THE EMPOWERING DEVICE

It's natural to want an antidote for brutally discomforting circumstances. We want internal or external power to deal with threats from someone or something. In gangs this desire is warped and can become deadly.

Amy, who joined The Satanic Cult (chapter 3), hoped the gang would teach her how to have power over her assaultive father. In the inner-city, youths join gangs for protection from the whims of the streets. In most skinhead and occultic gangs, youths act on the lie that by hating and exerting power over others—preferably isolated ethnic groups, which are easy to identify—one becomes powerful and important. Then one can bury one's own self-perceived insignificance or impotence.

The desire for an empowering device can also be expressed more subtly. The gang promise that "we understand you and will take care of you" in the absence of parental love and attention is very alluring. For some youths, the gang really is the first group that shows them attention, listening to and living through their day-to-day experiences. Andy Kriz (chapter 3) called his gang Down For Life because he wanted controlling power, a commitment that those in his gang would be together in mind, body, and spirit "even after we get older and retire." For Ivan Rock (chapter 8), running with the Gooners overpowered the vicious memory of being told to sit, while his father beat his mother. With the increased numbers of youth who come home to an empty household because one or both parents are working, the power-over-something lure can be tempting. (Nearly every youth poll since 1992 has indicated that over 50% wished their mothers didn't work and would be home to greet them when they returned from school.)

One student from a broken home gave the following rationale why she wore gang symbols as an empowering device.

"I don't know. To scare people I guess. People are just pretty much fed up with the people, with society in general. They just want to scare people. You know?"

"So gang symbols say: 'Keep your space'?"

"Yeah. That I'm mad at you and I can't believe that you would do this to me. Because if you really ultimately think about the generation that we have right now—the way that the adults treat us—it's pretty damn sad. And I think it's mean. Like when you think that there are a lot of men that run out on their wives, leave their kids. I mean, I have friends whose parents get stoned with them. What kind of thing is that? A lot of people, they throw their kids into institutions left and right. So I mean there's a lot of parents who don't care one way or the other about anything. People getting married four, five, six, and seven times and then expect their kid to do well in school. And then don't care about anything. My Mother's

not like that. You know?"
"What about your Dad?"
"Well, my Dad used to be. He's not like that anymore."
"You really don't think he is?"
"No. My Dad is nice now. He is very nice."
"Do you think he's changed?"
"Yes, I do. He has no money anymore. I think that's good. [Pause] *He used to have a lot, but he has none* [Long pause]. *He went bankrupt."*

This teenager saw the gang and its symbols as a way to pretend that she could have power over the source of her pain—a broken home in which her father was never around.

To engage youths who think gangs will give them power over their pain, the following must be done:

• Identify the *root* source of the pain.
• Point out immediate examples of those who also thought the gang would provide the power burst, but failed.
• Guide youths to those ways that one can legitimately deal with the source of their pain.

HOW THE PAYOFF TRANSLATES INTO GANG BEHAVIOR/ACTIVITY

There are four basic classifications for gang behavior in affluent communities—also applicable to inner-city gangs. They are:

• Social
• Thrill-seeking
• Delinquent
• Violent/Hate

Social—Not every affluent gang member will necessarily turn violent or commit crimes. Law enforcement across America has observed both occultic and skinhead gangs, for example, that commit few crimes. For these youths, gangs are a pop subculture venue to be different with friends who are like themselves. The temptation here is not to call them a gang, but rather a group of youths who are attracted to something which can become harmful. (The distinction of typing these groups as gangs must be retained, however, if crimes are persistently committed in a gang context.) Common expressions of social gang activity are: congregating together and "hanging out"; conducting meetings; and solely dating those of the opposite sex who are in the gang or who are at the periphery of the gang.

Thrill-seeking—Here, the emphasis is on doing something that is racy, on-the-edge—mischievous "fun." This is common in most gangs. In occultic gangs, for example, youths try to summon up hidden powers. In skinhead gangs, youths taunt those whom they claim they hate. In delinquent gangs, common expressions are drawing graffiti and "joy riding"—stealing a car for a wild drive or even setting it on fire.

Delinquent—In this classification a gang is focused on material gain through criminal activity.[2] This activity can include drug peddling, robbery, extortion, and even murder. Delinquent activity can be found in any of the three gang types identified in Section Three. It should be noted that just because gang members may buy drugs, doesn't necessarily mean that this is the primary activity of a gang. For example, a skinhead gang's primary focus might be ethnic hatred and violence, while the purchase of the drugs is simply to augment a gathering.

Violent/Hate—Behavior in this classification is manifested in a gang member who "seeks emotional gratification by way of violent behavior."[3] This activity can manifest itself in planned, target-oriented assaults against an ethnic group different from oneself or a rival gang. Taunting or criminal acts can also be spontaneous, fueled by too much to drink. Skinhead groups often manifest this type of behavior, but so can occult and delinquent gangs. In the future, violence and hate related crimes will probably increase or remain at unacceptably high levels, as indicated by escalating violence per capita among youth.

Which type of behavior is more dominant at any given time is likely to be determined by the degree of deterioration of local families. If families in a community, for example, become more stable and divorce begins to decline significantly, then within a few years gang activity will probably decrease and delinquent and violent/hate behavior will wane. In this scenario, social and thrill-seeking behavior will likely persist only until a new group of unaffected youths dominate the youth culture. If family conditions persist as they are today, then delinquent and violent/hate behavior will probably continue to escalate.

DEGREES OF GANG COMMITMENT

Four degrees of gang commitment have been observed in affluent gangs. While these degrees of commitment are also observed in inner-city gangs, the majority of affluent gang members currently embrace the second two degrees of commitment. Although the terms for these degrees have developed from the pop-lingo, they are useful when identifying a gang member's degree of commitment.

The terms for the four degrees of commitment to a gang are:
• Full-fledged
• Associate
• "Wanna-be"
• "Hanging out"

Full-fledged—This is a youth who has the highest degree of commitment to the gang activity, regardless of what type of gang activity the gang pursues. This youth is also likely to be the instigator of crimes and intimidation against those inside and outside the gang. In most affluent gangs, full-fledged members typically comprise 10% to 20% of the group. It is uncommon to find a majority to be full-fledged members. (The case of Andy Kriz [chapter 3] is an example of a full-fledged affluent gang member and Will Babylonia [chapter 16] is an example of an inner-city full-fledged member).

Associate—These youths have the second highest degree of commitment to the gang. Typically, these youths don't initiate the ideas to commit crimes and acts of violence, but easily become embroiled when trouble starts. These youths often like to intimidate those outside the gang, but without life-threatening violence. One tactic is simply to surround others and taunt. It is common for 30%-50% of a gang to be made up of these youths. (The Grapevine, Texas case, detailed in chapter 11, is an example where the majority of the youths were "associates.")

Wanna-be—This slang term, first used by law enforcement, characterizes youths who simply want to run along the periphery of a gang. Ivan Rock (chapter 8) was one example. These youths don't initiate crimes or confrontations, but are usually around when trouble breaks out, urging on their comrades or taunting the opposition. Aggression is often expressed through *subtlety*, rather than through a head-on confrontation. They are attracted to the visual raciness of the gang persona, but are afraid of committing violent crimes, and jumping into the foray of a fight. When they carry weapons, it is usually just for show.

Hanging out—This slang term, originally coined by gangs, specifies a youth who isn't in a gang, but who likes to "hang around" gang members wherever they meet and go. Shopping malls, homes, parties, locations near a school, music shops, etc. are typical locales for "hanging." "Hanging out" can act as a magnet for gang recruitment when observed by younger youths who want to join a gang (sometimes called "peewees") or at-risk youths who are new to a neighborhood.

PERSONAL REFLECTIONS

Unrelenting pain is exactly what it says—it hurts and it isn't pleasant. Helping a youth in pain can be equally painful. It isn't easy. It takes time, patience, and one-on-one attention. The fact that a youth is in this vice, however, *doesn't* relieve his responsibility to observe the law. It's like the story of the twin boys who had an alcoholic father who beat his kids. One boy grew up and became an alcoholic and an abuser and the other didn't. When they were thirty, they were both asked the same question: Why did you grow up and turn out as you did? They both replied with the same answer: With a father like mine, what could you expect?

As stated in chapter 6, the "my parent made me do it" defense is unacceptable. So too is the currently fashionable "urban survival" theory. Here, defense attorneys argue that inner-city youths who murder unarmed victims can do so because of their own fears of being harmed. Members of the Black community in Ft. Worth, Texas expressed their outrage when this was used as a defense tactic in the 1993 slaying of two Black youths by another Black eighteen-year-old youth, Daimion Osby. The theory was preceived as a racial slur. Osby was tried twice. The first trial ended in a hung jury. The second trial resulted in a guilty verdict and a sentence of life imprisonment.

As youths who are struggling must find ways to release their anger and repair their lives within the bounds of the law, so too must the juvenile justice system continue to sentence creatively those who truly want a chance. And so too must individuals unselfishly give of their time in their own neighborhoods. When dealing with deep, intense primal pain, the healing process is always a long one. Here, there is no place for quick fixes, because there are none.

CHAPTER 10.

From Reggae to Skin

He was sixteen and liked reggae—melodic Jamaican rock music, Bob Marley style. Like his idol, a Black Jamaican who died an untimely death in 1981, he let his brown hair grow long, fashioning it into dreadlock braids. At school in his middle-class neighborhood, he was considered rebellious and was told to cut his hair. School officials didn't want to promote the "hippie" culture. Long hair equaled counterculture in his neighborhood, and there was no tolerance for youths who didn't conform.

Angry, the youth rebelliously complied, shaved his head, adopted the fashion of the local skinheads, and eventually joined a gang. His music of choice now focused on unmelodic and blaringly harsh thrash, punk, heavy metal and "hate rock" which he watched on MTV-like music videos smuggled in from the West. He swapped idols, shedding Bob Marley, a Black singing artist, for White fascists. Where would a youth make a switch in music, fashion, friends, and heroes? California? Miami? Chicago? Try Warsaw, Poland. The city where, in the winter, even the snow is gray and Poles quip that the sky seems barely lit by a 40-watt bulb.

10.1. Zurich, Switzerland 1994. Poster promoting a reggae concert—a music form still popular in Europe—with a Bob Marley theme. This music form first inspired Kuba Belok to adopt a subculture façade. Photo—Dan Korem.

In 1983 Warsaw was a dismal place for a youth. Most people lived in bleakly constructed Communist-built apartment buildings—thin-walled guaranteeing that neighbors heard all enthusiastic conversations. "Polski in a box," one Pole called his dwelling.

Two years before, Gen. Wojciech Jaruzelski declared martial law. So the streets were dull. The Soviet Union had threatened an invasion of Poland in response to the yearning for freedom fanned by Solidarity, the Labor Union started in Gdansk, and led by Lech Walesa. Under state control, the milicja (police) were harsh and thuggish, using water cannons and whatever else was necessary to quell protests and curfews. If you were sixteen, you wanted to do something more than just huddle in a basement, drink beer, and talk about your anger. You wanted to have fun. You wanted to make a statement about the futility of your future; you wanted your parents to forget the past.

Germany crushed Poland during the war. Everyone bombed Warsaw into oblivion. Then the Communists took over and everything turned bleak. With a one-liner, people joked: "There will come a kind of Spring that instead of leaves hanging from the tree, there will be Communists hanging down."

Skinheads in 1983 weren't much interested in politics: just music and a hatred of the milicja, politicians, foreigners that might steal your job, and, of course, Jews. But why hate Jews? They were gone. There were 3.3 million before the war; now only 4,000 in the whole country. Those that didn't flee, were rounded up and shipped to concentration camps like Auschwitz and Birkenau. But Kuba, whose parents were divorced, didn't think about any of this in detail.

"I wanted to be a skinhead as a romantic notion. We defied the milicja. Everyone hated them. The girls thought it was exciting how we defied the milicja. I didn't care so much about hating Jews. I was too young to protest, so I resisted."[1]

All teenagers resist and rebel—even if modestly. It's time to begin moving towards being an adult. For a youth in Warsaw in 1983, this had a special meaning. There was the usual testing of parental authority. And then there was the "resistance" of the milicja, affectionately called The Gestapo, Polish-style. Young and old across Poland, wore small electronic resistors, less than an inch in length, on their sleeves—some youths wore them as earrings—as a show of defiance towards the totalitarian regime. Rebelling was fashionable, and for some youths, fun.

Thin and energetic, with a slightly nervous edge, Kuba was a guitarist, who easily flashed warm jovial smiles. Another youth wanted him in his band. Some of the hate rock music they listened to inspired unbridled hate.

For Kuba and his friends, just listening to and playing hate rock, though, wasn't satisfying enough. From lively discussions over beer, they decided, with four other skinhead youths, to do something even more thrilling: form their own government. Their model would be German: Führer, two advisors, Marshall, and Prime Minister. Kuba decided to let his friend be Führer. Why German? Weren't they the suspicious neighbors to the west who overran his country?

"We admired and followed the mechanism of the Nazis: they were very

orderly, powerful, well-dressed, and disciplined.

"I wanted to be patriotic, while having a good time resisting. But I wanted to be more serious than my friends. So I formed a political party that was informal, but with a sense of order."

Kuba wanted his small gang to be powerful like the milicja, but he abdicated the seat of power for himself.

"I wanted to be an advisor so if the Führer was caught, I'd be okay." Kuba was defiant, but he wasn't stupid.

They videotaped their meetings, discussed their political agenda and their distinguishing dress—red shoe laces and accompanying special knots. After a few months, the Marshall dropped out and attendance dwindled. Kuba and the Führer maintained their skinhead allegiance, until the skins from Łodz (pronounced: woodge), who knew the Führer, wanted to expand to Warsaw.

Łodz is an industrial city of one million, about one hundred and twenty kilometers to the south of Warsaw. The skins from Łodz—about 50, average age 16—weren't like Kuba. They really hated foreigners, especially Jews, who they said exploited Poles in the many textile mills they owned before the "cleansing."

10.2. Warsaw, Poland 1993. Kuba Belok—former skinhead (circa 1983) and now statistician for the Polish government.
Photo—Dan Korem.

"They were hooligans," Kuba remembers, an often used expression directed towards those bent on criminal activity. These skins were from poor sections of Łodz, and divided themselves into turf gangs. They organized and identified themselves by neighborhood and by the football (soccer) club their gang supported. They also distinguished themselves by the color of their shoe laces, like some American gangs. Step into their neighborhood or afront their football club, and bloody fists began swinging. Kuba didn't like the unpredictability of these menacing skins, who initially hated the milicja, but then focused their hatred towards foreigners. In Warsaw, a more cosmopolitan city, hatred of foreigners, such as Blacks, was not nearly as intense.

"I was scared when they beat people up and how it could get out of control. I wanted something that appealed more to

my ideals. The skins from Łodz were hooligans and not nationalistic types of people. The only reason they felt safe was because they could do anything they wanted."

Kuba became a skinhead, like many of his US counterparts, as a mask and distraction to *"impress girls and find a girlfriend, have friends to feel close to* [because he wasn't close to his divorced parents] *and to protest martial law."*

"I stopped being a skin," he recalls, *"because it wasn't fun anymore. I liked drinking beer and creating fictitious concentration camps where, in our minds, we sent the milicja, politicians, and anyone who tried to steal my girlfriend,"* he darkly joked.

But Kuba, like many US "associate" gang members, remembered, *"I was scared of getting hurt. I didn't like it when things got out of control."*

CHAPTER 11.

Youth Subculture ≤ Gangs: Similar Inspiration Points in the US and Europe

How Kuba Belok switched from reggae music and admiring a Black vocalist, to membership in a skinhead gang that took on its own brand of hate rock music as a coat of arms, is indicative of the youth subculture. It is fast-changing, fickle, and nearly always tied to music and the latest fashion. For Kuba, becoming a skinhead was first a fashion statement of rebellion, then a commitment to a gang. This is how trends often appear related to affluent gangs.

Music, fashion, and the current "rage" all stimulate youths and how they express themselves. There doesn't have to be a sense of logic attached to what draws youths, but what attracts them has to be *highly energetic*. Different, with an edge. For Kuba, living in Warsaw, reggae and the skinhead fashion were different relative to his Warsaw youth culture. In his mind, if he couldn't wear his hair the way he wanted, he'd take it to the *other extreme* as an act of protest. He'd shave his head. He didn't care about what it represented to others. He was too young to remember the terror of the Nazi regime. For Kuba, skinheads just represented something that school administrators and his mother were against.

Kuba had many counterparts in other countries at the same time. The simultaneous appearance of skinhead and occultic gangs in the early 1980s confounded many experts. The US, Poland, Austria, Germany, France, England, and even Yugoslavia all witnessed this spontaneous phenomenon. Many speculated that adult neo-Nazis were to blame for the *initial* formation and inspiration point for these gangs. Regarding occultic gangs, the theories abounded of adult satanic cults creating international networks. It was just too difficult for many to believe that youths *on their own* would form these kinds of gangs, never seen before in these countries.

As noted by sociologists and, more importantly, gang members themselves, the actual inspiration point for the appearance of each of these gang types and variants was the youth subculture, which included everything from new music forms and videos to new fashions to graffiti. What they each had in common is that they were all sensually driven.

In this chapter we will examine these inspiration points for gang activity and recent historical examples in America and Europe. Examples on both sides of the Atlantic will be examined because the youth subculture is influencing youths *in both directions*—some ideas originating in America, while others begin in Europe.

Identifying gang subculture inspiration points is very useful for those who interact with these youths. With this information we can:

- Identify specifically what inspires the context for each gang type and variant.
- More accurately predict future gang trends.
- Better relate to and interact with youths in the gang subculture.

SUBCULTURE INFLUENCES GANG VARIANTS

In the early 1980s skinhead gangs were popping up all over America and Europe, although in small numbers. In America this was an unprecedented trend. In Europe, the Nazi ideal was despised and feared, and in America, the political climate was far removed from that of a dictatorial state. Youths in these countries didn't have contact with one another, fueling speculation that adults were traveling throughout America and Europe recruiting youths to join these gangs.

It seemed to be a logical theory because the last time that fascism expressed itself through the Nazi ideologue in such countries as Germany, German adults directed its growth and recruited youths into such organizations at the Hitler Youth League. In the 1980s, it appeared unlikely that youths would decide on their own to form neo-Nazi gangs because youths typically rebel and do something that is different and apart from the past. They usually avoid associations with their parents' or grandparents' generation. But most youths in America and Europe formed their own skinhead gangs without adult supervision. Adult influence was a factor for some ideological hate gangs, but this influence didn't gain momentum until the late 1980s, *after* these gangs had already formed.

One example of a youth-formed skinhead gang was Kuba Belok's gang in Poland. It was isolated from a free flow of information because of Communism. He said that those in his gang were inspired to form a skinhead gang by the skinhead music—in both music video and audio-tape formats—imported from the West. Another similar example was former English skinhead, Nick Johnson, who joined a skinhead gang in the early 1980s. He too was inspired by the skinhead fashion, further described in chapter 13.

(It should be noted that not all skinhead gangs are racist or Fascist. Some are simply delinquent gangs that adopt the skinhead façade, as did Johnson's.) In America, similarly inspired youths also joined skinhead gangs, although most were of the ideological hate-variant type.

Paralleling the appearance of the skinhead gangs was the appearance of occultic gangs in America and Europe. This was also unprecedented and shocking. Disbelieving that youths could organize these type of gangs, there was much speculation that adult *conspiratorial groups* were recruiting youths, forming Satanic networks. Unlike the skinhead gangs, where adults tried to direct the activities of individual gangs *after they had formed*, adults never became a factor in directing the activities of these new occultic gangs— during or after their formation. As was true with the skinhead gangs, youths in these occultic gangs didn't have contact with youths in other countries. For many who studied these youths, it raised the same question: What or who gave these youths the idea at the same time to form this type of gang?

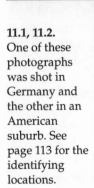

The answer was the youth pop subculture, which inspired *similarly at-risk youths* in America and Europe. This was done predominantly through music and fashion trends. Other inspiration points included such venues as magazines, concerts and rallies, spun off from heightened interest.

Before examining these influences in detail, it must not be assumed that subculture elements *by themselves* cause youths to join gangs. If music that espouses hate themes, for example, is

11.1, 11.2.
One of these photographs was shot in Germany and the other in an American suburb. See page 113 for the identifying locations.

"Danzig" in the lower right corner is the controversial German rendering of the Polish city of "Gdansk."

11.3. University of Greenwich, London, England 1994. Football fan who adopts a simple but decisive edge to his persona. Photo—Dan Korem.

11.4. London, England 1994. Spiked hairdo common among punkers in the US and Europe. Photo—Dan Korem.

played for a youth from a *stable home* that doesn't have a history of prejudice, it is unlikely that he will join a skinhead gang. But if the same music is played for an at-risk youth who is seeking release from internal pain, such a youth could be adversely influenced. This is evinced by the simultaneous growth of gangs in diverse cultures . . . and the fact that virtually all of these youths shared the same familial profile.

If similarly at-risk youths in America and Europe hadn't been *simultaneously* stimulated with the *same ideas* via the youth subculture, it is unlikely that skinhead and occultic gangs would have simultaneously formed in America and Europe. Youths in one country might have formed one type of gang, while those in another country or city might have chosen another context for their gang activity (if they chose to form any gang at all). For example, a gang in Nebraska might have formed a gang that spray-painted cows black, while a Hungarian gang might have chosen to slash tires in the shape of their initials.

The youth subculture has a *direct, dual* influence on gangs. The first influence acts as an inspiration point for which new gang variants form. This is particularly true of ideological and occultic gang variants. Only delinquent gang variants seem to *form* without significant influence from the youth subculture. For example, Andy Kriz's Minneapolis Gang and soccer gangs in England are both variants of delinquent gangs, yet neither variant formed due to influence from the youth subculture.

The second arena that seems to be influenced by the youth subculture, but which is more difficult to prove as a direct cause-and-effect relationship, is the potential for inspiring violent behavior.

Kenneth Lanning, a special agent in the FBI's behavioral science division, observes that some expressions of the youth subculture, such as music with overtly violent lyrics, contain "messages that are dangerous and anti-social when combined with displaced loners."[1] These manifestations of the youth subculture are clearly not a deterrent to criminal behavior, and for severely at-risk youths, they clearly have the potential for inspiring criminal behavior. With increasingly regularity youths tell of crimes they have committed inspired by long periods of listening to destructive music forms and viewing movies with mindless and exploitive violent themes. As a counterpoint, one never hears of gang members committing crimes after listening to Brahms or Bach.

Music

Music is often an *enhancer* of what youths feel, *mirroring* their energy level and their thoughts. In the 1960s and early 1970s, music that expressed rebellion typically shouted: This is what I think! In the late 1970s and early 1980s, the music shouted with even greater intensity and violence: *This is what I think and this is what I am going to do to you and what you think!* In the late 1970s and early 1980s, punk and skinhead dress fashions and music styles emerged from England. Thrash, hard core, and heavy metal music styles soon followed, emerging on both sides of the Atlantic. Youths in America and European countries adopted these new music forms.

Here are just a few examples of destructive music lyrics from the early 1980s that influenced youths:

Judas Priest

> Squealing in passion as the rod of steel injects
> (from "Eat Me Alive")[2]

Carnivore

> I sense that living human beings dwell below my feet
> an important source of protein you are what you eat
>
> ....
>
> broken splintered bones, boiling blood
> torn and bleeding skin
> blackened burning flesh melting fat
> amputated limbs
> eviscerated, lungs torn out
> heart ripped from the chest

decapitated, a meal of vagina and breasts.
(from "Predator")[3]

Suicidal Tendencies (a band)

Father forgive me
For I know now what I do,
I tried everything
Now I'll leave it up to you.
I don't want to live.
I don't know why.
I don't have no reasons,
I just want to die.
("Suicidal Failure")[4]

Slayer

I feel the urge,
The growing need,
To f— this sinful corpse;
My task's complete,
The bitch's soul
Lies raped in demonic lust.
(from "Necrophiliac")[5]

Venom

Sacrifice,
Oh so nice . . .
Sacrifice to Lucifer, my master.
Bring the chalice,
Raise the knife,
Welcome to my sacrifice;
Plunge the dagger in her breast,
I insist.
S-a-c-r-i-f-i-c-e . . .
Demons rejoice,
Sacrifice, sacrifice,
Name your price.

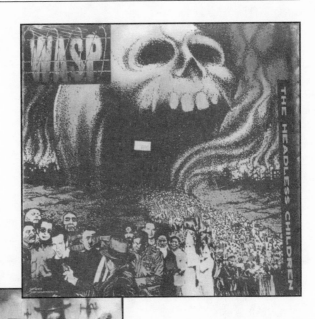

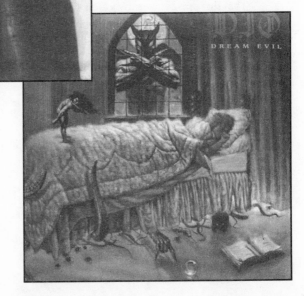

11.5, 6, 7. LP covers for US groups (circa 1980s) that display occultic and hate oriented motifs.

Here are some examples of groups that in recent years have lashed out with hate themes:

A CALL TO ARMS by Bound for Glory (a Minnesota based band)
Zionist illusions, state of confusions
Are decaying away my mind,
Feelings of hate, can't get it straight,
Am I the only one of my kind?

Massive inflation by the racial infestation
Has turned our streets to decay
Racial domination, swift termination
Has become the only way.

Close the border, start the New Order
Gather your guns, it's time to fight,
A call to arms![7]

SWASTIKA by Radikahl (German band whose name is a pun that combines the German words for radical and bald)
Give Adolf Hitler, give Adolf Hitler
Give Adolf Hitler the Nobel Prize
Raise the red flag, raise the red flag
Raise the red flag with the swastika.

Even as a boy, it was clear to me
That this symbol was my guide
And today I feel just the same
There's only one and you're it.

As on the German flags of old
It leads me down the right roads
For me, what matters hasn't changed:
Race and pride and swastika!

Everywhere I go you'll see it
Those who are different won't understand
There's no other sign that I like so much
Long may it wave for the entire world.[8]

WINTER IN THE F.R.G. (Federal Republic of Germany) by Endstufe (Final Stage)

Times are tough for the German people
Foreign troops still occupy our land
Forty years of calamity and corruption . . .

German culture—where is it these days?
We meet at a dump called McDonald's
Lust for profits and power poisons our environment . . .

It's winter in the F.R.G.
Will there ever be a Germany again
That's worth living in?

This tale is assumed of German history . . .
No matter what we say
The face of the government never changes . . .

We've got as many foreigners as grains of sand
Pimps, junkies—it's all forbidden
Believe me, Christians, praying won't do any good.

It's winter in the F.R.G.
Will there ever be a Germany again
That's worth living in?[9]

11.8. Budapest, Hungary 1993. Poster advertising the Hungarian heavy metal band, *Pokolgep*, which translates "hell machine," reminiscent of similar bands in the US and throughout Europe. Photo—Dan Korem.

11.9. Basel, Switzerland1994. Cross-cultural pollination of youth subculture trends is evident in both the US and Europe. Here, an older teen sports his *Metallica* heavy metal jacket—an American band. Photo—Dan Korem.

Rock-O-Rama, of Bruhl, Germany, was formerly the largest producer of "White power rock" in the world. In 1993, the German government began a crackdown on these forms of music, outlawing them and confiscating records, tapes, and compact discs. Rock-O-Rama had twenty-eight bands on its label, some of which have been under investigation for inciting racial hatred and related crimes or have been convicted of such crimes. The members of one such band, Tonstorung, "were sentenced for up to twenty-one months for inciting racial violence, including a 1992 attack on a Turkish wedding party after a concert in Mannheim."[10] Other such companies operating in other countries included: "Skull Records in Germany, Rebelles Européans in France, RAC Records and White Power Records in Britain, Resistance Records in Detroit and White Terror Records in Garden Grove, California." [11]

With the advent of modern media and technology, it has become possible for youths in diverse countries to hear the *same lyrics* and *see* the same groups via music video and MTV. (MTV is a music-video cable station based in New York, broadcasting worldwide music forms from pop music to some violent forms of what is called headbanger music, such as some heavy metal styles.)

Kuba Belok explained that he viewed music videos produced in the West via pirated music videocassettes brought to Poland. Some of these videocassettes he said were violent and humanly debasing forms of heavy metal broadcast into Europe via MTV and copied off the air. Researchers, such as Artur Kiviecien, a Polish documentary producer, have shown that the music culture was a key external force that provided the necessary catalyst for skinhead gangs to multiply initially in Poland.

Kiviecien, who produced a documentary on Poland's first skinheads, states that skinhead gangs emerged out of the punk style of dress and music in the early 1980s—similar to what happened in England during the 1970s. He said it took longer for skinhead groups to form in Poland than in Western European countries because Communism made it difficult for music and music videos to enter the country.

He observed that Poland's original skinheads were more interested in music, drugs, and parties than in politics. "Most skinheads," he added, "came from divorced, lower-middle-income families that had many children and common labor jobs."[12]

When MTV began broadcasting in Poland in 1988, Kiviecien said that the styles of youth subculture music that inspired youths to adopt skinhead attire accelerated, and music groups such as the Proletariat became popular in Poland. He and Kuba stated that this fueled the current increase of youths from more affluent Polish communities who have become skinheads—observing that today, a significant percentage of the new skinheads in Warsaw are from affluent families. Just a few weeks before my interview with Kiviecien, he said that he had only recently met a skinhead "from a wealthy family that had a huge villa."[13]

In Hungary, Maria Kopp also notes that during this same time period—the early 1980s—similarly at-risk youths were inspired by the music culture to form skinhead and occultic gangs.

Music media and music videos were the inspirational flashpoint that initially gave at-risk youths the idea or context of *how to rebel* and what type of gang to form. While music didn't always tell these youths *specifically* what to do in their gangs, music provided an ongoing, unifying vehicle so that at-risk youths were inspired to adopt a specific style of aggression and acting out. In some cases, concerts and music were the initial point of contact for similarly at-risk youths. Some of these concerts also acted as a breeding ground for acts of aggression, as evidenced by music forms, such as thrash, in which youths hurtle their bodies against one another, inflicting serious bodily harm. In the 1987 Dallas case in which skinhead and occultic gangs came together (chapter 5), the music factor acted as a magnet. It drew divergent groups of youths together who might have never met. What follows is a review of some important elements of that case.

POINT OF CONTACT

In Richardson, Texas, a north Dallas suburb twenty minutes from Carrollton, a counterculture music shop in the late 1980s tailored its selections to appeal to extreme subculture types. Skinheads, punks, hard cores, and youths in occultic gangs were common customers. Several youths I interviewed said that they were recruited into their occultic gangs through contacts made at the music shop. Some of these youths were reminiscent of Kuba, who first adopted the skinhead fashion when told he had to shave his head. They said that they first adopted the fashion of the counterculture, inspired by music videos they watched on MTV (and on videocassettes), magazines, movies, as well as what they observed others wear. Then they met similarly attired at-risk youths, who then recruited them into a gang, resembling how Kuba was recruited by the "Führer."

At the end of chapter 5, several questions were presented:
- The youths in the occultic gang weren't racist. Why would they hang out with youths who were?
- These youths were from completely different parts of town. Where did they meet? How did they meet?
- Was there a common identity that united them?

We know that their common identity was their family background—*the predictable profile.* The other questions were answered by Cindy, who liked to "hang" with the two gangs. She says that members of both gangs met at a rock concert that featured two different bands, which appealed to the tastes of the two different gangs.

"When we went to the concert," Cindy said. "The type of people that were there were into new wave music, like Depeche Mode [a band]. But there were also hard core people, like the skins, who don't mind Depeche Mode, but were there for the hard core act. Top Forty preppy kids were also there because they liked Depeche Mode."

In the late 1980s, new wave, industrial, heavy metal and hard core were in vogue and commonly shared depressive themes in their lyrics. Very different from the usual top-forty, they didn't often break into the top-forty unless the appeal was more diverse, like the song, "A Mind Is a Terrible Thing to Taste" by Ministry. Several youths associated with Cindy and those in both gangs described how they viewed each music style. Here is a compilation of their responses.

New Wave—More political and serious in its message—more beautiful and artsy; it's melancholia and desperation expressed artistically, not like rock and roll or heavy metal; a little bit like punk and a jagged form of rock with a little blues; lyrics may or may not be offensive depending upon the group and the particular song; new wavers like to wear black jerseys and black jeans and let people know they are artistic.

Industrial—Has a more high-tech sound; "It sounds like lasers;" has the same tone in its lyrics as new wave; attire is the same as new wavers.

Hard Core—Similar to heavy metal in that the themes deal with death, destruction, blood, suicide, and sex; discordant and not melodic; one new wave fan described it as "noise." "Punks," kids who spike their hair but are not violent like skinheads, are big fans of hard core.

Heavy Metal—Nonmelodic; a screaming sound; usually violent themes, such as hatred, death, suicide, victimizing women; skinhead attire and occultic symbols often part of dress for avid followers. Skinheads almost exclusively listen to this genre.

As a comparison, in hard core and heavy metal, the theme of *suicide* would be glorified and anguish expressed violently with reckless abandon. New wave forms would be more thought-provoking, addressing the same pain, but with greater sensitivity. Bands and concert promoters take these nuances into account, often combining music genres to draw a bigger crowd. The concert where youths from the occultic and skinhead gangs met packaged a new wave band with a hard core band as an opening act. Cindy's "artsy friends," who were more contemplative, came to hear the new wave band. The skinheads came to hear the hard core band that featured lyrics with guns and sex themes.

The connection between the youth subculture and what inspires at-risk youths is a consistent theme found in most *affluent* gangs. The harmful influence of extreme music expressions is what has led to calls for censorship in Germany. In America, MTV, in response to public pressure, has been more selective of the groups they broadcast, although the "Headbanger Show" (currently broadcast on Friday nights) is still considered by many social workers and juvenile officers to be too volatile to be watched by at-risk youths . . . if anyone at all.

As affluent communities are increasingly affected by gangs and violent expressions of the youth subculture, it is important that they discern the difference between a new subculture expression that doesn't inspire gang activity and those that do. One example took place in Grapevine, Texas, a northwest Dallas suburb, where the average price of a home ranges from $111,000-$187,000.

FASHION STATEMENTS

Doc Martens. They are a big, black, clunky-looking workman's boot that sometimes have a steel toe. They are the shoes of choice by skinheads. Manufactured by Griggs in the Northamptonshire village of Wollaston, England, *THE TIMES* of London, on November 6, 1993, reported that, "the British-made boots favored by punks, skinheads and other adolescents of both sexes—as well as just about everyone else—have briefly become victims of America's crusade to stop violence in schools."

Does this sound silly? Yes and no.

In England, most skinheads aren't racists. For most English youths,

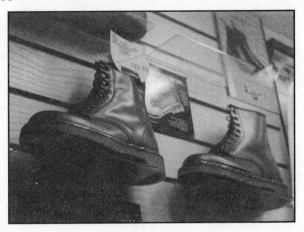

11.10. Cambridge, England 1994. A variety of the Doc Marten boot first worn by skinheads, and the subject of controversy in the Grapevine, Texas school district. Currently, Doc Martens are also worn as simply a fashion statement. Photo—Dan Korem.

dressing like a skinhead is a fashion statement. Nothing more. In America it has been a different story. Most youths who dress as skinheads typically identify themselves as bigoted against various ethnic groups. This differentiation between America and England was not commonly known by the British public; hence, their amusement with "America's" way of dealing with violence.

During the 1992–93 school year, racial trouble erupted at Grapevine High School. A number of youths adopted the skinhead attire, shaving swastikas into their closely cropped heads. An estimated 20-30 were described by police as "wanna-bes," while another half-dozen were avowed White supremacists. They were full-fledged members of skinhead gangs, and violence erupted on August 24, 1993.

Jonathan (his real name retained in court records) was threatened by a number of youths who came to his house. They wanted to fight. Many of these youths were skinheads. Jonathan, who is Black and typically nonviolent, testified that he had been previously threatened in face-to-face and over-the-phone encounters.

"They said they were going to kill me and rape my mother. They said they were going to rape me as well and burn crosses in my yard."

He fired one warning shot, then another, when one of the White youths, Martin Moberly (he insisted that his name be published in local news accounts) charged him. Moberly was wounded but recovered. On December 1, 1993, a jury cleared Jonathan of attempted-murder charges.

During the fall of 1993, several other incidents followed.

"There were other minor incidents where gangs 'got in the face' of a Black or Hispanic," according to Sgt. Sue Hanley of the Grapevine Police Department. "These took place after basketball and football games and in between classes at school." [14]

"The full-fledged skinhead gang members were from middle-income families. The rest of what we call 'associates' and 'wanna-bes' were typically very intelligent. They were very subtle about how they intimidated the ethnic youths—how they got in-their-face. Then the ethnic youth would lash out and the ethnic youth would get arrested. It wasn't fair, because the skins provoked the incident."

One incident, on October of 1993, did result in the arrest and conviction of Stephen K. Jarvis, 19, a self-professed skinhead. Jarvis, accompanied by ten other skinheads, made threats against two Hispanic and one Black teen who were with another friend, who was White.

On the heels of these incidents, the Grapevine-Colleyville Independent School District banned symbols of gangs, hate, and violence, including Doc Marten boots and Oakland Raiders football team jackets and hats. The jackets were often worn by other types of gangs. One city official thought that attire was being made the scapegoat, but many parents felt that this was a positive step in the right direction. Many of the 1,900 students disagreed and protested, which resulted in a revision of the dress code.

The school board adopted a policy that students could wear Doc Martens (of which there are many styles) and Oakland Raiders attire, but bandannas (often associated with violent inner-city gangs) and all steel-toed or military boots were not allowed.

By February 1994, tensions had abated. Sgt. Hanley observed, "It's died down now. The media is gone, the students staged their protest, and most of these kids [the skinheads] aren't really hard-core racists."[15] Regarding the school board's overreaction to banning all Doc Marten boots, she says, "You can't fault them for not wanting to encourage dress that identifies a gang, although it sure becomes easier to know who might be in trouble!"[16]

As in England, skinhead attire, according to teachers in Grapevine, is now principally a fashion statement and not necessarily an indicator of gang activity. However, because in America most skinheads typically have worn Doc Martens (up until 1993 they were the only students to wear this specific brand), it isn't unreasonable for local communities to take action to discourage gang attire. In Grapevine, bandannas were banned because inner-city gangs such as the Crips and the Bloods wear bandannas to signify their gang membership.

In the end, there is a balancing act between discouraging specific attire that identifies different gangs and unintentionally overreacting or creating a scapegoat out of a mere fashion statement. By acting prematurely, a *reverse reaction* can easily arouse youths who want to be different, but who aren't potential candidates for gangs. They might trumpet and cling to the "banned" attire simply to be different and rebel. Wisdom in these kinds of situations suggests that *before* taking action, inquiries should be made of those who most frequently interact with students, such as teachers. They can usually determine if a particular type of attire is solely linked to gang attire. If it is, then prohibiting such attire might be in order. If it isn't a substantive issue, then it is best not to take action, but continue to monitor the situation.

A final cautionary note: as Kuba Belok observed, "The idea for being a skinhead came from fashions you saw on the street and the music we listened to."[17] So it is the wise community that takes note when new fashions or music appear that have been similarly linked to destructive trends in other cities.

GRAFFITI

Intensification of graffiti in a community usually precedes gang activity. As far as graffiti is concerned, "John loves Mary" and "Lakeview Class of '94" obviously aren't a part of this discussion. We are looking for gang and subculture graffiti, extreme forms of personalization—a person's "I.D." The most common type today is called "tagging," and locations where graffiti is drawn is often shocking and highly visible. It's not just back-alley stuff anymore.

In Switzerland, for example, a country that traditionally has had little gang activity, graffiti is now found on beautiful buildings in commercial and upscale residential areas. This trend started just a few years ago. In 1992, I recorded in my journal that gang activity was probably not far behind. On returning to Switzerland in 1994, police officers confirmed that, although not chronic, gang activity in affluent communities was becoming more noticeable. (A very minimal number of skinhead gangs had been identified in the early 1980s, but was not a significant factor.)

11.11. Zurich, Switzerland 1992. Except for the language, this graffiti-filled wall is typical in appearance to non-gang graffiti drawn by US youths. The despondent phrase "ÄS GIT ÄS LÄBE VOREM TOD" translates: Is there life before death?
Photo—Dan Korem.

11.12. Zurich, Switzerland 1992. Young political dissidents defaced the beautiful city hall. Such practices, while akin to graffiti, are typically used to draw attention to a statement, rather than to mark out territory, common for gang graffiti.
Photo—Dan Korem.

Regarding the cross-pollinating influence of the youth subculture: While youths may embrace different music forms, individual youths don't usually create their own music. Graffiti is another matter. Youths create and draw their *own expressions*.

The photos in this chapter were taken over a period of two years in seven different countries, yet observe how it is difficult to distinguish in which country each graffiti was drawn. The graffiti on the flag first shown on page 99 and again below (PHOTOGRAPH 11.1), appear to have been scrawled in the US because of the use of English words, but the photograph was shot in the former East Berlin. The graffiti in PHOTOGRAPH 11.2, containing the German word *Danzig* appears to have been drawn in Germany, but was actually drawn by Dallas suburban youths who were members of the gang described in chapter 5. These two photographs clearly show the cross-pollination subculture effect now present between American and European youths.

11.1. Berlin, Germany (formerly Communist-controlled East Berlin) 1992. The English-speaking subculture influence is readily apparent here as an anarchist subculture group displays their flag in English. American youths in occultic gangs mistakening thought the anarchy symbol represented the "anti-christ," and used it in this context. Photo—Dan Korem.

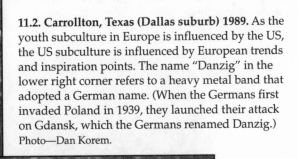

11.2. Carrollton, Texas (Dallas suburb) 1989. As the youth subculture in Europe is influenced by the US, the US subculture is influenced by European trends and inspiration points. The name "Danzig" in the lower right corner refers to a heavy metal band that adopted a German name. (When the Germans first invaded Poland in 1939, they launched their attack on Gdansk, which the Germans renamed Danzig.) Photo—Dan Korem.

Note the similarity and common use of the English word "skinhead" in PHOTOGRAPHS 11.13 and 11.14, shown below. The English language and the American culture presently have a powerful influence in youth cultures abroad. For example, the term "skinhead" originated in England, yet when this type of racist gang spread to Germany, German youths chose to retain the *English* word (as have youths in every other country) rather than develop a German translation of the word. In PHOTOGRAPHS 11.1, 13, 16, and 17 note the anarchy symbol, often used by anarchist gangs. In America, youths from occultic gangs mistakenly interpreted this as the sign for the "anti-Christ" and used it for this purpose.

11.13. Warsaw, Poland 1993. Skinhead and anarchist gang graffiti is displayed, including the names of two US subculture bands, *The Cure* and *Anthrax*. Photo—Dan Korem.

11.14. Belgrade, Serbia 1993. Although not a factor in the current war between Serbia and Bosnia, some skinhead youth gang activity was apparent. Note in this and in the one above the use of English words, which is common throughout Europe. Photo—Dan Korem.

11.15. Carrollton, Texas 1989. It is not uncommon for one youth subculture group or gang to mark over that of another. Here a youth first drew a peace symbol, adopted by one group of youths. Then some youths who later became skinheads drew a swastika over it. Finally, another youth drew a null type symbol over the swastika. *The Cult* was a popular subculture band at that time.
Photo—Dan Korem.

11.16. Budapest, Hungary 1993. Anarchist graffiti in one of Budapest's elite neighborhoods.
Photo—Dan Korem.

11.17. Salzburg, Austria 1992. Increasingly more common throughout much of Europe is garish graffiti in affluent and historical areas. Here, an anarchist subculture group left their graffiti in the serene Kapitalplatz next to the famous 12th century church, Dom St. Rupert.
Photo—Dan Korem.

Some of the common uses of graffiti in the gang subculture are:
• Identify a specific gang.
• Identify meeting places.
• "Tagging"—Here, a youth develops a personal identification mark, like a personalized logo. Although distinct, no one except himself and his friends know that it belongs to him. This provides a way for recognition without being arrested.
• Mark out and designate "turf."
• Provide a risk-taking activity—For many youths it is fun and racy to attempt to draw graffiti in a public place without getting caught.
• For some, it is an almost artful form of expression, particularly for secretive gangs that might leave elaborate graffiti in sewer tunnels, caves, etc. While this can apply to any gang type, this is especially true of some occultic gangs.

"Tagging" is one form of graffiti that has caught on in the last few years. It can be, but doesn't necessarily have to be, associated with a gang. Some youths "tag" on stationary objects, such as buildings and fences, while adventuresome youths do it on moving buses, trains, trucks, and cars. This can be dangerous and has resulted in a number of accidental deaths in America and Europe when youths have been run over. Interviews with taggers reveal that it is a fad that underscores a crisis of identity for youths. They are desperate to be known, but in a secretive way that is rebellious, while avoiding punishment. It's addictive. Most taggers are at-risk youths who are crying out for congratulatory slaps on the back from friends for the inventiveness of the "tag" and the number of tags a youth is able to leave.

When tagging is present in a neighborhood, it is wise to pay close attention because it is often indicates that the social fabric (family) is deteriorating and that gang activity is probably not be far behind. (Some communities, adopting a band-aid approach, simply attack the graffiti, leveling fines on business owners if they don't remove the tags within a prescribed period of time. This thinking is a tragic mistake. Yes, communities must address vandalism, but even more vigorously, individuals in a community must address the deteriorating family conditions that breed gangs.)

11.18. Zurich, Switzerland 1994. When asked why they tolerate the graffiti, local residents shake their heads and reply, "As soon as we take it down, it comes back again," or "We've just gotten used to it," or "It gives them an outlet and is better than the crime we see in the US." One Swiss retail business was alleged to have even encouraged some of the graffiti that left its name on bridges emulating a crude billboard. Photo—Dan Korem.

11.19 Zurich, Switzerland 1994. Note the absence of graffiti on this building located in an upscale neighborhood, which is directly across the street from the building shown above. I noted this in many different cities in Switzerland. It seems that when the greenery next to a building is higher than one's head, youths are discouraged from leaving their graffiti. To do so would require a ladder or climbing on someone's shoulders, which would increase the chances of one being spotted and caught. Local police, amused by my observation, determined to consider if this "principle" might be practically applied. Photo—Dan Korem.

11.20. Zurich, Switzerland 1994. It is not uncommon to see chronic amounts of graffiti in the finest neighborhoods in Switzerland, which has virtually no inner-city areas. This trend is increasing throughout Europe. Photo—Dan Korem.

11.21. Washington, D.C. 1994. The large cryptic graffiti shown here at a busy intersection next to the Department of Transportation is called a "tag." Not necessarily tied to gang activity, youths innovate their own "signatures." However, chronic tagging is often the forerunner of gang activity. It represents an aberration in the youth culture and belies an exaggerated need for recognition and attention, typically not received at home. Photo—Dan Korem.

GENERAL OBSERVATIONS

Those who work the most closely with youths will testify that youths are easily impressed by "what's new" and "radical." Regarding the youth subculture and how it relates to gangs, we can make these observations:

• Keeping abreast of new youth subculture expressions can help identify new gang activity, but it is not necessarily an indication of gangs. An example is the Doc Marten-American skinhead connection. Initially, the only students who wore these boots were skinheads, but this changed once Doc Martens became an accepted fashion.

• Different gangs often identify with different styles in the subculture as exemplified by the different types of music chosen by the skinhead and occultic Dallas gangs cited in chapter 5. It's useful to know *which* gang relates to which type of music or attire to facilitate the identification of the members of specific gangs.

• The youth subculture can be a *unifying factor* that draws similarly at-risk youths together. It can provide the first point of contact for a youth with gang members. In the Dallas skinhead/occultic gang case, music first helped to separate similarly at-risk youths into different gangs, but a music concert then provided the opportunity for youths from different gangs to meet.

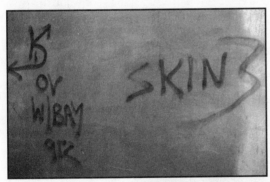

11.22. Whitby Bay, England 1993. Here, a skinhead tagger leaves both his gang's "tag" as well as his own. Photo—Dan Korem.

11.23. London, England 1994. A "tag" in an affluent London area. Photo—Dan Korem.

PERSONAL REFLECTIONS

Responsibility.

Gang members are responsible for their criminal actions. But remember, these are at-risk youths who are easily manipulated. Kuba Belok and Ivan Rock were. So too were the students in the Dallas occultic and skinhead gangs.

Many in the American press applauded the German government's censoring actions against hate rock, initiated after significant internal and international pressure. People remembered the consequences of a people listening to Hitler's messages of hate spewn through propaganda films and mass rallies—a sort of adult rock concert for that age at which grown women swooned at the Fürher's words, as observed by William Shirer, author of *The Rise and Fall of the Third Reich*. Similar censoring actions in the US would be considered unconstitutional. While I am not in favor of censorship, I certainly don't endorse the cowardly hesitation in the US entertainment and news media to make a strong case for restraint. In the US, we flaunt our ability to say whatever we want, regardless of the inspirational consequences. It seems that we only applaud restraint when it takes place in *someone else's* country and *not* our own.

Thematic exploitation of rebellion, violence, and bigotry will reap its own rewards. If uncontrolled juvenile violence and gangs continue to grow, as will probably be the case for at least another ten years due to the present condition of Western families, at some point people are going to cry out, "Enough!" And then it is predictable that the ire of the people will be hurled at the first thing they see. And the easiest thing to "see" will be media groups and participants who, for years, have inspired generations of youths without regard for the consequences.

Gangs are a manifestation of a cultural insanity—irrational groups out of control.

The English film producer of Academy Award-winning *Chariots of Fire*, David Putnam, passionately told the *New York Times*, when asked about the current state of his industry: "It seems an act of total madness to create a society you don't want to live in."[18]

Music, films, magazines, and concerts with overtly destructive themes don't *force* youths to commit crimes or join gangs, but they certainly do *inspire* at-risk youths towards that which is evil. The spontaneous appearance of the same gang types internationally is testimony to that. The only acceptable media response is unapologetic restraint.

Section Three

---◆---

GANG TYPES AND THEIR ACTIVITIES

CHAPTER 12.

Delinquent Gangs

I van Rock (chapter 8) ran with a delinquent gang. So did Andy Kriz (chapter 3). Although the profile of youths and the primal payoff they seek is the same for most gang members, the *context* in which criminal activity is carried out changes. In this chapter, after a brief discussion of *gang typology*, the following about the delinquent gang type is explored:

- A brief "snapshot" is provided as a helpful guide.
- General observations.
- Pre-gang activity.
- Inner-city comparisons.
- European delinquent gangs.
- Possible future trends.

PURPOSE OF TYPOLOGY

Each affluent gang has its own characteristics. Breaking down gangs by types helps us to predict with greater accuracy and understand a particular gang's behavior.[1] Skinhead gangs, for example, don't operate in the same way as Andy Kriz's gang, which specialized in burglary. A gang qualifies for one of the *three types* if the majority of criminal offenses are carried out in a *specific context*, although it isn't necessary for every youth in a gang to actually *believe* in the context. It is only important that the gang commits offenses in that specific context. For example, a youth might join a delinquent gang just to "run" with some fellows and not actually want to be a part of or party to criminal acts. While this youth might *not* actually believe in the context in which his gang commits criminal acts, his gang would still qualify for classification.

One of the risks of typing is the possibility of *stereo*typing; that is, stating that every gang in a particular type is the same. To avoid stereotyping, one must read the specific *actions* of a gang. The purpose of this and the following three chapters is to provide an *initial framework* to interpret what type of gang is operating in a given neighborhood or community based upon its actions.

If the affluent gang trend continues to grow and diversify, it will probably necessitate developing more types. For example, if gangs surface across America that primarily carry out their assaults in the context of *sporting events*, it might be useful to develop a new type called *sports gangs*. In Europe, football hooligans are common and are considered an individual type. In America, this type of gang hasn't appeared; therefore, for the purpose of this discussion, a football hooligan gang is listed as a *variant* of a delinquent gang. The decision to list them under delinquent gangs is for the purpose of providing greater insight into the mind-set of *affluent delinquent gangs*. (It could also be argued that Ivan's gang should be classified as an ideological gang because it committed assaults in an ideological context that said "Arsenal is good." But overall, his gang was just looking for a good fight, similar to suburban youths who "duke it out" in a parking lot after a football game. For this reason, his gang has been typed a *delinquent* gang.)

Because the affluent gang trend is a new one, there isn't a long track record of behaviors to evaluate. Inner-city gangs are a different matter and numerous sophisticated typologies have been developed. For example, researcher W. B. Miller broke down the various law-violating youth gangs and groups into types. Here is a partial list: turf gangs; regularly associating disruptive local groups/crowds; solidarity disruptive local cliques; gain-oriented gangs/extended networks; fighting gangs; etc.[2]

As already stated, for purposes of orientation and understanding, the types of affluent gangs have been broken down by the *context* in which they commit criminal offenses. These contexts are:

- *Delinquent Gang*: Desire for profit and thuggery.
- *Ideological Gang*: Attachment to a specific ideology, which may or may not be political.
- *Occultic Gang*: Attachment to beliefs in occultic powers.

Naturally, these contexts overlap. For example, in chapter 3 was presented a case of an occultic gang that also sought economic rewards by selling drugs—a typical factor in delinquent gangs. One might also find an ideological gang, such as a skinhead gang, that adopts some occultic beliefs as a part of its persona. Technically, such cases might be classified as combination types. (For an in-depth look at typology, please see *Juvenile Gangs* by Covey et al.). As a helpful guide, a brief "snapshot" summary of each gang type is provided.

SNAPSHOT OF A DELINQUENT GANG

The lure of delinquent gangs is typically financial, physical or sexual assaults, and thrills—the rush of doing something on the edge that gets the adrenaline going. Affluent delinquent gangs are the closest parallel to most inner-city gangs, thriving off of greed and thuggery: they either want their own way or what doesn't belong to them. The key distinguishing factor of delinquent gangs is that they don't attach themselves to complicated ideologies and occultic belief systems. For this reason, they are typically easier to understand; their behavior easier to predict. The delinquent gang has not yet solidified into concrete and specific variants, as have the other gang types (i.e., skinhead and anarchistic gangs are variants of the ideological type), but this type has the potential for the greatest growth and appeal because one doesn't have to subscribe to a particular ideology or abstract/esoteric belief system, as is common in ideological and occultic gang types.

OVERVIEW OF DELINQUENT GANGS

The mind-set of the delinquent gang is usually the most transparent and easy to understand of the three types, enabling one to identify quickly specific motivations and activities. There usually aren't a lot of surprises.

The story of Andy Kriz and Ivan Rock, taken together, provide a panoramic picture of a typical delinquent gang member. Andy was a leader and Ivan was a follower. Andy's gang wanted money and all that goes along with it. Ivan wanted a fight and something that was certain and unchanging. Both realized after they ceased their gang activity that the rationalization they used to justify their actions was flawed. Each also agreed that no one could have simply talked them out of their gang activities. Of the two, Ivan made the right moves and turned his life around and avoided jail. Andy wants to "make good," but he is already incarcerated. Together, they represent the face of affluent delinquent gang members we are likely to see in the future.

What qualified Andy's gang as a "delinquent gang" is that its criminal activity was carried out in a context of delinquency. They formed their group to steal. This is different from many US skinhead gangs that commit crimes in an *ideological context* and assault ethnic groups.

The frequency or type of criminal activity doesn't qualify a particular gang as a delinquent gang type. Ivan Rock's gang engaged in occasional assaults that were typically not life-threatening. The reason his gang qualifies as a delinquent gang is because they committed crime with some frequency, even though it was irregular. Andy Kriz's gang easily qualifies as a delinquent gang because they engaged in burglary on a repetitive basis. If either gang had committed only one offense after getting drunk one night, they might better be classified as a *pre-gang* group—if classified at all. This would also apply if only *one member* of a group committed an isolated criminal act(s).

Delinquent gangs across the board haven't yet broken down into different variants. Only the ideological and occultic gangs have taken on specific variants (such as skinhead gangs). (I have refrained from any detailed discussion of cases that don't particularly represent a trend, but rather represent isolated cases of thuggery, such as the Spurs Posse gang in Lakewood, California [1993], whose members bragged about their sexual conquests. These kinds of isolated gangs have always been present and are more akin to groups of youths who might meet after a football game for a rumble and sexual conquests; although in the case of the Posse, some individual youths were arrested for credit card theft and sexual assault. For this reason, gangs, such as Andy Kriz's DFL, which engaged in theft, burglary, and assault are the focus of this text.)

PRE-GANG ACTIVITY AND YOUNGER GANG MEMBERS

Pre-gang groups are common in inner-city gangs. Some are consciously developed by inner-city gangs to groom new recruits. Other pre-gang groups spontaneously form by youths too young to participate in gang activity, but who want to emulate their older counterparts (chapter 16 provides one example). This kind of pre-gang activity has been observed in affluent communities, but it usually forms without the inspiration of older gangs in a neighborhood. One example was a group which called themselves the PIGS: People In Important Groups. (Never mind that the letters don't perfectly match their name.)

Surfacing for a few months in a north Dallas suburb, about a dozen youths, aged 12 and 13, formed a club-like clique. To become a member, a youth had to commit an outrageous, but not necessarily criminal, act. Two members, though, decided to burn down a "Port-O-Potty," an outdoor outhouse at their school. This kind of "malicious mischief" doesn't qualify as gang activity, especially because it was an isolated incident. However, the mind-set of the offenders was worth monitoring by the local juvenile officers. The reason is simple: other delinquent gangs were forming in the neighborhood.

One youthful subcultural group that has been noted to provide a context for pre-gang activity are "skaters." Skateboards have been a source of recreation and fun dating back to the sixties. Since the early 1980s, though, for some youths (typically ages 10-15) skateboarding becomes a launch pad for gang involvement. In the Dallas case cited in chapter 5, the youths who killed a Black male were members of the Confederate Hammerskins. Some of the youths in that gang had been skaters for a couple of years prior to their skinhead activity. (An adult parallel are biker clubs versus biker gangs, such as the Hell's Angels. One activity is recreational, the other turns criminal.)

Some skaters sport extreme youth subculture symbols on their skateboards—the anarchy symbol, skulls, upside-down pentagrams (often associated with occultic gangs), and so on. Many who attach themselves to these expressions often come from at-risk home environments. Because of these visuals, often accompanied by comparable attire, these youths are easy to identify by local gangs and are susceptible to recruitment overtures. As already noted in chapter 11, the presence of such subcultural expressions doesn't necessarily mean that a youth is at-risk of gang activity, but it can indicate a need for closer scrutiny. One often follows the other.

Presently, it is commonplace for youths in delinquent gangs to be as young as 13 or 14 years old. In fact in many affluent communities, one is more likely today to find youths in grades 7-9 participating in gangs than in grades 10-12. One theory that suggests itself from interviews with these youths is that they operate more out of their emotions and react more violently when the Missing Protector Factor (chapter 7) is operative in their lives.

An example of a gang comprised of solely young at-risk teens occurred in an affluent part of Lancaster, Pennsylvania in 1992. It was called the BDP: Beat Down Posse. (The BDP was not connected to the 1993 Spurs Posse case in Lakewood, California.) The BDP took its name from the slang "beat down," a slang expression used by youths when they are going to assault and injure someone. The Lancaster youths, ages 10–14, most of whom came from broken homes, threatened youths, assaulted others, and were caught shoplifting. A few were sent to a local juvenile correction center. Because they were young and law enforcement responded quickly, the gang was quickly broken up.

INNER-CITY CONNECTION

As already stated, of the three gang types, the *delinquent* gang is most like an inner-city gang. (The exception are those instances when inner-city gangs take on an ideological bent, as described in chapter 13). The Andy Kriz and Ivan Rock stories sum up what many youths in inner-city gangs want: a sense of esteem and permanency, plus some cash in their pockets. Like in the inner-city, criminal activity centers around *physical assaults, the buying and selling of illegal substances, theft, and burglary.* The difference is that in affluent communities youths are not affected by economic blight; they simply rebel in a context of greed.

Affluent gangs initially formed on their own without direct influence from inner-city gangs, as noted in chapter 4. It was not common for inner-city gangs to spawn gang extensions comprised of affluent youths in affluent communities. What has been more common, however, is for gang activity from a lower-income area to *spill over* into an affluent community. That is, nonaffluent gangs engaging in illegal activities in nearby affluent communities. This occasionally occurs when a low-income area that has gang activity borders an affluent community. The lower income area may be in the same town or city or is adjacent to it.

In chapter 1, the 1992 shooting death of Sean Cooper was referenced. It occurred in the Dallas suburb of Richardson, Texas, population over 50,000. Richardson is an affluent community with one low-income area. It also borders another low-income area within the city limits of Dallas. The gang that shot and killed Sean Cooper was from the former area and the shooting was an isolated incident.

In those cases when inner-city gangs have influenced the growth of affluent gangs, the following factors have been observed:

- Youths, who are either new to a community or are isolated from other youths, such as Andy Kriz (chapter 3), are approached to join or form an *extension* gang.
- An affluent suburb is adjacent to a lower income area in which there are other gangs.
- A youth from another city who was involved with gangs, moves to an affluent community and forms his own gang. This factor is not common, but one such example occurred near Bucknell University in Milton, Pennsylvania, population 70,000. *Pre-gang* activity was observed as well when a youth from New York with former gang ties moved to Milton. Quick preemptive action averted gang formation and violence.

Common in many affluent delinquent gangs is the incorporation of hand signals used by inner-city gangs as a part of the gang persona. On these two pages are some examples of hand signals as demonstrated by former gang member, Will Babylonia, whose story is detailed in chapter 16.

12.1. This hand signal signifies membership in the Latin Kings, one of the largest gangs in the US.
Photo—Dan Korem.

12.2. Hand signal when two Latin Kings greet one another. One gang member presses his hand to the hand of another gang member, representing a "crown." Photo—Dan Korem.

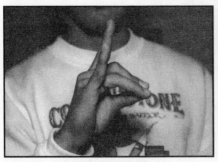

12.3. Hand signal to identify the Insane Dragons, of which Will Babylonia was a former member. The shape of the signal is to represent a dragon. Photo—Dan Korem.

12.4. A later innovation to indicate a member of the Insane Dragons. Photo—Dan Korem.

12.5. Signifies membership in the Imperial Gangsters, representing a crown. Photo—Dan Korem.

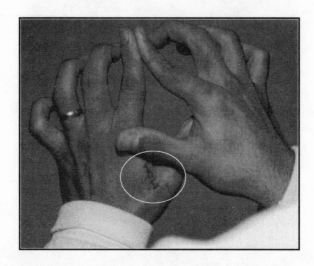

12.6. Will Babylonia's elaborate variation of the Imperial Gangster "crown," which was never adopted by the gang. Note the tatoo, "MOM," near the left thumb, representing "mind over matter."
Photo—Dan Korem.

EUROPEAN DELINQUENT GANGS

Delinquent gangs, like Andy Kriz's that focus on *theft*, are not a common phenomenon in affluent, European communities, but they are common in lower-income areas. As noted in chapter 4, after the fall of Communism, delinquent gangs proliferated in most Eastern and Central European countries from Russia to Hungary. Law enforcement experts, sociologists, and journalists have observed that repressive regimes had kept a cap on juvenile gangs. They were held in check or never had a chance to develop. Now that the authoritarian controls have loosened, they can more easily thrive. This doesn't mean that repressive regimes should be embraced. They do, however, have a palpable effect on juvenile gangs. This can be exploited for political purposes, making it appealing for people to embrace and welcome an authoritarian regime during times of chaos.

In affluent suburban areas of England, pre-gang groups, such as skater groups have been observed in Shirley, a suburb of Solihull just outside of Birmingham. Here, family social conditions similar to those in America are evident, although not as chronic in England. This is evinced by a five-fold increase in divorce rates since 1960 and a 300% increase in adolescent suicide.[3] And, as in the US, recent English polls reveal that one of most feared trends is the increase of youth violence.

In Switzerland, pre-gang groups, such as *taggers* are very common-place. Here too family social problems are increasingly evident as evinced by the increased divorce rate. In 1940, the divorce rate as a percent of the total marriages that year was only a 9.5 percent, but in 1992 that percent more than tripled, climbing to 32.2%.[4]

This sampling of increases is consistent throughout Europe and pre-gang groups are now a common phenomenon. As in the US, the European countries in the next few years will begin to experience an increase of delinquent gangs in affluent neighborhoods.

To date, the football hooligan delinquent gang variant is the most common in Europe and these gangs are often comprised of both affluent and low-income youths and young adults. Even in Russia, football gangs, called "fanaty," have been common since the 1960s and are comparable to a cross between British football fans and American inner-city gangs.[5]

In England, although incidents of juvenile violence have increased and not declined, violence at football matches has markedly declined since the early 1990s according to University of Aberdeen sociologist, Richard Giulianotti, an expert on football hooligans.[6] Some of the reasons for this as explained by Giulianotti and others include:

• Coordinated efforts by police to anticipate and disperse violent crowd behavior. Ivan Rock described how police helped to curb violence during the "taking of the end": "You just get into an end. Go to one side of it. Chant. And the next thing the police are in the middle, there's been no fighting, and they take you in."[7] One of the reasons that police action has been an effective deterrent is that their activities revolve around sporting events which are predictable, giving police time to plan and take effective action, unlike inner-city drive-by random shootings which can take place anytime.

• The elimination of "festival seating" behind a goal. Here, fans don't sit in designated seats, but rather stand because there aren't any seats. This encouraged the "taking the end" sort of mischief described at the beginning of chapter 8. (In the US, many rock concerts that feature violent or extreme forms of music have abandoned festival seating after youths in different cities were trampled to death, such as the 1991 incident in Salt Lake City in which three youths died.)

• Increased ticket prices discouraged many younger youths from attending. Those who are 13-16 are typically some of the most violent "bobs," because they strive for the attention of the gang boss. They also feel the least powerful in responding to personal domestic unrest, thus creating a more volatile situation.

FOOTBALL HOOLIGANS IN AMERICA?

One bizarre twist to the football hooligan phenomenon is that many skinhead gangs attach themselves to football clubs. This is seen in most European countries. In Budapest, for example, skinheads "support" the Ferençuáros Torna Club. It's customary to see football hooligans, skinheads, and hard-core fans all together, mixing it up in a melee after a game. This is a strange brew to an outsider.

The photo below is one that I took in a well-known platz in Gdansk, Poland. Gdansk is noted as the birthplace of the shipyard union, Solidarity, where some of the first effective protests took place paving the way for the fall of Communist regimes in Eastern Europe. Gdansk is also the city on which the Germans launched their first strike to commence WW II.

A local football match had just concluded. These youths, who had been drinking, swaggered loudly through the platz. To take this shot, I urged my wide-eyed translator to ask for their permission to take their picture. He told them I was a football fan from America who was very enthusiastic about Polish football. He explained that, Krys Sobieski, who was formerly the goalie for one of Warsaw's best teams, Legia, was a personal friend of mine. They cheered the request, then patted me on the back after I photographed them.

12.7. Gdansk, Poland 1994. Hard-core and run-along "football hooligans" in Gdansk, Poland. Note the skinhead in the middle inspiring the rest to lift the Nazi salute. Photo—Dan Korem.

The moment captured in this photograph depicts the exuberance of youths burying the day in cavalier excitement. Like Ivan Rock, there was a seductive charm about them. If you ask a European football hooligan, "Are you a hooligan?" he gleefully affirms. Although the term seems pejorative with a derogatory ring to it, *hooligan* becomes an emblematic badge of honor—something to boast about.

A similar delinquent gang variant that could emerge in America is a gang that attaches itself to a *sport* around which it can rally, similar to Ivan Rock's Gooners gang. This could be very appealing to affluent youths. Colorful team uniforms and insignia create an immediate identity. Weekly games provide an opportunity to gather before, during and after a contest. Chants and secretive hand signals are a part of the ritualized activity. Unlike inner-city gangs, where one must sustain a life-threatening beating to disengage, here the challenge is to keep up your nerve to stay in, like a game of chicken or "I dare ya."

If such a trend *does* occur, it is unlikely that these gangs will attach themselves to *professional* teams, which travel from coast to coast outside their home cities. Transportation would be too costly except for a very small minority of affluent youths, counterpointed with travel in Europe, where trains are relatively inexpensive and one only has to ride a few hours on a Saturday to and from a match. In America, *local* or *regional* nonprofessional sports teams would be more likely candidates, making travel more accessible. (This is not to suggest, of course, that sports and clean competition are unhealthy activities and should be discouraged, curtailed, or eliminated.)

During the last thirty years, there has been a deluge of the antihero type in the youthful subculture. A twist of timing could cause youths to latch onto something new that also has a flavor of victory attached to it—something easy to exploit and distort. A possible *catalyst* could be a new band that latched onto a sport or team. Or a group of youths might look at football hooligan gangs in Europe and think: No one has ever done that before. Let's call ourselves . . . The Lancaster (name of their city) Hooligans.

FUTURE TRENDS

A temptation is to interpret isolated cases, such as the Spurs Posse in Lakewood, California as the appearance of a *specific* new trend. There have always been isolated cases of affluent delinquent gangs. These isolated gangs ordinarily don't tell us much about a societal trend, just like an isolated serial killer doesn't tell us much about crime at large.

During the coming years, the delinquent gang type will probably spawn more variations and greater numbers than the other two gang types combined. The youth described in the chapter 1, who fired off gang signals at me, was typical of many youths drawn to delinquent gangs: They aren't sophisticated about what they believe or don't believe. To be involved in most delinquent gangs, one doesn't necessarily have to be able to think through complex issues, possess an above-average IQ, embrace a complicated, thought-provoking ideology or dark system of metaphysical beliefs. Most American youths aren't preoccupied with these kinds of things. They prefer something more direct and not intellectually taxing. For this reason, delinquent gangs can more easily attract the "wane" and "slackers"—those who want to run along the periphery and live at the fringes of society.

Increasing the number of "wanna-bes" through the vehicle of less complicated gang enticements has a multiplying effect. A larger group of youths are now available who might be converted to hard-core members; and leaders of a gang get part of their "juice" from the number of youths who follow them. Increased notoriety adds to the persona of the leader and the gang, which can attract attention from rival gangs, increasing the possibility of violence. These factors demand that prudent communities *carefully monitor* the delinquent gang-type when it appears.

Another dimension of the delinquent gang type that must also be closely monitored is if the number of at-risk youths remains chronically high and upscale gangs continue to persist and grow in number, developing ongoing infrastructures. If this occurs, the affluent youth who is drawn to the delinquent gang type is the most logical choice for inner-city gang recruitment. Andy Kriz (chapter 3) is one example of this phenomenon. Currently, inner-city gangs recruiting affluent youths into their folds isn't a dominant trend, but it could be for urban gangs desiring to extend the reach of their profit centers. If the affluent gang trend is not preemptively addressed, it is not implausible to imagine urban gangs franchising extensions in suburban communities to groups dominated by affluent youths who would know their own territory, increasing illegal drug trade, theft, burglary, associated violence, etc. Given collective estimates of urban gangs in the hundreds of thousands (precise data is not available because of varying definitions of a *gang* and reporting mechanisms across the US) and the current large numbers of at-risk youths (typically around 25-35%) in affluent communities, it is reasonable to expect that more direct influence from inner-city delinquent gangs is likely to become a dominant trend in the future. If this occurs, then it is also reasonable to expect some institutionalization of these gangs in affluent communities which will make them far more difficult to address because they will be supported by *both* local affluent *and* external urban gang structures.

Another potential variant that could appeal to a youth seeking a meatier intellectual challenge is what has been popularly dubbed the "cyberpunk" gang. Presently, this gang variant isn't common, but it has the potential for vast devastation.

Briefly, the word *cyberpunk* is an invention of those on the fringe of the "information highway," computer lingo for persons with formidable computer skills who might band together to perpetrate acts of terrorism from the sanctuary of their terminal-lit bedrooms. This type of gang has the potential of becoming the most disruptive and unpredictable of any gang variant seen to date. The possibilities for an intelligent youth are sobering: hackers can use computers and modems to sabotage mainframes and shut down a power plant or part of a phone company's operations. They can alter a company's records affecting inventory control, manipulate medical records, and perform cash transactions from one account to another. Thankfully, only isolated cases have been spotted. The FBI is closely watching this trend as cyberpunk gangs (or whatever future term might be ascribed to them) are likely to be comprised of very intelligent and crafty youths who can invisibly wreak havoc. It sounds like science fiction, but FBI special agent, Al Brantley, states that this is one possible gang-variant that must be very carefully monitored.

The profile characteristics of such a youth might include: highly intelligent, secretive, reclusive, critical, and, in some cases, have an event in his/her life that fostered a deviant desire to inflict harm on a particular industry or group. Locales that should be monitored are newer suburban areas that have high-tech industries and where youths from "new money" families are observedly unsettled and feel unconnected to their community. A sampling of potential suburbs can be found in *Edge City: Life on the New Frontier* (1992) by Joel Garreau. Additionally, whether or not a suburb has an overall high crime rate will not necessarily be a factor if this gang variant appears because youth crime often grows and shrinks independently of the adult crime rate.

CHAPTER 13.

Ideological Gangs: Part I Overview, History, and Hate Gang Variants

When I originally outlined this manuscript, the second gang type was to be defined as a "hate" gang, specifying a gang type that committed criminal acts in a racial-hatred context. The decision to develop a broader type was influenced by a trip to Poland (March 1994) and after an in-depth interview with sociologist, Barbara Fatyga. She noted a surge in ideological youth gangs in Poland, ranging from skinhead to anarchistic and even ecological gangs, in which youths adopted the ruse of protecting the environment to justify acts of thuggery. She discovered that youths in these gangs came from both low and high income families; and many of the gang variants she described could easily appeal to intellectually astute youths in affluent communities in the United States, given the current social climate.

As detailed in chapter 11, youth subcultures quickly influence and easily inspire new variants in the United States and Europe. Presently, the hate gang variant is the most common ideological gang in the United States, but this could change. Youths rebelling in the context of a gang in affluent communities prefer to find *new* contexts to do so, and unlike their predecessors, they want *unique ownership*. Thus, the ideological type provides a broad umbrella to entail any new gang variant that might appear and attach itself to a specific ideology.

The dominant focus of this chapter will be the hate gang variant because presently it is the most common. Two examples have already been presented. The first was Kuba Belok's gang (chapter 10). His gang adopted a serious and direct political protest against a repressive Polish regime. A subtext was hatred towards the Jewish minority group, even though there were less than 4,000 Jews living in Poland at that time. The second example was the three Dallas skinheads convicted of a drive-by shooting in

137

Arlington, Texas (chapter 5). They possessed little long-term commitment to their ethnic genocide ideology, but they randomly committed murder while out drinking. These two stories demonstrate that skinhead gangs can be diverse. Some invest significant intellectual currency in what they believe, yet limit themselves to few non-life-threatening criminal acts. Others, however, with a minimum of heartfelt beliefs commit crimes, including murder.

In chapter 14, potential candidates of new variants that might appear in the United States are presented along with a summation of current European trends. Extraordinary and invaluable insights from the research of sociologist Barbara Fatyga is also presented as her research is some of the most helpful for use in the US and in Europe.

SNAPSHOT OF AN IDEOLOGICAL GANG

The lure of the ideological gang is that one can believe in a particular ideology—racial, political, etc. From the context of the specific ideology, gang members commit and, for some, justify criminal acts. The ideology is a surface, uniting factor for the gang members. Leaders of these gangs are often looking for a greater intellectual challenge than those in delinquent gangs. Nonleaders may or may not seek intellectual challenge, but they often boast of their "knowledge." For those who possess substandard intellectual skills, when compared to their nongang peers, participation in the gang feeds a warped sense of self-esteem because in their minds they "understand" issues their nongang peers don't. Presently, variants in the US are limited to the *hate* gang variant. In Europe many other variants are apparent, such as *anarchistic* and *ecological* gangs, and new US variants are likely to be inspired by European variants.

OVERVIEW OF IDEOLOGICAL GANGS

Ideological gangs are not a new phenomenon. They commit and justify criminal activity because of a defined and sometimes not-so-defined ideological belief-system or social cause. As Covey, Menard, and Franzese document in *Juvenile Gangs*, in the past, Black street gangs have been the most likely to adopt an ideological/political bent. The social protest movement of the 1950s and early 1960s didn't witness this phenomenon, but in the late 1960s, various Black gangs such as the Black Panthers took on an ideological context. They killed in the name of racial protest. Most gang members in this gang variant were young adults (18-28) and they didn't last long. Another example, the "Crusaders" (1968–69) had 200 members who typically came from "lower-class backgrounds and single-parent families."[1] Currently, some Black delinquent gangs are attempting to become a strategic ideological force, as evinced by the growth of the Gangster Disciple Nation network of gangs in Chicago comprised of over 30,000 gang members.[2] (Although he was White, Andy Kriz (chapter 3) was a member of a predominantly Black Gangster Disciple gang in Minneapolis.)

In 1992, masterminded by their incarcerated leader, Larry Hoover, the Gangster Disciples adopted an agenda to seek political control in areas in which they operated in Chicago. Chicago police undercover cameras captured gang members stating their intentions to obtain political muscle. To this end, they formed 21st Century Vote, a door-to-door canvassing operation to register people to vote—ostensibly for the politicians designated by the gang. Their show of force was impressive, recruiting over 25,000 people for mass rallies that even paraded through the downtown district.[3] Many of those who participated were gang members who didn't even know why they were there. They were just told to "show up."

Dogged by the past effects of sometimes abusive Chicago police investigations into Black Power and anti-war groups in the 1960s, Chicago Police Commander, Robert W. Dart, observed that 21st Century Vote is a ruse to shield the Gangster Disciples from criminal investigations. "If they say it's political, we can't investigate."[4] That the Gangster Disciples is a real threat is evident by the fact that they control one-third of the drug trafficking in Chicago and have over 150 chapters and affiliates throughout the US. FBI special agent, Ken Piernick, observed that, "They are many, many times larger than the Mafia. They are the Mafia of the future."[5]

The Gangster Disciples venture into the political arena, while driven internally by nonideological factors, could eventually qualify as a *delinquent-ideological* gang type. Although unlikely, without a severe splintering effect, if the leadership decided to abandon most of its financially driven criminal activity and focus instead on crimes designed to forward a social agenda, then they might qualify for consideration as an *ideological* gang.

Obviously, there can be difficulty when defining the difference between a social protest movement, in which an isolated criminal act is committed, and an ideological gang that forms and frequently commits criminal acts. It seems reasonable, though, that many of the campus protest-riots of the late 1960s, for example, would be better classified in most situations as criminal acts associated with social protests. At Tulane University, for example, students burned an ROTC building in 1969 to protest the Vietnam War. This action would probably best be classified as a criminal act committed by a social protest group. (I attended Tulane the following year, and none of the participating students engaged in similar subsequent criminal acts.)

A more difficult classification would be the anarchistic gang-like group of which Katherine Ann Power was a member in the early 1970s. One of the most sought after fugitives by the FBI, Power was finally apprehended in 1993 when she surrendered to authorities for her participation in the 1970 shooting death of a Boston police officer associated with a bank robbery. Because her group had plotted various criminal acts as a form of social protest, it is reasonable to suggest that this group would be better classified as an ideological gang. Others may disagree, suggesting the social protest label.

In most instances involving youths, however, youth gangs that commit crimes in an ideological context should be typed as an *ideological gang*. As noted, the most common type of ideological gang in the US is the *hate gang* variant. The majority of people in the United States do not espouse the skinhead, ethnic-hate philosophy; therefore, few would have difficulty classifying crime-committing skinhead groups as gangs. But what if the gang is an *anarchistic* gang, the counterpart of a skinhead gang? Anarchistic gangs are common in Europe, and, unlike their skinhead counterparts, are not nationalistic. Anarchistic gang members typically believe in diminishing laws and social controls, committing low-level types of crimes in the name of their ideology. Should they be typed as an *ideological* gang or as a social protest movement that commits crimes? There will be cases when it will be difficult distinguishing between anarchistic gangs and anarchistic social protest groups that do not *persistently* commit crimes. Admittedly, there will always be some latitude in individual situations for making a case against classifying a specific group as a *gang*, but for referential purposes in this text, such ideological groups of *youths* who display a degree of persistence when committing crimes will be classified as a *gang*.

SNAPSHOT OF HATE GANG MEMBER

The lure of the hate gang is power over others and a mechanism to release pent-up anger. Many youths often display paranoia and the gang is often driven by fear. Much of the activity of hate gangs is predictable in its nature, although specific acts are often unpredictable. Leaders of this gang variant often take on cultic qualities and some of these gangs can cross the line and become cults, as defined in chapter 4. In fact, it is not uncommon for leaders in these gangs to be typed as Random Actors, which is one of the most dangerous performance/decision makers. (Random Actors are characterized by individuals who make decisions out of fear and their actions are unpredictable,[6] common in many cult figures.)

OVERVIEW OF AMERICAN SKINHEAD GANGS
Demographics and Violence

Skinhead gangs are the most common ideological youth gang in the United States that fits the hate gang variant, and they are growing in numbers. There were 1,000-1,500 skinheads operating in 12 states in February

1988.[7] By June 1993, only five years later, 3,300-3,500 were spread across 40 states.[8] Exact numbers are difficult to come by because of a lack of centralized reporting by local communities. In New Jersey, for example, in 1994 there were an estimated 400 skinheads, which appears staggering compared to the rest of the US, but state officials point out that New Jersey is one of the only states with a system to report bias crimes.[9] By comparison, in 1993 approximately 300-400 skinheads had been identified in Texas,[10] a far more populous state, and in both states skinhead gang members are present in affluent communities. (Additionally, some statistics vary due to reporting procedures, while some research organizations tamper with some statistics to further a particular perspective.[11] The statistics quoted in this text, however, have exhibited consistency among sources, are not inflammatory, and are reliable for referential purposes.) In most states where skinhead gangs are present, they have been closely associated with the dramatic escalation of hate crimes.

In 1993, 2,232 hate crimes were committed by neo-Nazis, skinheads, and other right-wing extremist groups—according to the FBI, which, beginning in 1994, by law must compile a report on hate crimes.[12] This figure, however, is considered "a small percentage of the problem"[13] as local police departments are not compelled to supply hate-crime data. From 1987 to 1990, six murders were committed by skinhead youths. This figure jumped to 22 murders between 1990 and 1993,[14] and affected communities from Clearwater, Florida to Pittsburgh, Pennsylvania to San Jose, California. Donald Thomas of Arlington, Texas was one of the twenty-two slain (chapter 5). By comparison, in Germany, where skinhead activity is more prevalent, about 7.7 people have been killed a year since 1990 according to the 1994 FBI report. (It should also be noted that hate crimes are no longer limited to Whites against other ethnic groups. In 1992, 46% of all racially committed murders were committed by Blacks against those who were White, Asian, or Hispanic, according to Klanwatch, a watch-dog project of the Southern Poverty Center, which monitors hate crimes in the US and abroad.[15] Klanwatch also noted that only one such murder was committed by a Black person in 1990 and none in 1989.[16] Also, of all 7,684 hate crimes reported in 1993, which included assualts against persons and property crimes, the motivating factors broke down as follows: race, 4,168; religion, 1,189; sexual orientation, 806; national origin or ethnicity, 583.[17]

While most United States skinhead gangs haven't committed murder, nevertheless the *threat* is ever-present. The literature skinheads read-and-heed is severely inflammatory propaganda, and direction by adult groups is always a possibility. Add the heightening and distorting effects resulting from drug use and the results can be terrifying and often tragic.

In respect to the potential for violence emanating from the skinhead-gang culture worldwide, Mark S. Hamm, a criminologist at Indiana State

University and the author of the comprehensive book, *American Skinheads* (1994), states that one must be careful to examine the *geography* and *cultural tradition* in which a skinhead lives. He notes that in Canada, for example, that very few, if any, local skinheads commit crimes. In Germany, on the other hand, between 4,000-5,000 neo-Nazi skinhead youths were imprisoned for committing serious offenses.[18] Hence, Germany is a country which has a more entrenched tradition of racism than Canada. So, criminal acts committed in a racist context are more likely in Germany than in Canada. Similarly, one expects more acts of racial violence in the United States than in Canada for the same reason.

Historical Roots

The roots of the skinhead movement can be traced to England in the 1960s. It was comprised of young toughs who worked in factories and wore heavy steel-toed boots and braces (English term for suspenders). English skinheads in the early years didn't have a racist bent and actually frequented all-Black nightclubs listening to ska, a forerunner of Jamaican reggae. Skinheads didn't espouse a cohesive ideological philosophy and not all joined gangs. Similar to the Black street gangs mentioned earlier in this chapter, those who did join a gang, first formed delinquent gangs many of which later changed to ideological gangs. Thus, youths who joined skinhead gangs and didn't embrace an ideology, but committed crimes, would best be classified as members of delinquent gangs.

By the 1970s, extremist skinhead factions took on an ideological bent, adding nationalistic purity to its baggage. These new gangs that operated in this mode are better typed as an *ideological* gang. By the mid-1980s, the skinhead movement had taken root in the United States—inspired by music and fashion in the youth subculture. Neo-fascist adult groups, such as the Aryan Nations, then exploited and in some cases directed these gangs and individual skinheads. In the fall of 1989, for example, skinheads provided protection during a rally sponsored by the Aryan Nations in Polaski, Tennessee. Similarly, in England, Derek Beackon, a member of the neo-fascist British National Front (BNF), enlisted skinhead gang support and was elected to local office in London in the wake of the skinhead killing of an Asian youth in 1993. In March of 1994, Russian extremist and political aspirant, Vladimir Zhirinovsky, visited Poland and his "security" was provided by Polish skinheads carrying *American* baseball bats.

Unlike other examples in history of racially motivated hatred—hatred passed down by family, ethnic, racial, or national tradition—this youth phenomenon in the United States was different. Many weren't like the "Brownshirts" of Hitler's Third Reich. They weren't taught since birth to be prejudiced. Some latched on to this hate-trend after reading literature passed out in local high schools and junior highs. Other youths first contacted skinheads through other means such as a party or drug buys. The emergence of these extremist youths was unique in history. Internationally, Hamm observed that: "Never have we had in the history of the nations of the world nonstate, military, right-wing extremist youths take to the streets in paramilitary garb armed with firebombs, baseball bats and guns and attack the citizenry until the early 1980s."[19]

Hatred and criminal activity directed against *Jews* is a common constituent in most skinhead groups throughout the United States and Europe, while hatred towards other minority groups varies from country to country. The key, unifying aspect found in most of these gangs is that their hatred is focused against isolated and/or easily identifiable groups. For example, in Germany criminal acts against Turkish immigrants have been more prevalent than against Blacks. In fact, there is little racial hatred expressed towards Blacks in Germany because Turkish immigrants are viewed as a threat to the German job market. In the United States, however, criminal acts directed against Blacks and Hispanics are more common, whereas criminal acts against other ethnic groups—Turks, Italians, etc.—are uncommon.

Danny Welch of Klanwatch and others speculate that the most recent roots for skinhead-hatred directed at Jewish people in the United States and Europe was fueled by neo-Nazi hate group reaction to highly publicized and internationally celebrated events: the 40th commemorative anniversary of the Holocaust (1985) and the 50th anniversary of Kristallnacht (1988)—when the Nazis terrorized the German Jews, burning Torahs, smashing shop windows and furniture in homes, and killing many of them. On November 10, 1988, more than sixty US incidents of anti-Semitic vandalism, assault, and harassment were reported.[20]

What frightened officials is that while the skinhead attacks accounted for 8% of the 1,432 anti-Semitic attacks in the US in 1989, "none of the acts were related to each other in an organized fashion."[21] Abraham H. Foxman of the Anti-Defamation League observed, "It makes it more sinister, more dangerous, because it is more unpredictable. Violent acts associated with skinhead activity, like inner-city gangs, inspire fear because of the randomness of the acts and the inability to predict when it will strike next."[22]

If one has a minority ethnic background, this is especially terrifying in light of history's dramatic examples of genocide and recent "ethnic cleansing" in the former Yugoslavia and in several African nations. One can't feel truly safe when such gangs are present in a community. In 1991, members of the Dallas skinhead gang singled out Donald Thomas solely because he was a Black man enjoying a summer evening with two White friends.

Common Characteristics of Affluent Skinhead Gangs

Types of Youths Attracted—Presently, most skinhead youths are more prone to thuggery than youths in occultic gangs or delinquent gangs that focus on thievery. Physical displays of machoism are more common, visually keyed by skinhead regalia—chains, black leather jackets, etc. Most are of average intelligence and aren't able, with eloquence, to define their beliefs, often rambling angrily when challenged to a debate. The often poor presentation of their disseminated materials is evidence of this. Regarding leaders, some possess eloquence, others don't.

Spontaneous Acts and Minimal Long-term Commitment to Adult Groups—The three Dallas skinheads who murdered Thomas were typical of skinheads from affluent communities in the United States. They "act out" spontaneously, are not necessarily devout in their beliefs and usually don't develop long-term relationships with other groups, such as the Ku Klux Klan (KKK) or other extremist, fascist groups. The Dallas shooting illustrated the spontaneity of these gangs. A February 1994 Klan rally in the north Dallas suburb of Plano, Texas, a thoroughly cosmopolitan city, exemplified the *absence* of long-term devotion to adult fascist groups.

Plano is home to corporate giants such as Frito Lay, EDS, and J. C. Penney. It has one of the lowest overall crime rates for cities over 100,000 in the state of Texas. The 1994 Klan rally, held at the quaint gazebo near the old downtown district, drew only a few of the more than twenty local skinheads. Klan organizers, no doubt, hoped to draw out affluent youth sympathizers, but failed, even though skinhead activity had been persis-

13.1. Plano, Texas (Dallas suburb) 1994. The Ku Klux Klan sponsored rally in a quaint park next to the quiet downtown area drew few of the 20 area skinhead youths. Photo—Sandy Korem.

13.2. Plano, Texas 1994. Black-hooded Klan member attempts to attract the attention of lazy Saturday afternoon traffic, but only garnered stares. Photo—Sandy Korem.

tent in that area for several years. (According to the local FBI field office, of the one-hundred-plus Dallas skinheads in 1993 and 1994, most lived in the affluent, north Dallas area.[23] Supporting this opinion was a 1993 report by the Anti-Defamation League [ADL] that a large number of skinheads were concentrated in affluent communities like Plano, the Woodlands near Houston, and Arlington, home of the Texas Rangers baseball team.)

Although difficult to quantify, comparative opinions suggest that *affluent* youths in these gangs express a less committed long-term attachment to neo-Nazi/hate ideology and are less prone to recurrent acts of violence than skinhead gang youths from less affluent communities. They seem less inclined to perpetuate the hate tradition into their adult lives. The varied reasons for this include—greater affluence permits greater mobility and the ability to change orientations; youths attend college and are separated from former friends; and affluent communities have more resources to thwart the creation and proliferation of such gangs. As with other gang types, the gang façade is usually a reaction to a broken home, and thus, extremist ideology often sloughs off as a youth gets older.

A young French woman, whom we will call Valerie, was a part of the drug subculture in Zurich in the late 1980s and early 1990s. She knew many members of skinhead, anarchist, and other variants of the ideological gang type. Her observation mirrors the experience of many who deal with skinhead gang members here in the United States. She said, "Punks, skins, and anarchists always talk *first* about their terrible family and then politics when they first meet you. Their political view is simply their mask."[24]

Extremist Ideology and Equally Extreme Variability. Although US *affluent* skinheads aren't as prone to violence or to long-term commitments, a quick scan of the materials these youths ingest will temper any tendencies to dismiss the threat that they might pose. Below are examples of skinhead hate literature distributed in North Dallas suburban schools in 1989–90 by Dallas skinhead gangs to youths, ages 12-17.

We're sick and tired of the Zionist Occupational Government—ZOG—that runs this country. *From literature distributed by White Power Confederate Hammer.*

The Confederate Strikeforce Skinheads are working class Aryan youth. We oppose the capitalist and communist scum who are working to destroy our once proud nation. We also realize that the parasitic Jewish race (who control the American mass media) is at the heart of our problem, as well as the traitors of our own race who willingly do the Jews bidding. Join our fight to save our WHITE HERITAGE before it is lost forever. *From literature distributed by Confederate Strikeforce skinheads.*

You enjoy living in this clean, White suburban neighborhood! That's why you spend a little extra time trimming the lawn and you pay higher property taxes, to ensure that your standard of living will prevail. With each passing day, however, the hordes of Blacks, Puerto Ricans, Mexicans, Chinese and Jews are moving in a little closer and threatening your way of life. *From literature distributed by Confederate Hammerskins.*

Lost your jobs due to "AFFIRMATIVE ACTION"?
Denied earned promotions due to "AFFIRMATIVE ACTION"?
Denied jobs because you are WHITE?
Are your wives, mothers or sisters dreading to walk the streets for fear of being disfigured or raped? Would you rather be sovereign White MEN as were your forefathers? . . . Are you willing to sacrifice as did your Forefathers, for Liberty under the LAWS OF GOD? *From literature distributed by Confederate Hammerskins.*

13.3. Washington, DC 1994. Skinhead flyer pasted on a railing next to FBI Hoover Building. Photo—Dan Korem.

13.4, 5, 6. Dallas, Texas 1989. Examples of skinhead literature confiscated in a Dallas suburban junior high (grades 7-9) where it was being distributed to recruit new gang members.

Most skinhead material, like the above, is adapted and photocopied from other sources ranging from historic personages to neo-Nazi groups such as the KKK. In addition to the examples presented in chapter 11, here is another example of the kind of music that inspires skinhead activity.

MERCENARY by Störkraft

> He is a mercenary and a fascist
> He is a murderer and a sadist
> He has no friends and loves only himself
> A human life means nothing to him
> He has no soul, he has no mind
> He has no scruples, he has been banned
> Mercenary, he is a mercenary!

He is a skinhead and a fascist
He is bald and a racist
He has no conscience or heart
Hatred and violence mark his face
Mercenary, he is a mercenary!
He loves war and violence
And if you're his enemy he'll waste you
Mercenary, he is a mercenary![25]

These kinds of materials and lyrics illustrate one stream of the skinhead culture—those bounded by hatred towards ethnic groups. But there are other skinhead gangs who direct their hatred towards *other* skinhead gangs. One such variant is the SHARPS—Skinheads Against Racial Prejudice. They are *anti-racist* and engage in assaults *against* skinhead gangs that *are* racist. Although smaller in numbers and not as severe a criminal threat, SHARP members in Dallas occasionally assaulted members of other Dallas skinhead groups that were racist in the late 1980s. The SHARPS also have individual nongang followers as well as gangs in England that are like their ethnic-hating counterparts. They too seek a release of pent-up anger against an isolated and easily identifiable group. Only in this case, they direct this anger towards other racist skinhead gangs.

Another unusual variation of the skinhead gang found in England are those comprised of gang members who are homosexual. This is an anomaly because many of the skinhead groups are manifestly opposed to homosexuality. (In Germany, it is not uncommon to find homosexuals who are a part of the neo-Nazi movement, such as Nationalist Front leader, Michael Kühnen, who died of AIDS in 1991.[26])

Perversion of Traditional Spiritual Concepts—It isn't uncommon for some skinhead gangs to manifest bizarre perversions of traditional spiritual beliefs. In one extreme, there are skinheads who embrace Satanism to justify their own moralistic order. In the opposite direction are devotees of the Church of the Creator, a spin-off of the Church of the Identity, of which Hamm has written. In brief, its adherents use *The White Man's Bible* (1971) as its guiding text. It reinterprets the book of Genesis, claiming that the White man was God's ultimate creation on the seventh day (all other "inferior" races were created on the *third* day). They teach that White people are descendants of a lost tribe of Israel, the Tribe of Manasseh, which they claim migrated to the British Isles and then later to America. Most importantly, their dogma permits them to "redefine the meaning of sin as it relates to violence,"[27] similar to alleged "Christian men" of the KKK justifying burning fiery crosses and Hitler rewriting the Bible, deleting all references to Jews, paving the way to justify genocide.

13.7. Warsaw, Poland 1994.—Skinhead graffiti left by a Legia fan, Warsaw's most popular soccer club. Note the different elements: 1. Celtic Cross and White Power (written in English)—a person with anti-skinhead sentiments later drew a gallows attached to the cross. 2. The circle with the "L" and a crown on top represents Legia. 3. A foaming beer mug. 4. A smiling sun. Warsaw sociologist, Barbara Fatyga, when told about the graffiti, laughed and said: "It had to have been drawn by an anarchist. There's too much of a touch of subtle irony to have been drawn by skins. Skinheads aren't that subtle. They lack a sense of humor." She did acknowledge, however, that it might have been drawn by a skinhead youth from a more affluent community, as had been observed in Warsaw. Photo—Dan Korem.

Subculture Influence

Researchers such as Hamm, Fatyga, and Kopp have observed that youths are often drawn to the skinhead culture through music from the youth subculture. An example was the White Aryan Resistance [WAR] started by Tom Metzger. It was the "first American hate group to build its organization on the emotional appeal of rock and roll music."[28]

One of the dominant neo-Nazi, skinhead music forms which originated in England is called Oi (pronounced oy and sometimes spelled Oj), which some say is a word derived from an old English battle cry meaning "ready to fight." Others say it is an old Gypsy term used by cockney workers that meant 'Hey!'[29] Bands named Skrewdriver and Brutal Attack were representative of this style. *The Blood and Honor Movement*, a British neo-Nazi-like publication in the early 1980s inspired other bands that touted the racist hate theme. The music served as "a recruiting tool, a propaganda weapon, a celebration of the gang ethic and a clarion call to violence."[30]

Throughout the United States and Europe the Celtic cross has been a common symbol seen in skinhead graffiti. It is also one of the most common graffiti symbols seen throughout Europe. Ironically, when asked about the symbol, most Europeans don't know its significance. An example of the Celtic cross is shown in PHOTOGRAPH 13.7. The shaved-head fashion and skinhead dress also originated in England. From here, the skinhead ideology spread and has twisted into many variants in Europe and the United States.

A darkly amusing fact is that the term "skinhead," which originated in England, was coined to identify youths who shaved their heads. In Germany, youths adopted the same term and didn't bother to translate skinhead into their own language. This seems odd because these German skinheads are extremely nationalistic, yet it didn't occur to them to change the name to reflect their nationality. When skinhead activity spread from Germany

**13.8.
England
early 1980's.**
Nick Johnson and his gang on their mopeds.

13.9. England 1987. Nick Johnson sporting a "Psycho-Billy" look.

13.10. England 1988. Shot at the time when Johnson was consuming over 50 pints of alcohol a week.

13.11. England 1989. Youth subculture statements rarely are static, even within the same subgroup. Here it is apparent that the fashion statements of Nick Johnson, a former English skinhead, varied over a period of years.

13.12. Solihull, England 1994. Nick Johnson today. Photo—Dan Korem.

the term to a Polish name so that they could distinguish themselves from their German counterparts, even though Germany invaded Poland in 1939—providing further evidence of the power of the youth subculture. In the same way, other façades of the skinhead culture were amusingly spread.

In Plano, Texas, the members of one skinhead gang rode red mopeds. It was emblematic of being a member, along with their Doc Marten boots. It was wildly incongruous. You would expect a skinhead youth to radiate a tough-guy persona, riding something like a beefed up Harley Davidson motorcycle, as commonly done in many biker gangs. It wasn't until 1993, when I interviewed Nick Johnson, a former English skinhead in the 1980s, that the reason for selecting mopeds was revealed. Johnson explained that in England, many youths who adopt the skinhead fashion and run in skinhead gangs ride mopeds because they are cheaper than other makes. They can't afford Harleys, which they would ride if given the chance. In Plano, American youths saw their British counterparts riding mopeds in magazines and assumed that there was a special reason, a cool, possibly arcane purpose behind riding mopeds; therefore, they bought and rode mopeds.

Johnson also provided additional insight into the skinhead culture in England. Neither he nor any of those in his gang were racially prejudiced. They adopted the fashion, listened to nonracist skinhead music (similar to punk and thrash music styles), committed a few minor crimes, engaged in fights, but didn't adopt a racist or nonracist ideology. They used the pose and antisocial dress, coupled with shocking but relatively benign intimidating behavior to release suppressed anger, hostility, and frustration. Technically, their gang would be classified as a skinhead *variant* of a *delinquent* gang.

"We had a lot of fights and were like a turf gang,"[31] he explained, adding that a majority of the skinhead gangs in England are similar to his. While in the United States most skinheads are racist, a nonracist and nongang trend appears to be taking shape in the United States as evidenced by some of the youths in Grapevine, Texas (chapter 11) who adopted the skinhead *fashion* but didn't participate in gangs nor were they racist. Therefore, like other youth subculture movements, the skinhead culture is likely to continue to mutate and change as youths seek new venues in which they can creatively rebel.

Misleading Stereotypes

Because hate gangs are intimidating to outsiders, some false stereotypical impressions have formed about skinhead groups. Common and salient examples are:

Skinhead gangs only form in lower-income communities that have chronic unemployment. Beginning in England in the 1970s, this was originally true (although many weren't racist, as explained later in this chapter). However, beginning in the late 1980s, skinhead youths started appearing in affluent communities in the United States and Europe. This is illustrated by the 1991 conviction of three Dallas skinheads from suburban neighborhoods. Skinhead gangs can just as easily form in affluent as in lower-income communities. When I was in Berlin in 1993, skinhead activity had actually become more common in *affluent* western Berlin (the former West Berlin) than in economically depressed and dilapidated eastern Berlin (the former Communist-controlled East Berlin).

Skinhead activity in a community implies that the community is racist. This might be true in some rural areas, such as isolated regions in Idaho where neo-Nazi groups like the Aryan Nations have been operative. But in many affluent communities, such as the north Dallas suburbs, this isn't true, where racial incidents of any kind are rare.

Skinhead gangs initially formed in the United States because of the urgings of adult hate groups such as KKK. In the beginning, US skinhead gangs formed in copycat fashion, modeled after English skinheads. It was the youth subculture that spawned the skinhead movement in the United States. In England, youths formed their own gangs first and later were exploited and directed by extremist politicians, such as Derek Beackon and his neo-fascist BNF. In the United States, a similar phenomenon unfolded as youths adopted the skinhead façade and *then* groups like the KKK began to exploit fully these youths in the early 1980s, in some cases requesting that skinheads provide "security" for their meetings. *But the growth of skinhead gangs was actually inversely proportional to the size of KKK groups.* While skinhead gangs have increased in numbers since the early 1980s, KKK membership actually *declined* during the same time period from 11,500 in 1981 to 5,000 in 1985.[32]

It is important to reemphasize the following progression: 1) Skinhead youths typically come from similar family backgrounds, and like youths in other gang types, a primary, unifying force in their lives is seeking release from the pain from a broken/ruptured stable home-life. 2) For affluent youths, inspiration to become a skinhead typically originates with the youth subculture, not outside groups like the KKK. 3) Adult direction typically occurs *after* a gang has formed, if it occurs at all.

Once this predictable progression is recognized, *prevention* and *disengagement* strategies in a community can attack the true source of the problem, rather than false-lead factors.

There is a uniform hatred in all skinhead gangs towards ethnic groups. An "expert" who testified in the conspiracy to commit murder trial of Dallas skinhead, Daniel Brosky, stated, "All skinhead groups have an intense, gut-level hatred, not only for African-Americans, but for all other ethnic groups. They uniformly hate Blacks and believe there is no place for them in this country, or on this planet."[33] As already referenced, some skinhead gangs are actually *antiracist* and commit assaults against other skinhead gangs that are racist, while other *groups* of skinheads can't even be classified as a gang because they don't commit crimes. In fact, in the Dallas case, in which youths from the Confederate Hammerskins freely met with youths from the Carrollton occultic gang (chapter 5), there was one youth of a racially mixed background who actively sought to be a member of another local skinhead gang!

Confused?

Remember, skinheads are a youth subculture phenomenon. Youths are impressionable and are capable of spontaneously "acting out," driven by something as simple as the latest fashion. Kuba Belok, one of Poland's first skinheads who engaged in minor assaultive acts against the Polish police (chapter 10), decided to become a skinhead and shave his head because he was told to cut his hair by school authorities. He simply chose a radical way to obey and rebel at the same time. His impulse was driven by music videos and tapes of groups, such as TSA and CAT, that espoused the skinhead philosophy.

The Adult Hate-Group Threat

Although the relationship between affluent skinhead youths and other adult groups has remained a low-level threat in the United States—when compared to the volume of crimes committed by other types of gangs— this could change. There are many on the fanatical, lunatic fringe who are ready and eager to find a youthful following. Here are a few of the many possible examples:

• Tom Metzger, formerly of the White Aryan Resistance (WAR), in 1989 led an "Aryan Woodstock" in Napa County, California for skinheads who "came equipped with semiautomatic weapons, including an AR-15, and AK-47, automatic pistols, and shotguns."[34] (Metzger was later found liable for the 1988 beating death of an Ethiopian immigrant. A Portland, Oregon state court leveled a $12.5 million wrongful-death verdict against Metzger and WAR, effectively shutting down his cable talk show *Race and Reason*, his publications, computer bulletin boards and telephone message lines designed to reach and recruit adult and youthful followers.)

• In 1991, KKK leader Dennis Mahon from Oklahoma traveled to Germany and led a cross-burning gathering of German skinhead youths, attempting to be a catalyst for developing a cohesive movement there.

• Annette Lévy-Willard, a senior political writer for the French newspaper, *Libération*, produced a 1984 documentary, "The Other Face of Terror," in which she chronicled the collaborative efforts of neo-Nazi groups in England, Belgium, France, Spain, Germany, and the US. These included both adult groups and youth gangs that murkily fed off one another.

If deteriorating family trends continue to persist in affluent communities, it is very likely that more of these groups will isolate and exploit the kinds of youths now present in skinhead gangs. What is particularly troubling about this possibility is that these youths potentially have access to more money with which to pursue gang activity than youths from lower-income communities. But there is a positive side. The fact that the skinhead culture in Europe, and now slowly in the United States, is diversifying and is not as unified, makes it far more difficult for such an undifferentiated, loosely knit group to be directed and exploited by adult groups.

In addition to the reasons listed earlier in this chapter that explain why affluent youths haven't been observed to maintain long-term commitments to the skinhead hate ideology, here are some other reasons why sustained adult direction may not be effective:

• The natural tendency of youth gangs to remain independent from adults.
• The violent reputation of a specific adult group fosters fear in youths who fear that things could get out of control (similar to Kuba Belok, chapter 10).
• Adults in affluent communities can fund legal resistance, scaring off adult leaders from openly recruiting.

If this type of activity is suspected in a specific community, contact with local police and research groups, such as Klanwatch and the ADL, is recommended as they often maintain up-to-date databases of the latest recommended as they often maintain up-to-date databases of the latest groups, trends, and strategies for response.

———————◆◆◆———————

The nature of the ideological gangs—that they are attached to a specific ideology—could have great appeal to affluent US youths, especially if bouyed by a catchy subculture expression. To date, the hate gang variant as expressed by skinhead gangs is the only ideological gang that has emerged in the US. For potential inspiration points that might affect future trends, it is wise to become familiar with the ideological gang topography in Europe. For this reason the chapter that follows has been provided. It reviews the current European ideological variants and suggests which trends are more likely than others to take root in the US.

Skinhead perpetrator or victim?
See page 167.

CHAPTER 14.

Ideological Gangs: Part II
Present European
and
Future American Trends

In this chapter we will first examine variants of ideological gangs present in Europe which may affect affluent American communities. Then we will look at current US trends that might affect future affluent gang variants.

EUROPEAN SKINHEAD GANGS

In Britain, where the skinhead movement began, up to 70,000 racially motivated attacks and over 70 murders were reported yearly until 1985, a year marked by the Brussels soccer riot, in which 38 died and 200 people were wounded.[1] Many of these attacks and the 1985 riots were attributed to skinhead incitement. Worldwide attention didn't completely crystallize the events, until the skinhead movement spread to other European countries. This incited great fear.

One of the first countries where youths adopted the skinhead hate line outside of Britain was in the former East Germany. Skinhead gangs formed there in the early 1980s, but the repressive communist regime precluded the possibility of many overt criminal acts. One open display of defiance—not reported in the East German press—occurred at a soccer match in 1988, attended by Erich Mielke, head of the communist secret police. Skinhead youths in unison stood up, hoisted the Nazi flag, and shouted, "Sieg Heil," after which a brawl broke out between the gangs and police.[2]

By 1990, 246 attacks against foreigners were reported in Germany; in 1991, 2,247; in the first half of 1992, 1,443[3]—injuring 700 and killing 10.[4] In the first nine months of 1993, 1,480 attacks were recorded, 22 times the level of such attacks in 1983.[5] (In the first three months of 1994, an alarming

157

4,163 crimes linked to extremist right groups were reported.[6]) Then in June of 1991, in Dresden (pop. 520,000), located in eastern Germany, a skinhead gang burned down a bordello. It was the first highly publicized criminal act by a skinhead gang in the newly united Germany. The youth gang had been led by Rainer Sonntag, a thirty-six-year-old neo-Nazi, who had been gunned down and killed only days before. He had declared war on sex shops and homosexual bars in Dresden, an economically ravaged city from forty-five years of communism. (As already noted, skinhead groups in Europe typically endorse hatred towards homosexuals, ethnic groups, and leftists/anarchists). Sonntag sought to rally his gang behind a cause that was already favored in Dresden. It was one of the first times that Nazi slogans had permeated the Dresden night air since the communist's seized control after World War II. Similar incidents had occurred in East Berlin in April of that year when skinhead youths disrupted a homosexual festival, and in May when a bar in East Berlin's central Alexanderplatz was attacked. Neither incident, however, received much coverage in the national press.

The next year, in August of 1992, skinheads firebombed a refugee hostel filled with Vietnamese immigrants in Rostock, near the Baltic Sea in northern Germany and received much support from the local adult population. Numerous other attacks had occurred during two years prior, resulting in over thirty deaths, including another arson attack which killed five Turkish people in Solingen in May of 1993.[7] Even attacks against the handicapped were reported. Those in wheelchairs were accosted by thugs, spitting on them and taunting: "Under Hitler you would have been gassed."[8] Currently, the number of similar acts of violence remains as high.

Up until the Rostock attack, most of the international attention on ethnic attacks by skinheads and neo-Nazis was minimal. Because of mounting internal and international pressure for the Germans to quell the increased number of acts of terrorism against ethnic groups by skinheads, the German government in 1992 took the extreme measure to ban certain songs and bands that spewed neo-Nazi hatred in its lyrics (as noted in chapter 11) as well as three neo-Nazi groups—the German Alternative, National Front, and National Offensive. Later, in 1994, the German government banned the 400-member fascist organization, the Viking Youth. Led by thirty-year-old Wolfram Harath, dubbed the "federal führer," they advocated Jews wearing yellow stars, sterilizing "inferior beings" and distributed Nazi song books.[9] Although the Viking Youth (established 1952) had not been formally charged with specific acts of violence, authorities said that they had attracted a large skinhead youth following.[10] Similar to the German actions, in 1991 the Austrian government banned widely distributed video games for youths that had neo-Nazi themes; in 1992 it outlawed public denials of the Holocaust; and in 1994, Austria's leading neo-Nazi, Gottfried Kuessel, was convicted and sentenced to eleven years imprisonment for insurrection.[11]

Up until 1992, many in the international community viewed the skinhead phenomenon as an "eastern" German problem, solely brought on by depressed economic conditions wrought by communism. Social/ family conditions were rarely, if ever, mentioned. Even though skinhead gangs appeared across the European map—from France to Hungary and even a handful in Holland and Switzerland—their arrival was initially disregarded in Europe, in part, because it was difficult for many to accept the fact that youths would adopt the Nazi racist line, which had destroyed whole sections and peoples of Europe. Nevertheless, skinhead gangs grew and so did their acts of violence. And like in the US, many incorrectly assumed that these gangs primarily appeared because of the urgings of adult fascist groups. The actual story was the same as that in the US: skinhead gangs typically formed first followed by adult group attempts to recruit, guide, and direct.

In Europe, as the skinhead gang trend was initially downplayed or disregarded, skinhead gangs made their appearance in affluent communities in the United States and Europe.

When I was in Berlin in February of 1993, local gang experts noted that a new trend was emerging—skinhead gangs had been forming in the affluent west sector, the former West Berlin, since the Berlin Wall came down in 1989. In Poland in 1993, former Polish skinhead, Kuba Belok, and Warsaw sociologist, Barbara Fatyga noted the same trend in Warsaw. Fatyga observed that the trend of drawing in youths who were affluent was not just limited to skinhead gangs, but to other variants of ideological gangs, such as anarchistic gangs. Of those who have studied the gang phenomenon in Europe, her studies are some of the most comprehensive in scope and depth of understanding.

IDEOLOGICAL GANG VARIANTS

Fatyga personally conducted over fifty in-depth interviews with skinhead gang members as well as with numerous other gang member variants. She also kept a detailed journal of which variants attended which rallies, protest marches, and demonstrations. Although the youth culture she has observed was Polish, Polish youths have shown themselves to be just as easily influenced by the youth subculture as youths in the rest of Europe and the United States. (One interesting distinction between Poland and the US was revealed in a 1993–94 informal written survey of Polish high school students by youth worker, Dan Potter. He noted that in the US youths typically express that their greatest needs are help with coping with peer pressure, sex, etc. Polish youths, however, expressed that their greatest need was learning how to assume *personal responsibility* and making decisions about their future.)

What follows is a short synopsis of some of Fatyga's research, which she shared with me in March of 1994, and hopefully will soon be published in the West via a team of sociologists at Harvard University.

Anarchistic/Leftist Gangs—Virtually unknown in the United States, anarchistic gangs are present throughout Europe. Fatyga characterizes youths involved in this gang variant as follows:

- They listen to specific forms of music, such as punk, industrial, thrash, etc.
- They have an intense hatred towards those who are nationalistic—demand national, ethnic or racial purity—and/or who embrace hatred towards ethnic, or isolated groups. Skinheads and adult neo-Nazi groups are a favorite target of derision.
- Typically very literate, they embrace literature more readily than those in skinhead gangs.
- They embrace freedom of the individual.
- Criminal activity is limited to drug selling and assaults against skinhead gangs.
- While they do engage in fights at protests, many of which are planned, most "don't run through the streets with bombs in their pockets," although some extremist gang members can be excessively violent.
- The symbol often seen in anarchistic gang graffiti is a circle with a large "A" inscribed inside it. As noted in chapter 11, in American suburbs, youths who had seen this symbol, used by many rock groups in the United States and Europe, mistakenly assumed that it was the sign for the "anti-Christ."

14.1, 2. London and Cambridge, England 1994. Posters protesting the growth of the extremist British National Party (noted as the British Nazi Party) which attracts many English skinhead gangs with neo-Nazi ideals. Photo—Dan Korem.

14.3. University of Greenwich, London, England 1994. Anarchistic flyers pasted on campus. The upper flyer in part reads: Stop McHunger. Organize now for a better world. People and Nature—Not Profits. The lower flyer in part reads: Direct Action Movement. Anarcho Syndicalists. Photo—Dan Korem.

14.4. Warsaw, Poland 1994. Comparatively, Poland was noted in 1993 and 1994 to have far less graffiti than other countries such as Germany and Switzerland. This graffiti depicts skinhead and anti-skinhead sentiments. Additionally, anti-Semitic sentiments have diminished as there are less than 4,000 Jews left in Poland as a result of the Nazi reign of terror in WWII. Photo—Dan Korem.

14.5. Gdansk, Poland 1994. Anarchistic graffiti. Photo— Dan Korem.

14.6. Zurich, Switzerland 1994.
An anarchistic leaning group of
youths and young adults took
over this small run-down
section of a street (which is
uncommon in Switzerland)
near the downtown area.
Photo—Dan Korem.

I inquired of hundreds of youths throughout Europe regarding the
above characterization of anarchistic gangs, and they unanimously accepted
Fatyga's observations.

Fatyga observed that in the early 1980s anarchistic gangs took part in
fights in the streets against police and were *pro* "something." This changed
in the early 1990s when they became more pacifistic, but still retained their
hatred of skinhead youth gangs. She notes that there are even different
variants under the anarchistic label, such as those gangs that engage in
low-level criminal acts to protest such issues as foreign investment, abor-
tion, and even environmental and ecological issues. These variants were
first observed in Poland about 1989. It might be hard to imagine that youths
would form gangs that would take on this kind of façade, but the tradition
in Europe of multiparty political systems lends itself to this kind of expression. Youths often hear parents complain about their ills and vent their
anger directed at a specific party, rather than placing the blame on a government collectively. Thus, youths are more accustomed in the European
community to venting their frustrations in the context of some *issue* and in
relationship to a particular *political philosophy*.

Regarding the possibility of ecological gangs in the United States: This isn't as far-fetched as it might seem. Presently there are extremist adult environmental gang/groups who "spike" trees. Here, the assailant drives a large spike into a tree and then covers the entry hole with a piece of bark. When the tree is cut down or when it is sent to a mill to be cut into planks, both chainsaws and saw blades explode like shrapnel, killing logging and lumber operators. These groups hope that by this kind of "protest" they will prevent deforestation in the United States and further damage to the environment.

Skinhead/Fascist Gangs—In the early 1980s, Fatyga noted few skinheads in Poland, as was comparatively true in the United States. She also noted, as have others, that it was an "imported subculture."[12] She characterized skinheads as follows:

- Serious.
- Not subtle, like anarchists, and more prone to violent acts.
- Xenophobic.
- Intensely nationalistic.
- Have direct hatred towards specific groups, such as Jews, Arabs and Gypsies.
- Intensely want someone to listen to them. Often, she said that they say little at the beginning of an interview, but once they knew they could trust the interviewer, they rarely wanted to leave the interview once it was over.
- Most of the original skinheads were nonpolitical: "Just tough guys who were very tense," who frequently asked what other people thought about them personally. Now, skinheads have become a menacing force in nationalistic politics. Nationalistic political groups openly court them, such as the National Renaissance of Poland (NRP) and the Polish National Party, led by ultra-extremist B. Tejkowski. These political groups use skins to increase support and as a "protective force," similar to how the KKK used skinheads as "protection" in Polaski, Tennessee.
- Today skinheads are broken down into three categories: "skin-hooligans" who adopt the fashion and aren't political but would be classified in the delinquent gang type; "skins-sports fans," much like Ivan Rock in chapter 8; and "nationalistic" skins who are political.
- As in the States, the skinhead movement is *not* "correlated with unemployment among young people,"[13]and the number of skins has grown steadily since the mid-1980s.

Throughout Europe, as in Poland, there is a constant "turf battle of the mind" expressed in confrontations between anarchy and skin gangs. In the United States, such "turf wars" aren't present in affluent communities. This is a distinct possibility, however. In affluent communities, physical turf isn't as important as it is in the inner-city because affluent youths have comparatively more mobility. If gang rivalry were to become present in affluent communities, ideology could become an appealing "turf" in which to stake one's sovereignty.

Observations on the Nature of Ideological Gang Activity—One of the most important ideas suggested by Fatyga's research is that when an *object of protest* is absent, gangs will be driven *more* by the youth subculture than by an *issue* that is popular in the adult population. In the early 1980s, for example, many of the activities of skins were in reaction to the repressive regime, exemplified by Kuba Belok's low-level assaults against the state police. Although the formation of the gang was influenced by the youth subculture, its activities were driven by the current political climate. But by 1989, as the oppressive nemesis abated, most criminal activity, such as fights and drug dealing, took place in the street. It was *not* driven by current issues but rather the youth subculture. Clear structure and divisions between many of the ideological gang variants began to dissipate and often blurred, similar to what occurred in Dallas, Texas when an occult and skinhead gang co-mingled. But in the early 1990s, with the rise of nationalistic extremist parties, the activity of many skinhead gangs were again fueled by *political forces*. This time, however, the political influences were extremist forces and not the politics of the general population as was the case in the early 1980s.

It is crucial to recognize that in today's mass-media environment, in which ideas, both political and nonpolitical, can be communicated quickly, it's likely that youth trends will continue to change quickly, expressing a seemingly fickle nature. Therefore, sometimes youths will be in step with the protest politics; other times, they won't. (For a brief encapsulation of Poland's gang/protests trends during the 1980s until the present, see Source Note #1 at the end of this chapter).

FUTURE TRENDS

As is currently true of inner-city gangs, Danny Welch of Klanwatch notes that what makes the skinhead hate variant noteworthy "right now is their random violence."[14]Currently, there is a universal potential for explosiveness in the youth culture in the United States and Europe, and there are no signs that this will diminish.

There is a perilous bias that trends in Europe can't appear in the States because we are isolated. This is misguided thinking. Even in a neutral and historically isolated country like Switzerland, with a completely different tradition than other surrounding European countries, activity that fore-shadows *affluent gangs* is present.

As observed by Fatyga, ideological gangs form due to inspiration from the youth subculture and are driven either by political or individual youth subculture *agendas*. For those attempting to thwart the growth of these gangs, it will be important to note which factor is the most dominant.

If ideological gangs develop new variants in affluent, American communities, in the beginning they will probably continue to be *distinctly different* from delinquent or occultic gang types, as has been true in Europe. If a blurring effect occurs, it will most likely take place among ideological gang variants as well as with occultic gangs. Hybrids of ideological/delinquent gangs are unlikely because these youths would need to have greater ideological sophistication, which is currently not a part of the youth subculture. Also, as stated in the last chapter, new ideological variants probably won't be as popular as delinquent gangs because of this same need for ideological sophistication. Leaders of new ideological variants, however, are likely to be more articulate and intellectually astute than delinquent gang leaders, possessing an ability to define and rally gang members around a *particular cause*, which is more abstract than something concrete like burglary or drug dealing. This means that while delinquent gangs will create political headaches for those seeking to reduce crime, ideological gangs are more likely to drive and attach themselves to specific political agendas.

Traditionally, youths gangs typically prefer to shun older adult leadership. It is often a part of the rebellion factor. In recent years, the ideological gang type has shown itself to be an exception in the United States and Europe, as evidenced by youths attaching themselves to the political agendas of political aspirants and fringe extremists. (Hamm, who conducted the first survey of skinheads in the States, notes that among skinhead gangs, adults, 25-30, are sometimes seen to be leaders of hardened gangs.[15])

In 1992, for example, David Duke, a Louisiana KKK leader who came from a severely dysfunctional family in which his mother was an alcoholic, made a failed bid for the governor's office of Louisiana. During his campaign he garnered the admiration of many skinhead youths. Poland, England, and Russia are other countries that have also witnessed comparable associations. Adult political aspirants like Poland's Tejkowsky and Russia's Zhirinovsky not only offer an ideology and a context in which a gang can thrive, but the visibility of these political fringe aspirants provides the thrill and self-importance factor many youths are seeking. Rallies and media exposure perform some of the same functions that are apparent at fringe music concerts—youths can gather together under one banner, express interest in the ideas, and release their pent-up anger at something or someone. Additionally, if deteriorating family conditions persist, the ideological gang type has great potential for accepting adult leadership, providing the hero role of a surrogate "parent" or "big brother" for at-risk youths.

David Duke was from Louisiana. But what if he had come from Iowa and his ideological message had an anarchistic twist, which would better relate to a broader spectrum of affluent disenfranchised youths? Such a person might quickly amass a large youth following. Violent, terrorist-bent anarchistic groups appeared among US university students in the 1960s. Katherine Ann Power, referenced in chapter 13, was one such example. Why not younger American youths, like their counterparts in Europe?

Although speculative, it seems that if ideological gangs grow in America, the two most likely variants will be of the hate or anarchistic variant. The former will probably continue to attract a youth who is more overtly violent and less sophisticated intellectually, while the latter would likely attract youths who express aggression with greater subtlety, although either one could be just as lethal for those who get in their way.

PERSONAL REFLECTIONS

It is wise for those in the US who grapple with gangs in affluent communities to maintain a current understanding of ideological gang trends in Europe. If one type of gang persists on either continent, it will keep alive that variant for all youths because of the cross-pollination of the youth subculture.

In August of 1994, a Mannheim, Germany court reaffirmed the one-year probationary sentence against Günter Deckert, chairman of the 5,000 member ultra-right National Democratic Party of Germany. He was sentenced for "sedition, incitement to racial hatred and calumny to the memory of the dead,"[16] but was described by the court as "a reasonable person of clear beliefs."[17] Before and after the hearing, both skinhead gangs and left-leaning gangs, described as "punks" (a subculture group), took to the streets resulting in hundreds of youths being detained throughout the country. Over 600 youths were detained, and yet there was little coverage of this in the US national press. The international edition of Time published in Europe carried a full-page story, but in the US, nothing. This type of gang/mob activity present in Europe should be closely watched because it could inspire youths in other countries, including the US. Although on the surface these gangs say they are attached to an ideology, much of their criminal activity is irrational—mob-like rampages preceded by drunkenness—as is true in the US.

The youth subculture is sensually driven. Reason is often abandoned. Sometimes, though, youths can be shocked into awareness. The photograph inserted at the beginning of this chapter is shown in its entirety at right. It is an 8 x 10 glossy, shot by concentration camp guards, of a Polish youth

14.7. Eighteen-year-old Polish youth who died at Auschwitz I in 1941.

9368
SUBIX-BISIER JERZY
ur. 8.9.23,uezeń
przybyt: 10.1.41, zginął: 17.11.41.

14.8. Krakow, Poland 1994.
The kantor of the oldest synagogue in Krakow. Upon meeting this man, it was hard to imagine skinheads in the US or Europe indiscriminately hating someone like this. The kantor noted that when his synagogue was occupied by the Nazis, they deliberately removed the Torahs from the Ark and guns were placed there instead as a deliberate act of desecration. (Not far from the synagogue is the late Oskar Schindler's factory, which is still operating. Schindler, a Nazi industrialist, helped save many Jews, and his efforts inspired the noted book and movie, *Schindler's List*.) Photo—Dan Korem.

who died at Auschwitz I. Auschwitz is the German rendering of the Polish town, Oswiecim, which is about an hour's drive from Krakow. There are two former concentration camps there: Auschwitz I and Auschwitz II, the latter called Birkenau, the German rendering. At Auschwitz I, several of the barracks have been converted into compelling museums. In the Polish barracks is a long hallway filled with hundreds of 8 x 10 photographs taken by the Nazis of each prisoner before they were slaughtered. This Polish teen was only 18 years old when he died. Forced to shave his head, he might pass for a skinhead youth today. If a skinhead youth were shown this youth's photo without a description, might he not realize for a moment the frightening similarity between victim and perpetrator? That he might stop and consider the logical consequences of unwarranted hatred? That the unbridled hate he unleashes may one day consume him? Might he stop before unleashing terror on someone, such as the kantor of one of Krakow's synagogues, shown above?

SOURCE NOTE #1

Progression of Youth Gangs in Poland

1968—The first eruption of youth protests was observed as a legitimate protest against socialism. It was the first time that students, both university and pre-university students, stood up without being led by adults. (This youth trend simultaneously occurred in many other western countries, such as the US and Switzerland, as already noted. These protests were driven both by the subculture as well as politics.) In Poland, the catalyst was the March 8, 1968 censoring of a classic Polish play, "Dziady" by Adam Mickiewicz, which had anti-Russian elements in it. From ensuing protests, students were banned from continued studies. Additionally, some government revisionists stirred anti-Semitic sentiments and a number of Jewish professors were dismissed. Simultaneously, supportive students were Jews, anti-Communists, and hooligans. About 20,000 Jews left Poland, reducing the number to the current state of about 5,000.

1968–80—Nonconformist youths joined political protests in Poland. Solidarity formed in August of 1980, and the Student Independent Union formed that same year. Here youth activity became more diverse due to the pressure of the political and social climate and youth subculture influence from the West. It was during this time that the "new youth culture was born." Rock music with violently destructive lyrics appeared in 1981 (similar to what was seen in the US), which the government tried at first to suppress, but then decided to allow as a "safety valve." The basic opinion was: "let them cry out and they won't revolt." Simultaneously, Polish family relationships deteriorated.

Early and Mid-1980s—Skinhead gangs appeared and martial law was leveled in 1981. Many of the gangs that protested this move were much like Kuba Belok's; they lashed out because of true political factors. Freedom and independence were common themes. Most of the gangs were against the police but were *pro* something. For this reason, they were viewed as more part of the mainstream by adults because they were siding with the issues heartfelt by most adults. (Delinquent punk gangs from 1980 till the present became more "civilized" and interested in literature.) The principal motivating factors that spurred gang growth were the deterioration of the Polish family, an increase of adults who withdrew from helping at-risk youths, and inspiration from the youth subculture.

1988—Dramatic increase of youth gangs was observed, including the appearance of numerous variants of anarchistic gangs. Some sociologists, with specific political leanings, said that they formed because of strikes that year. While political factors did inspire the nature of some of their activity, the deterioration of the family and inspiration from the youth subculture were more important factors.

1989—Gang protests and street activity overlapped because many were against the same issues, such as environmental issues and foreign investment. Also, beginning in the late 1980s, youths from slightly more affluent families than the mainstream joined punk gangs, a delinquent gang variant. These gangs became less dangerous and violent because of more emphasis on intellectual protests and pursuits.

1990—The first symptoms of anger after change from Communism were observed. Gang confrontations reflected this context. For youths, changes didn't come instantly, familial discontent was still chronic and lack of expedient change of conditions was used as a scapegoat for discontent.

1991—Fewer protests driven by the left or the right, rather gang "protests" and criminal activity were driven by their own issues, youth subculture agendas. They took on a more negative tone than in the early 1980s when many gangs were pro freedom, independence, etc. More anarchistic gangs became pacifistic and apathetic.

1992—Ideological gangs continue to become more distinct from each other after the government changed. One target against whom they could all protest against wasn't present.

1993–94—More skins from more affluent communities are observed, similar to the US.

CHAPTER 15.

Occultic Gangs

O ccultic gangs have spawned the most amount of panic, hysteria, and false rumors than the other two types combined.

Since the mid-1980s, numerous adults have reported that they were the victims of "Satanic ritualistic abuse," now known as "SRA" cases. Without substantiating facts, thousands of adults claimed that both as children and as adults that they had been forced to participate in gruesome sacrificial rituals and even murder. Almost without exception, these cases were fabrications. Some of the most popular "SRA" books have been exposed as complete fictions. The most significant factor that inspired the SRA hysteria, apart from social conditions (see Source Note #1 at the end of this chapter), was the fact that youths since the early 1980s, without adult participation, were independently forming occultic gangs. Additionally, this trend emerged in Europe simultaneous to when skinhead gangs became a force. What both trends shared were youths with a twisted desire for power. When the occultic gang trend became visible, numerous adults adopted the SRA line, fostering their own imaginative stories. Many people believed these stories to be true. After all, what other explanation could there be for the fact that youths in diverse places across America and Europe were involved in occultic gangs? The actual catalyst that fostered these theories, however, was the *youth subculture and gangs.*

Youths involved in occult gangs focus on some occultic entity or practice, such as Satan or an Ouija board, to whom they "swear their allegiance" and/or from which they hope to derive *power*. It is in this context that crimes such as drug dealing, animal killings and mutilations, and rape have been committed. Murder has also occurred, but with great rarity. Just because a youth expresses *devotion* to some entity or occult practice, however, of course doesn't mean that he or she will commit a crime. The material in this chapter addresses gangs who actually commit crimes in an occultic context. Examined are general observations concerning occultic gangs, an example of a *fabricated* story, common characteristics of these gangs and some *legal perspectives*. Additional information addresses recent historical observations concerning alleged occultic activity and crime is provided in Source Note #1, and Source Note #2 briefly examines the relationship between those who seek paranormal power and cults/gangs.

GENERAL OBSERVATIONS

Since the early 1980s, delinquent and ideological gangs started to appear—*first* in lower-income communities, then in affluent communities. The occult gang trend, however, rooted itself first in middle- and upper-middle class communities. While there are exceptions, this type of gang is far less common in lower-income communities, with the exception of rural, isolated areas.

Officer Lee Reed, a juvenile officer in Abilene, Texas, offered the following hard-edged observations regarding affluent youths who join occultic gangs.

"There are three reasons that you don't see poor kids getting into [occultic gangs]. First, they have enough street smarts to know you don't get something for nothing, and that is what Satanism promises: worship Satan and you can have power for free. Second, street kids might take orders from an older kid or young adult who can pound their face in, but they're not going to bow down to some self-styled Satanic priest and the like. And third, they don't like to have to read and study and memorize all that junk."[1]

A quick check of youth officers across America and Europe will reveal that occultic gangs are an *affluent* gang phenomenon. The common exception are occultic gangs that sometimes form in rural areas. An example was a 1989 drug-related case reported by Officer Rodney Cromeans of the Round Rock Police Department, located just outside of Austin, Texas. A youth, arrested on drugs and weapons charges, showed officers where he and other youths sacrificed a dog and spray painted "Devil Child" in a deserted house. In a recent 1993 case in West Memphis, Arkansas, three youths (16, 17, and 18), who professed a belief in the occult and sacrificed animals, raped and murdered three eight-year-old boys.

It seems that literacy and the ability to read and retain extremely abstract thoughts is a key contributing factor why occultic gangs appeal to those in middle- and upper-middle-class communities. Many of these youths purchase books on the occult from which they eclectically derive their gang's rituals, chants, and beliefs. This means that the youth must have a propensity and capacity for literacy. This is often found lacking among many lower-income youths. For this reason, it is not uncommon to find academically above-average students participating in these gangs; and many tend to have an artistic bent, which they use to express their rituals and anger. Some artistic renderings culled from various US cases are shown below:

Occultic gangs first emerged on the West Coast (California and Washington) in the early and mid-1980s, but became a visible presence in many diverse affluent communities across America and Europe in the mid- and

15.1. A youth's drawing reflecting the persona of occultic gangs and subculture groups since the early 1980s.

late-1980s. (Researchers, such as Hungarian sociologist, Dr. Maria Kopp, noted that occultic gangs first appeared in European countries in the early 1980s.) Currently, it appears that this gang-type reached the peak of its appeal around 1992 and has since declined in popularity. In 1990 it might have been easy to identify several different occultic gangs in a community, but today only one or two occultic gangs might be present. This doesn't mean that the trend has disappeared. It has been observed that this gang type may diminish in a community for a year or two, then return. It can work like this:

One generation finds this type of gang appealing, then tires of it, discarding it. Nobody sees any activity or manifestations. Remember, occultic gang activity isn't institutionalized as it is in the inner-city; therefore, there isn't any long-term motivation to keep it going, such as the drug trade in inner-city gangs. If the family conditions in a given neighborhood remain the same, when a younger group of youths reaches the age of about thirteen (the onset of adolescence), they latch onto ways to rebel against their parents and all authority. They seek ways to make their confusion intelligible and to mitigate their pain. I observed this phenomena in the community of Carrollton, Texas (chapter 5). Many in the community thought they were rid of this type of gang, but they didn't address the *root source* of the problem—the chronic breakdown of families. Two years later, new gangs surfaced.

Although occultic gang activity is unique to affluent communities, not all affluent communities experience occultic gangs. For example, in the spring of 1990 when occultic gangs were at the height of their popularity with the youth subculture, William Manning, a patrol officer with the Los Angeles Police Department, wrote:

> I have been working with the Los Angeles Police Department for approximately eight years, two-and-a-half as a full-time officer. I have worked in six different areas of the city: Devonshire (upper-middle class); Foothill (lower- to middle-class); Van Nuys (lower-, middle-, and upper-middle-class); Southwest (lower-class); Rampart (lower- to middle-class); and West Los Angeles (middle- to high-upper-class).
>
> In my experience as a patrol officer, I have never seen any activity or aftermath of any activity that could even remotely be considered Satanic. Neither have I heard of any such [occultic] activity happening [in my patrol area]."[2]

In a subsequent interview on August 21, 1990, Officer Manning said that he had inquired of other police stations in his area and said there were confirmed and scattered reports of mutilated animals, apparently by teen gangs, but there were no reports of felony crimes like rape or murder.

That same year, Janet Maitlen, the assistant director of Orange County Animal control, said that out of 113 reports that came to her office, half of which were necropsied, nearly a dozen revealed "human kills." She said, "One cat in Rosamore was tied to a door knob, and three cats were found in Costa Mesa in a shed with Slayer (the name of a heavy metal group) painted inside, and in another city a cat was found nailed to a cross."[3] She said that the majority of "kills," however, were coyote-related in which the genitals, heart, and liver were sometimes missing although the rest of the corpse was intact. This fueled a panic that occultic gangs were running rampant, exaggerating and distorting the actual problem.

"The reason that only certain parts were eaten was due to the fact that when meat is plentiful, these coyotes eat more nutritious and high-protein parts," Maitlen explained. "When owners didn't find blood, this was due to the fact that coyotes are very efficient carnivores. Once we papered the area last fall [1989] with flyers and told people to keep their cats inside and the lids on their garbage cans, the number of reports subsided. Now we are primarily picking up 'flat-cats,'" alluding to cats run over by cars.

This case and others like it beg another word of caution regarding this gang type.

As already noted, *of the three types of gangs discussed in this book, the occultic gang has stirred more exaggeration, hysteria, and controversy than the other two types of gangs combined.* This is partly due to the nature of these gangs and their sometimes grisly acts. For this reason, extra caution must be taken by those who are asked to respond to *claims* of crimes being com-

WARNING

ALERT

On Friday, June 15, 1990, two mutilated kittens were discovered on two front lawns of residents on Raintree. These cats were definitely killed by humans. Several hundred animal mutilations have taken place in various parts of Orange County over the last two years. If you see suspicious activity *in progress* in your neighborhood call 911. If you have *any* information about these killings that have plagued Orange County, call T.R.A.K. (Tustin Residents Against Animal Killers) at ████████ We Tip, Inc. is offering a reward for information leading to the arrest and conviction of the Orange County cat killers. You may call We Tip, Inc.—24 hours a day—anonymously at 1-800-███████████

ANY ANIMAL OUT AFTER DARK IS A POTENTIAL VICTIM.

PLEASE KEEP YOUR ANIMALS INDOORS AT NIGHT TO SAFEGUARD THEM FROM THESE VICIOUS CRIMINALS.

15.2. Tustin, California, 1990. Frightened residents, reacting to the mutilation of cats by youths, posted this bulletin. While some cats were mutilated by youths, more were killed by coyotes, fueling a panic. Photo—Dan Korem.

mitted by this type of gang. Otherwise, it can lead to the unnecessary fueling of panic and the creation of "urban legends." All this obfuscates the facts for bona fide criminal investigations.

Before examining the characteristics of these gangs, let us examine one other representative case which is extracted from taped interviews that were conducted over a two-day period. The case is told in a narrative form to capture the essence of how such stories affect those who hear them.

SACRIFICIAL MISTRESS

"Stan wanted me to be his mistress, and he showed me this little white dress—it looked like a wedding dress with a long pretty train."

Trish is talking, one arm folded across her tall and slender fifteen-year-old frame. It was June 1989. When most kids were enjoying their summer vacation, Trish was on the run. She thought she would be killed. Two men who said they kept her in hiding for her safety, asked me to talk to her. As she told her story, fear registered in her deep, blue eyes. Her young face was framed by long brown hair.

Her hometown is Denton, Texas, a thriving college town thirty miles north of Dallas. She first ran away in 1985 when she was twelve. Back then, everyone called her Pat, until her father abused her. "That's when Pat died and I started calling myself Trish," she said. (Her proper name was Patricia.)

Terrified of repeated sexual abuse from her father, she became a perpetual runaway, ending up at Stan's "hang house," in a run-down part of town, where young teen runaways—usually from middle-class families—hung out and were swept into the vortex of the drug culture. Other times the cops picked her up and left her at juvenile detention where she was soon released back to her parents; Denton County caseworkers didn't believe the stories of abuse, which Trish said led to her first of three suicide attempts—taking an overdose of Tylenol 3. Now she wasn't running from abuse, she was running from Stan—and for her life.

Blonde and in his late twenties, Stan liked to wear silk suits, preppy outfits and gold jewelry. He offered Trish an exploitative refuge, when one of her friends introduced her to him in December of 1985. The safe haven he offered was a mixture of drugs and kinky sexual misadventures.

Bounced around from one foster home to another, Stan (at age sixteen) declared his hatred of God and chose to worship the Evil One. It was in the basement, where the furnace burned, that he placed an antique marble table: his altar.

"The dress was so pretty, and everyone was standing around us in black robes and Grim Reaper hoods. Stan had a white robe with a black pentagram on the back," she said with a glazed stare as she spoke of the June 1987 rite. "I asked Stan if we were getting married, and he said, 'Something like that.'"

"I had already seen them sacrifice a calf and drink its blood," but being made Stan's mistress was even more special.

"He handed me a chalice filled with something that tasted like wine. Everyone repeated some verses—which I didn't understand. They then bowed, and I asked Stan, 'Is that it?'" And he said, 'Yeah, that's it.'"

"I wasn't afraid of Stan hurting me because I knew he loved me." What did shake her bravado was what happened in the basement in September.

"This plump girl with long stringy red hair—she must have been about 15—brought her baby," Trish said with the same fixed gaze, her hands now clutched in front of her. "There were all these people kneeling around Stan holding red and black candles. I had finished off two primos (a marijuana joint with cocaine) and smoked some rock (rock cocaine), so I was buzzing. He made everyone call him Jason, his other person, whenever he got weird."

"He took the baby from the mother—it was wrapped in a blanket—and he used his gold-handled dagger and cut off the baby's little finger. I couldn't watch. I turned away as I heard the baby scream, and I never asked what happened to it. That's when I made up my mind to leave Stan and the hang house."

Trish did leave Stan for several months and even spent Christmas at home. From there she ran away again and was put in a youth home. She ran from there and in March of 1989 she asked Stan to take her back, but he said he didn't trust her and she would have to prove her loyalty to him.

"Well, what do I have to do?" she asked.

"I don't care, I'll leave that up to you," he replied menacingly.

"After we talked," Trish continued, "I smoked a $50 rock (rock cocaine), snorted three nickel lines (pure cocaine), and smoked a primo (marijuana and cocaine). I was flying—really buzzing. So I took one of the dogs and went for a walk like I always did."

Just up the road from the hang house was the Deluxe Inn, a budget-type but clean motel. Trish liked to walk each of Stan's nine great danes down the service road that ran parallel to the Interstate. She stayed near a wooded area so that the cops, who regularly patrolled that area and knew her by sight, wouldn't see her.

It was there that Trish saw a small skinny girl, about nine— Tracy. After she worked up her courage, Tracy said, "That's a big pretty dog. Has he ever bitten anyone?"

"No, put your hands out and let him sniff you," Trish offered, and Tracy stroked Shadow's thick mane.

"Do you think I could ride him?" Tracy boldly asked.

"Yeah," said Trish as she hoisted the light little girl onto the tame steed. The two girls talked and exchanged names.

After a while Tracy said she had to run home, back to the Inn where she and her mom lived and her mom worked. "We waved good-bye, I put the leash back on Shadow, and Tracy said she hoped she could ride the 'doggy' again sometime," Trish recalled with girlish glee.

"I came back home, and I told Stan about this pretty little girl who rode the dane. That's when he got this look in his eye—like when he wants to be called Jason. He told me I had to bring her back to the house."

When Trish resisted, *Jason* said, "It's either you or her." The next day Trish went back to the wooded area with one of the female dogs, which were easier to ride. "There she was with her strawberry blonde hair, hazel eyes, and no front teeth," Trish remembered in detail. "She was in a short suit like jams that had big flowers—red violet and pink—and her cap shirt didn't have a back and had two straps. Her Keds and her socks were white."

Trish invited Tracy over to her house to play with her dog, and Tracy cheerfully said, "Okay, but only for a little while or my Mommy will get mad."

At the hang house, Stan was waiting. After giving her some candy and a shiny silver dollar, he distracted her from the dogs and showed her some slides in his bedroom that he had shot around Denton. Stan only liked girls who were eighteen or younger. Older girls threatened him. Coyly, he asked Tracy if she liked to dance.

"Yes, I am a good dancer," the little girl answered confidently, and so she "taught" Stan how to dance. Scared and angry, Trish left the house and took some "rock" with her, hoping to escape out of her head. She knew nothing would happen to Tracy while it was light.

When Trish returned, it was dark, and the recitation of unintelligible and frenzied chanting rose from the basement. Descending down the wooden steps, she saw her little friend, now groggy, silhouetted by the dim candlelight, lying on the cold marble altar, her limbs pinned down by robed figures. As the dagger approached her neck, Tracy's dilated pupils spun crazily. Even the drugs hadn't numbed the terror. Tracy's nostrils flared hard to take in air; her small mouth was taped.

From the back, hidden behind the fleshly curtains of black, Trish's eyes locked on the carbon steel edge as it slipped beneath Tracy's skin—her diminutive chest heaving. Trish started to flee. Oblivious, Jason's fingers started to peel back the soft skin, and Trish fled and never stopped running. . . .

Sounds Convincing, Needs Facts

On the evening of June 8, 1989, in the conference room of an office building, I met with Trish and two men in their twenties. She had convinced them that her life was in imminent danger. The next morning we met in the room of a local motel. The two men said that they stayed in the room with her for fear that she might be attacked or that the police would return Trish to her father, whom she said had molested her. I finished Trish's interview in the office of a local Dallas pastor. Since I didn't know if Trish, a minor, was telling the truth, I chose the pastor's office to insure that she didn't invent a story that I or anyone else had made advances to her.

I have interviewed a number of rape victims, a task that requires sensitivity and compassion. As the victim is able to answer questions, you try to find the facts. This is how I approached Trish. I didn't have any previous bias about the case or that she may have been lying. She wept convincingly. But it turned out that Trish's tale was completely fabricated, and her "story" followed a pattern, an almost predictable plot. This genre of a tale has been falsely spread since the late 1980s by youths and adults.

Trish's *real* story was undeniably sad, yet typical. She was a fifteen-year-old perpetual runaway from Oklahoma. She had lived in Denton, Texas, and was now "on the streets" in Dallas. The Denton police said that they had picked her up many times.

Her tales of sacrifices and rituals were graphic and well-acted inventions. Stan, whose alter personality "Jason" was presumably taken from the teen horror movie *Friday the 13th,* was also a familiar figure to the Denton Police.

It only took a few phone calls to realize that her story—at least the part about the little girl, Tracy—was fantasy. First, there were no missing persons reports at

15.3. 1989—Trish in front of a motel after relating her story, which was discovered to be a fabrication. Photo—Dan Korem

the Denton County Sheriff's Department that even came close to matching Tracy's description. Second, no one ever worked and lived with a little girl at the Deluxe Inn. Trish also said that Stan threw a hand grenade in a car at the Triangle Mall, blowing it up. The mall manager said this never happened. Given Trish's penchant for storytelling, it's a safe bet that her other stories like the calf killing and the mistress ritual were also inventions.

The details of alleged sexual abuse by her father were more compelling, but never confirmed. It is possible that she may have invented the story of the little girl, Tracy, as a metaphor of her alleged abuse to minimize her psychological and emotional trauma. This is not uncommon. Though Trish lied about her Satanic episodes, if she had been abused I wanted to find that out—not because I was interested in doing a story on sexual abuse, but so she could get help. State and county agencies, however, are prohibited by law—which they should be—from confirming that kind of information. When I called directory assistance for the town in Oklahoma where she said she lived, there was no male in that town with her father's name, listed or unlisted.

I explained to Trish that I had no choice but to take her to the juvenile authorities. A local law enforcement officer facilitated this. Sadly, this is the way many juvenile cases end. When I later called Denton County Juvenile Detention, they couldn't acknowledge that she was there. She had disappeared as abruptly as she had appeared.

When confronted with this kind of story for the first time, whether real or imagined, listening to the grisly accounts and the expressions of emotional trauma can put anyone on edge and make lucid interrogation difficult. It is facts, however, that determine what is real and what is illusion. If the claims are true, emerging facts will support them. Then you must determine what to do about such incidents. If there is a satisfying conclusion to this story, I was relieved to know that no one was murdered. No life was sacrificed or lost.

Despite the many fabricated stories like Trish's, one fact resonates: *occultic* youth gangs *have* recurrently existed in affluent communities. In the case of the Dallas youths in chapter 5, there were many individuals, including other youths, parents, teachers, and law enforcement officers that could confirm various elements of the case. Even so, there were elements that *never occurred*. One male teen, for example, told of seeing a man decapitated in a ritual. As already detailed, investigating the background of one of the gang leaders revealed that he had previously *staged* a very convincing decapitation sequence for a local civic group at a "haunted house" set up in a warehouse as a Halloween fund-raiser. In the nearby suburb of Garland, another panic was fueled that was partly based upon fact and the rest on rumor.

Remember the gang, The Satanic Cult, in chapter 3? They specified that new recruits should have blonde, red or black hair and blue eyes. Through the rumor mill this got around, exaggeration followed and prompted a panic that an occult group was going to *abduct* a young blond-haired, blue-eyed child for a sacrifice. Police and school officials did their best to investigate and quell the fears of the community, which they did. On the next page are the memos sent out that aided the process.

Those who must contend with this type of gang or claims that this type of gang activity is present, are urged to use extreme caution before accepting stories as factual. The occultic gang, because of its highly sensationalistic nature, requires extreme prudence and a relentless probing of the events before coming to a conclusion that the "stories" are authentic.

September 28, 1989

To: Dr. Gerald Hill
Director, Elementary Operations

From: Dr. Michael Richey
Principal, Luna Elementary

Re: Student Safety

I just wanted to update you since our last phone conversation. My phone calls are becoming pretty regular now from parents about the kidnapping rumors. They want to know what we are doing as a school. My reply has been: All teachers have spent class time going over safety rules with their children. All of my staff have been made aware of the rumors and all outside doors will remain locked during the school day (except the front door). Visitation policy has been gone over with teachers. I will be sending home a letter just asking parents to go over their family safety procedures. (This letter will be sent home September 29). Police have been notified by me. The central administration has been made aware of the problem.

If you have other suggestions, will you please let me know. Thanks.

cc: Steve Knagg
Dr. Jill Shugart

15.4. Garland, Texas, September 28, 1989. Internal school memo reviewing safety precautions.

15.5. Garland, Texas, September 29, 1989. Letter to parents that avoids any mention of the rumor abduction, but does encourage parents to review safety procedures with their children.

September 29, 1989

Dear Parents,

This past week we have been working on safety. Teachers have focused on safety at school and at home. I am asking your help in reinforcing this with our children. Would you please take some family time this weekend and sit down with your children and stress safety rules. Go over the things that you expect as a parent of your children. Remind them of your procedures about playing in the neighborhood, walking to school, how to use the telephone in an emergency, what to do if approached by a stranger, etc. Also, if you have time, practice a family fire drill. Make sure your children know correct routes out of your home and what to do once out of the house.

We are all concerned with safety and making sure our kids are safe. I hope you will take time to discuss safety procedures this weekend. Thank you for your help in letting our children know that this is important.

Sincerely,

Michael V. Richey

Michael V. Richey, Ed.D.
Principal, Luna Elementary

October 2, 1989

TO: All Principals

FROM: Mary Ellen Marnholtz
Coordinator of Communications

RE: Rumored Cult Activity

This week we have heard rumors of suspected cult activity in a neighboring community. These rumors include the possible abduction of children from the Luna Elementary area to be used in cult activities on or around Friday, October 13. The Garland Police Department has not been able to validate any information concerning this rumor.

Garland ISD administrators are aware of the situation, and we are taking the appropriate precautionary steps. We are working with the Garland Police Department and have begun a three point plan to deal with the situation.

1. Patrols by the GPD have already been increased around Luna Elementary.

2. Dr. Richey has met with his staff to explain the situation and to ask them to be extra cautious and to help keep the building secure. He has also heightened the student's awareness about safe conduct going to and from school.

3. A letter from Dr. Richey has been sent home to all Luna parents urging extra caution at home and asking them to discuss safety procedures with their children (a copy is attached).

Although these rumors apparently do not target any other GISD campuses, it would not be unwise for all principals to follow steps similar to 2 and 3 listed above.

Attachment

15.6. Garland, Texas, October 2, 1989. Memo to all principals regarding "Rumored Cult Activity," indicating the rumor is unconfirmed, but that it "would not be unwise" for principals to keep buildings secure and send a letter to all parents.

COMMON CHARACTERISTICS

Nature and Size—Occultic gangs tend to be smaller than other types of gangs (typically less than 10 members), due to their obsessively secretive nature. Regarding female members, occultic gangs are more likely to have *more* female members than the other two gang types. This may be due to the allurements of power conveyed through the *verbal* activity and the abstract aspects of occultic gang activity—what is said (chants) and by what constitutes the beliefs—which are less *physically aggressive* than acts such as stealing a car, shooting a gun, or beating up someone of another ethnic group. The sexual overtones of some occultic beliefs also attract both males and females and are recruiting incentives. In the case of Amy, chapter 3, sex was something she felt she *had* to participate in to receive "power." In other gangs, sexual activity may be present, but isn't a part of the integral context of the gang. One female gang member I interviewed stated that the physical intimidation—power device—of the gang is what appealed to her. "I felt a need to scare people, so they'd leave me alone. I just wanted everybody to get the f— away from me. So I'd give off this bad impression." For additional insight into the desire for paranormal powers that can translate into gang and cult activity, see Source Note #1 for another case which resulted in the murders of a number of people in Matamoros, Mexico.

Beliefs—For many youths, there is an expectation of receiving or controlling some kind of paranormal or supernatural power. Some of the beliefs and practices common in an occultic gang are: Satanism; paganistic practices; worship of specific gods and goddesses; and the practice of "New Age" beliefs, such as tarot card divination, the use of healing crystals to heal and Ouija boards to predict the future. Each group's beliefs are unique and change rapidly, typical of most subculture expressions. For example, the occultic gang cited in chapter 3 spray painted a pentagram in the grass in which sacrifices were performed. Lit candles, incense, and assorted occultic symbolism were also incorporated with chants inspired by *The Satanic Bible* (1969). In other gangs, the focal point of the gang's allegiance could simply be a rock in an isolated location doused with animal blood, as a sign of allegiance to some entity. Some youths even pledge allegiance to a pagan god or goddess that they believe protect the earth. One youth I interviewed told me that the idea to pledge his allegiance to a "pagan goddess" was inspired by the ecology movement and how "man was raping the earth," reminscent of ecological terrorists that spike trees (chapter 14). He hoped that his self-styled rituals, gleaned from books on the occult, would protect his wooded meeting place.

Sometimes these gangs can be classified as cults but most don't qualify because of a lack of clear leadership or the use of thought reform techniques.

Use of Trickery—Regarding the issue of "calling up powers," none of the scores of gangs I have investigated ever presented real proof that they could summon up such powers. What is common, however, is the use of trickery to convince youths that dark powers exist.

In one case in Rockwall, Texas, in the late 1980s, a youth used a very clever trick to convince gang members assembled at the edge of a watering pond that he had powers. Late one summer night, gathered at a remote, rural location, the youth, an older teen who was the leader of the gang, shouted, "If you don't do as I *say*, this is what will descend upon *you*!" As he leveled his threat, the pond *behind* the gathering burst into flames, terrifying everyone. He created the fire-bolt illusion with the aid of a youth, who was hidden in the tall grass, surrounding the pond. As the leader spoke to the group, the concealed teenager, poured highly flammable fluid from a fifty-five gallon drum into the small pond, covering its surface. Then, timed with the leader's threat, the boy threw a lit match into the pond, and the pond burst into flames—ostensible proof of the leader's powers. Everyone was frightened and awed.

Just as certain individuals, events, or books have *triggered* interest in occultism over the years, other people, incidents, or works have served to (1) *decrease* the public's interest in the attainment of powers and (2) promote reason over hysteria. One work in the second category was the famous treatise, *The Discoverie of Witchcraft* (1584) by Reginald Scot (1538-99). It was an important work in its time because it started the wheels in motion that brought the witch hunt craze of the Middle Ages to a conclusion. Scot, who believed in the actual existence of Satan, exposed in his text many of the sleight-of-hand tricks and the psychological dodges that occultists use to convince their prey that they had supernatural powers. (For further discussion on the mindset of this type of power faker, see Source Note #2.)

Merging with Other Gangs—If an occultic gang is going to merge or mingle with another gang, this will more likely occur with an ideological gang than a delinquent gang. This is because most occultic gangs focus on an exchange of *ideas*—the exception is drug-selling gangs, such as the one cited in chapter 3. The essence of an occultic youth gang is its eclecticism. Delinquent gangs, such as the one in which Ivan Rock (chapter 8) and Andy Kriz (chapter 3) were participants, are not likely to be compatible. They are action-oriented, more direct, and less cerebral.

Inspiration Points—Tracking which neighborhoods might be prone to occultic gang activity in the late 1980s and early 1990s was often as simple as visiting the neighborhood chain bookstore.

Consistently, bookstores that experienced unusually high numbers of sales of *The Satanic Bible* (1969) to youths also had occultic gangs in nearby communities. What was ironic is that the author, Anton LaVey, wrote the book as a hedonistic *spoof*, since he stated that he didn't believe that Satan existed. This didn't stop thousands of youths from purchasing the book by LaVey, who was a former carnival barker and crime-scene photographer in the 1950s for the San Francisco Police Department. Here are some excerpts from LaVey's book that many youths accepted as the gospel of evil:

> I dip my forefinger in the watery blood of your impotent mad redeemer, and write over his thorn-torn brow: The TRUE prince of evil— king of the slave![4]
> Behold the crucifix; what does it symbolize? Pallid incompetence hanging on a tree.[5]
> Blessed are those that believe in what is best for them, for never shall their minds be terrorized—Cursed are the "lambs of God," for they shall be bled whiter than snow![6]

In his "Nine Satanic Statements," LaVey writes:

1. Satan represents indulgence, instead of abstinence!
2. Satan represents vital existence, instead of spiritual pipe dreams!
3. Satan represents undefiled wisdom, instead of hypocritical self-deceit!
4. Satan represents kindness to those who deserve it, instead of love wasted on ingrates!
5. Satan represents vengeance, instead of turning the other cheek!
6. Satan represents responsibility to the responsible, instead of concern for psychic vampires!
7. Satan represents man as just another animal, sometimes better, more often worse than those that walk on all-fours, who, because of his "divine spiritual and intellectual development," has become the most vicious animal of all!
8. Satan represents all of the so-called sins, as they all lead to physical, mental, or emotional gratification!
9. Satan has been the best friend the church has ever had, as he has kept it in business all these years![7]

And from LaVey's chapter on human sacrifice:

The use of a human sacrifice in a Satanic ritual does not imply that the sacrifice is slaughtered "to appease the gods." *Symbolically*, the victim is destroyed through the working of a hex or curse, which in turn leads to the physical, mental or emotional destruction of the "sacrifice" in ways and means not attributable to the magician.

The only time a Satanist would perform a human sacrifice would be if it were to serve a two-fold purpose; that being to release the magician's wrath in the throwing of a curse, and more important, to dispose of a totally obnoxious and deserving individual.[8]

Performing what is popularly called the "black mass" is simply an urban legend—the result of rumor and innuendo that has been passed down over a period of time and eventually accepted as fact. Recent history in the past three centuries confirms that there have been an isolated few who have committed crimes under the guise of Satanism, but there is no evidence that there has been an *ongoing formalized* "Satanic tradition" over the centuries. Unfortunately, most youths don't know this.

The extreme expressions in *The Satanic Bible*, coupled with the kinds of music lyrics cited in chapter 11, are common inspiration points for youths in occultic gangs who have committed crimes. For many, it was the final excuse to break the law, but the Satan-made-me-do-it defense doesn't wax, as further discussed later in this chapter. This defense has been justifiably met with objections by those in law enforcement when Theron "Pete" Roland, a member of a small teen gang in Joplin, Missouri, received a reduced sentence for the 1987 killing of a classmate. Roland came from a broken home and was abused. He and two other classmates, Ron Clements and Jim Hardy, "sacrificed" a high school classmate, Steven Newberry. They beat him to death with baseball bats, then dumped his body in a well dubbed "the well of hell." The three testified that they "ritually" sacrificed animals, were obsessed with heavy metal music with Satanic lyrics, defecated on Bibles—mimicking fabled Black Mass lore, and dealt drugs. Other less volatile inspiration points for youths not already detailed in chapter 11, include:

- The writings of occultist Aleister Crowley
- The *Necronomicon*, an invented occultic manual which even youths in Salzburg, Austria thought was authentic
- "New Age" and other assorted books on occultism and metaphysics
- Runes, an occultic fortune-telling practice sold as a kit in mainstream bookstores
- Movies with occultic/horror themes such as *The Exorcist*.

Drugs—The most common criminal activity currently found in occultic gangs is the using and selling of hard drugs. In the occultic gang case cited in chapter 3, youths took drugs to escape from their problems. Drugs were also sold as a source of income. The young adult, Terry, who directed the gang's activities, used the occultic gang context as an opportunity to sell drugs. Most youths in his gang wanted power, whereas he wanted money and illicit sex with minors. The occultic gang context, which is secretive by nature, was ideally suited for carrying on illegal activities.

A number of researchers note that gangs that focus on drug *use* are typically short-lived[9]—although they can still pose a deadly threat. This seems to be the case with most occultic gangs, particularly those with a

15.7. Two books, *The Satanic Bible* (1969) and *Necronomicon* (1977) were believed by many youths to contain actual "satanic" liturgy. Both in fact were farcical, and Anton LaVey, author of the former, denied a belief in Satan. Photo—Dan Korem.

15.8. Salzburg, Austria 1992. "NECRONOMICON" is painted on a side wall of the famous 12C church, Dom St. Rupert, by youths of a local gang. Photo—Dan Korem.

15.9. Brandon, Florida (Tampa suburb) 1990. In an abandoned house, an occultic drug-selling gang performed self-styled "rituals." Candle drippings, mutilated birds, and graffiti were evident before the house was razed. Photo—Dan Korem.

15.10. Gdansk, Poland 1994. Even though many Eastern European countries, such as Poland and Hungary, were isolated from the West prior to the collapse of Communism, youth subculture influences have been evident through the underground distribution of recordings of bands, magazines, and clothing fashions. Photo—Dan Korem.

strong drug orientation. While reasons are speculative, this is perhaps due to the illusory nature of the occultic-drug context, which ultimately doesn't fulfill its members. In the end, the gang doesn't grant wish-fulfillments nor deliver what youths hope to receive.

The blend of the occult and drugs is not unique nor new. In the New Testament, the Greek word *pharmakos*, which is sometimes translated as "sorcerer" or "magician," referred to an occultist who gave potions—magic elixirs—and simultaneously cast spells. (It is from the root word, *pharmakeia*, that we derive the word "pharmacy.") The idea was simple. The occultist gave drugs—potions—and cast spells to create the illusion in the believer's mind of supernatural spiritual powers. This same line of illusory behavior is usually operative in most occultic gangs.

Gangs that focus on *using* drugs should not be confused with the institutionalization of inner-city gangs brought on by the infusion of *selling* drugs. The selling of various cocaine derivatives has played a big part in establishing the economic underpinnings of many gangs. In affluent gangs, however, drug selling has not had the same kind of economic impact on youths to extend gang membership through one's young adult years because of other means of earning income. As previously noted, availability of jobs and the prospects of a college education are some of the factors that undermine the financial lure common in lower-income urban areas.

Likely Locations Where Occultic Gangs Gather—Where occultic gangs are likely to meet is more predictable than the other two gang types because occultic gangs prefer secrecy and natural elements, a harkening back to pagan practices. The following are common sites or places but don't entail every possibility.

Bridges and Tunnels—I asked a sixteen-year-old teen what was the kick about meeting underneath a bridge. He replied: "We laughed at people as they drove over us, because they never knew what we were doing. It was getting away with it right underneath their noses." For this youth, the "rush" of meeting under a heavily trafficked bridge increased the thrill: the thought of getting caught made the activities seem even more daring.

A bridge for youths is like a modified enclosure—an outdoor clubhouse. Furthermore, bridges are readily identifiable landmarks that one can easily find at night. They also are an ideal location for graffiti. Some bridges are located near water—which conjures up images, inspired by occultic books, of the elements of earth, wind, and fire giving birth to powers. Splashes of light from the moon, headlights, street lights, flashlights, and candles all add additional atmosphere to an already highly charged environment that stirs the imaginations of youths and arouses their passions.

Tunnel-like passages found in sewer, water, and drainage mains are possible gathering points. The buried, womb-like enclosures provide a mystique of concealment for gang members.

Woods, Lakes, and Streams—Places that are secluded and are associated with nature are inspiration points for youths to write chants to "mother earth" or other entities. Because many occultic books celebrate the mystique of woods and the earthen elements, it is prudent to check out nature-oriented areas when occultic gang activity has been confirmed in a community. On more than one occasion I have located youths secretly meeting in this type of an isolated location. Our local police department once asked me to assemble a list of likely locales that this type of gang might meet. When I pointed out one wooded area, they said that they had already observed occultic gang activity at that location.

Old Buildings and New Housing Developments—Abandoned houses and buildings are likely locations that should be checked out as well as new housing developments. Both offer isolation and a place to meet without being observed. Old buildings are usually preferred because new developments are often patrolled by police to protect against vandalism. The woods and fields near a new subdivision are also likely sites because of their accessibility. They are more desirable to youths than woods in a settled neighborhood because they are more isolated.

Malls—Shopping malls, where kids can hang out, are locations where they can make contacts to sell drugs and to identify recruits. Rapes and animal sacrifices obviously don't take place at malls, but they are neutral ground where kids from one part of a city can go to meet kids from other sections of the city.

Science Fiction Fairs, Esoteric Conventions, and Occult Bookstores and Shops—One must use discernment when considering this list. While many youths who aren't at-risk sometimes go to each of these, these kinds of locations and gatherings often attract kids with creative imaginations looking for powers, and is thus an potential place to find recruits. One type of occultic shop that has become popular in recent years is called a "botanica." Here one can purchase animal bones, herbs, and other necessities for the practice of Santeria, a Cuban form of voodoo.

"SATAN MADE ME DO IT" DEFENSE

As referenced by the 1987 Joplin, Missouri killing, on occasion there has been an uneasy prejudice by courts to consider criminal acts committed in an occultic context as something special, providing some convicted defendants with lighter sentences.

As suggested by Robert Hicks, crime analyst for the Virginia Department of Criminal Justice Services, a crime should be investigated and tried based upon a criminal act and not based upon a person's belief or absence of beliefs. He provides the following example:

> When I was a police officer, a guy walked into a Seven-Eleven store and tried to hold it up. He put a gun to the cashier's head and said, "This is a stick up." And as it turned out, the cashier who had just been robbed the week before, rather than get scared, got angry. In an instant he grabbed the gun and whacked the guy across the face, and captured him.

> When we interviewed the suspect, I asked, "Why did you go do this?" And he said, "Because I saw a sign."

> I said, "What sign?" He said, "3152." I said, "What's 3152?" He said, "It's the future of mankind."

Well, it turned out he had seen a license plate with the four numbers 3152 on it. In his head it clicked, "Ah, I am given a sign to rob the store." He made much of this during the interview. We asked ourselves: "What's the prosecutor going to do with this?" The prosecutor was faced with, "Can we do a criminal prosecution as we should. What do we do with this extra bit of information and his whole rationale for the robbery?"

The prosecutor decided just to do a straightforward robbery investigation, but the defense wanted to offer up an insanity defense to mitigate the guy's conduct.

As it turned out, the court didn't buy it. And after giving this guy a battery of psychological tests and interviews, the conclusion was that he was making it up.

For our purposes we investigated it as a robbery. The prosecutor decided, "Well, let's go with it as a robbery, straightforward robbery and see what happens." The defense made much of this motivation, saying, "Well, this mitigates the guy's conduct, because he clearly doesn't really understand consequences of his own actions."

Now take a different abstract example of somebody saying, "Satan made me do it." Kenneth Lanning of the FBI [Behavioral Science] makes the point that to get preoccupied with this sort of motivation, is to hand a defense attorney an excellent argument to get the guy off. So it doesn't really serve a law enforcement interest to pursue [Satanism] as a part of the case.

All of criminal law is based upon the Mensrea concept [Latin for criminal mind], that you have a free will and you can act. And if you commit a criminal act but have not established the free will to go with that, it mitigates the offense.[10]

Hicks's point is clear. Criminal acts must be prosecuted *as criminal acts.* A person should not be set free because they said, "Satan made me do it." People are responsible for their own actions, regardless of whether a friend suggested that they commit a crime or if they were inspired by something like *The Satanic Bible.* When suspects are genuinely insane or have experienced some form of thought-reform negating the Mensrea concept, then the court can pursue another course of action. Related to occultic gangs, youths who commit crimes should not be freed or be given preferential sentences anymore than youths in hate gangs who commit murders should received reduced sentences because they plead "Hitler made me do it."

Additionally, Kenneth Lanning, adds that murder should simply be called murder, not a "satanic" or "occultic" murder because of the belief of the perpetrator. Referring to the case of John List, who, in 1971, murdered his family of six because he claimed he was afraid that they wouldn't go to heaven, Lanning asks, "Can we say that this is a Christian killing, simply because the man claimed to be a Christian who wanted to protect the salvation of his family?"[11] The obvious answer is no.

Lanning adds:

> Neither would we consider a "Christian crime" any of these other criminal acts: A child molester reads the Bible to his victims in order to justify his sex acts with them; or parents starve and beat their child to death because their minister said the child was possessed by demonic spirits.[12]

When crimes are committed by an occultic gang, prosecutors are best advised not to focus much attention on the *context* in which the crimes were committed, except when such perspective and information can be useful to pursue an investigation. For example, to penetrate the secretiveness of an occultic gang, it's sometimes necessary to uncover the points for its inspiration which might reveal *how* youths are likely to act out their beliefs, where they might meet, and in what kind of context.

PERSONAL REFLECTIONS

While occultic gangs are likely to persist into the future in America and Europe, if current family conditions persist, it is impossible to predict with specificity—in one or two year increments—at precisely what times they will be popular. Youths tire quickly of subculture trends and jump to something new. The continued expansion of mystical "New Age" thinking, telephone "psychic hot lines," and so on will probably contribute to the idea of attaining *personal* paranormal powers. This, in turn, fires youthful interest as it relates to gang activity. Also, when societies approach the end of a century, it often engenders the apocalyptic mind-set. As we approach the year 2000, it has been predicted by many, including myself, that groups, gangs, and cults will continue to focus on the pursuit of personal paranormal powers and extreme acts, such as the suicidal self-immolation of the Branch Davidian cultists in Waco, Texas in 1993. In this same vein, it won't be surprising if there is a sudden resurgence of occultic gangs as we approach the year 2000.

SOURCE NOTE #1

Historical Observations

As noted in the beginning of the chapter, the appearance of occultic gangs was accompanied by undue public hysteria. In addition, there was outright exploitation of this hysteria by various media.

Several contributing factors in the early- to mid-1980s were:

• The appearance of occultic youth gangs.

• The release of several widely read books in which authors fabricated stories of how they were adult "survivors" of Satanic cults.

• The appearance of heavy metal bands that espoused occultic themes in their lyrics, fashions, and stage presentations.

• An explosion of criminal and civil cases related to allegations of Satanic ritualistic abuse (SRA) that in fact never occurred, such as the McMartin Preschool Case (late 1980s through 1990). Few convictions of any kind were handed down in these cases, although some youths were charged with committing violent crimes, including murder, in an occultic context. (It should also be noted that many people during this same time period started surfacing claiming that they had been abducted by UFOs, including a best-selling author, Whitley Streiber, whose book, *Communion*, details his alleged abduction.)

• A Mexican drug gang in 1989 in Matamoros, Mexico, murdered over a dozen people while they practiced a deviant form of Santeria.

It appears that the youth occultic gang trend, especially the gangs that identified themselves with Satanism, triggered fear in adults who assumed that the youths must have been organized by *adults*. Many concerned parents whom I interviewed openly expressed this opinion. It was beyond their comprehension that for the first time in American history, youths, *on their own*, without adult encouragement, would all of a sudden come up with the notion of forming an occultic gang in an *affluent* neighborhood. Adding to their horror were the visible displays by heavy metal bands that used Satanic themes. In fact, American and European youths engaged in this type of activity, inspired by these same heavy metal bands. In Hungary, for example, Dr. Maria Kopp observed in the mid-1980s small numbers of youths engaging in this activity, inspired by the *themes* of these bands. In reaction to this, exploitation materials began to circulate freely that talked about massive, adult conspiratorial groups worshipping Satan as they committed crimes.

One example was the book, *The Edge of Evil* (1989) by youth evangelist Jerry Johnston. In his book he reported that up to 50,000 people a year were being slaughtered as sacrifices by Satanic cults. Most of his book was based on news clips and *secondhand* reports. For example, he wrote:

Dr. Al Carlisle of the Utah State Prison System has estimated that between forty and sixty thousand human beings are killed through ritual homicides in the United States each year. This statistic is based upon an estimated number of Satanists at the level where they commit ritual human sacrifices times the frequency with which these would be done during a satanic calendar year.[13]

When later interviewed, psychologist Dr. Al Carlisle stated that he had never spoken to Johnston and that while he thought the figure to be true initially, he recanted before the publication of Johnston's book, stating that the figure was "highly inflated."[14]

Because of the exploitation of the "Satan at your door" theme by some ministers, some have incorrectly speculated that youths who were brought up in fundamentalist Christian homes were prone to become involved in this type of gang activity. At first blush, it seemed a likely possibility: Reject your parents, who are living like hypocrites—then reject their religion and rebel by embracing the *opposite* of what they believe. But this simplistic theory was erroneous. Typically, at-risk youths of this type comprised a small minority in these occultic gangs. Abuse of drugs and alcohol were found to be a far more common venue to rebel for these youths, not gang activity.

Other books during the mid-1980s appeared, written by supposed Satanists. The three most widely read were: *The Satan Seller* by Mike Warnke; *Satan's Underground* by Lauren Stratford; and *He Came to Set the Captives Free* by Rebecca Brown, MD. Each of these writers were later exposed as having written fictious accounts. Collectively, their books sold over 200,000 copies. Mass-media aided and fueled the hysteria.

In 1988, Stratford appeared on the *Oprah Winfrey Show* and a clip from Warnke's film on Satanism aired on the ABC news show *20/20*. Then tabloid talk show host, Geraldo Rivera, hosted his own special, *Devil Worship: Exposing Satan's Underground* on October 25, 1988, just prior to Halloween. Rivera's special earned the highest Nielsen TV ratings (26) of any show of its genre. Based upon

15.11.1990. A sample of the kinds of promotional materials used by purported experts on Satanism, circa 1990.

15.12. October 1988. Tabloid talk show host, Geraldo Rivera, hosted a 1988 two-hour television show, *Devil Worship: Exposing Satan's Underground*. The show garnered the highest Nielsen rating to that date (26) and fueled needless speculation and panic in neighborhoods then affected by occultic gangs. Photo—Dan Korem.

15.13. Matamoros, Mexico 1989. Shack in which occult/drug gang leader, Adolpho de Jesus Constanzo, tortured and killed over a dozen victims. Gang members chained those they tortured to the bedframe shown. In the box are candles that were used in rituals. Photo—Officer Rodney Cromeans.

a handful of isolated murder cases committed in an occultic context, Rivera called for Congressional hearings to quell the rise of these Satanic groups committing untold numbers of murders. In response, Jerry Johnston released his "Satanist Item Check List for Parents," warning parents "to search for these occultic items" including: "ferns, mirrors, and a preference for being alone."[15]

Added to this false wave of hysteria, the famous McMartin Preschool Case ended in an acquittal of Raymond Buckey (31) and his mother Peggy McMartin Buckey (63). The McMartins had been accused of 52 counts of child molestation. Parents believed that they were Satanists who secretively molested their children. In reaction to the verdict, one distressed mother pleaded to the lens of a CBS *60 Minutes* camera crew, "Fourteen-hundred children in this community have been ritualistically abused. . . . Doesn't that hit you?" She was outraged that the January 18, 1990 outcome of the longest and costliest criminal trial in American history—33 months of testimony, 6 years of legal proceedings, $13 million dollars of legal bills, 124 witnesses, and over 60,000 pages of transcripts—ended with an *acquittal on all charges*.

Additional fuel for the SRA scare were a small number of isolated cases where small groups of drug dealers or youths had actually committed murder in an occultic context. One of these cases occurred in Matamoros, Mexico.

On March 14, 1989, a University of Texas student, Mark Kilroy, disappeared while on spring break in Matamoros, Mexico. His mutilated corpse was discovered in a mass grave behind a shack in Matamoros. Along with Kilroy's body were those of over a dozen other people murdered as human sacrifices by a drug gang. The gang believed that by ritually killing their victims that they would have supernatural protection from the police. The gang's leader, twenty-six-year-old Adolpho de Jesus Constanzo, was the son of Cuban refugees who settled in Miami. In his early teens, he conned neighbors into believing he possessed psychic powers; that he could predict the future through his practice of Santeria, an Afro-Caribbean form of occultism. (Santeria's origins can be traced to the Yoruba culture of southwestern Nigeria. It was brought to the New World by slaves, where it combined with elements of Catholicism, and is characterized by divination, chants, candles, seeking favor from patron saints, and animal sacrifices.) As Constanzo grew older, he combined drug trafficking with elements of Palo Mayombe, an Afro-Caribbean form of voodoo (also spelled "vodun," which means god or spirit). This practice was brought over to the Caribbean by slaves from the Congo (Bantu) region of Africa where, like Santeria, it combined with Catholicism. (Palo Mayombe is characterized by rituals in which practitioners, called Paleros or Mayomberos, try to derive power from the spirits of the dead in order to have power over others, and human bones placed in a cauldron, a *nganga*, are believed to be a source of that power.) Constanzo also seemed to borrow from an Aztec practice of disembowelment as a means to attaining supernatural power. (The Aztecs believed that the heart absorbed the energy of the sun and had to be sacrificed to appease the gods.) His gang members claim that the reason Constanzo wanted to sacrifice a college student, was that an *intelligent brain* would give them greater power and protection. When police closed in on his apartment after the discovery of the mass grave site, Constanzo's "protection" deserted him, and he ordered one of his own gang to kill him, rather than to surrender.

In the US, a small handful of youths from different locales were convicted on murder and other felony charges committed in an occultic context or by those who simply *claimed* to be adherents of occult beliefs. In addition to the Joplin, Missouri case, another youth was convicted in a high profile case in Oklahoma City.

Seventeen-year-old Sean Sellers, a resident of Oklahoma City from a broken home, was convicted of the September 8, 1985, "thrill killing" of an Oklahoma City convenience-store clerk. He was also convicted of the March 5, 1986, shooting deaths of his mother and stepfather. Sellers said he shot them point-blank, while they were sleeping, with a .44 revolver.

Now on death row at the Oklahoma State Penitentiary, Sellers claimed that the reason for the killings was that, "In my own demented mind, I opened myself up to Satan."[16] An avid reader of *The Satanic Bible* and a player of D&D, he says that he nearly carried out his own suicide after he broke up with his girlfriend. Opinions about Sellers were diverse.

"He was more of a pseudo-Satan worshiper," said Oklahoma City Police Detective Bob Jones. "He was just full of bull. That [Satanism] was not the cause. That was just another symptom of his twisted little mind."[17]

Wayne Van Kampen, chief pastoral officer of Denver's Bethesda Hospital Association, who testified on behalf of Sellers, said, "He was very deeply engrossed in it [Satanism]. There was no question from what I read of his notebooks and journals. There was a close bonding with Satan and Lucifer, and a commitment to serving them. Sean had a very clear focus on death as the ultimate goal."[18]

Collectively, the above factors and phenomena created the scare. A combination of a small number of actual murders, the Matamoros case, heavy metal music videos with Satanic themes beamed on MTV, a few opportunists who wrote books that were later exposed, the McMartin Preschool case, and the appearance of occultic youths gangs, and exploitation of all this by the tabloid media, fostered an unfounded Satanic ritual abuse (SRA) hysteria.

SOURCE NOTE #2

Aberrant Groups and Claims of Paranormal Powers

An alleged psychic, James Hydrick confessed in a television documentary that I produced, "Psychic Confession" (1993), that his mind-over-matter demonstrations were a fraud. A twenty-two-year-old with a third-grade education, Hydrick had convinced many on national television that he could move objects by telekinetic powers—the alleged, but unproved ability of the mind to exert energy by influencing the movement of inanimate objects. Far more revealing than *how* Hydrick tricked his followers were the reasons *why* he wanted people to believe that he had powers.

Hydrick was severely abused as a child and shuffled to various foster homes. Between the ages of 9 and 17, he was confined in a South Carolina institution for the mentally retarded, even though he wasn't retarded. While confined, he developed an obsession with obtaining and developing paranormal powers. When he failed, he sought to *trick* others into believing he had such powers. The result—in his mind—was the same. He also legitimately developed martial arts skills and performed extraordinary strength demonstrations, such as an ability to balance his entire 200-pound, six-foot-one-inch frame on *one thumb* and perform push-ups.

On February 24, 1981, on the ABC television program, "That's Incredible," Hydrick fooled millions of viewers with his demonstrations of telekinesis. When he confessed to me in a two-and-a-half hour videotaped interview that everything was a deception, he revealed a warped, dual need for recognition: He wanted to put a safe, neutral space between himself and anyone he perceived to be a threat, helping him manufacture his own self-esteem. Here is a part of his admission/confession.

"You were on "That's Incredible" a few months back. You tricked them." "Tricked the whole world," Hydrick replied.

"You tricked them really good. Do you remember how impressed they were with you? What did it make you feel like?"

"It's like a hand reaching out for recognition. I guess I just wanted to be known. I needed to be recognized. All my life I've been kicked around. I wanted to see if these people were really intelligent and (if) I was really dumb. . . . All these doctors that I went through said, 'Yes, he is retarded; put him in a school. He's no good for the public.' All I'm saying is: 'Hi, dummy. Look where I am now.'. . . My whole idea behind this in the first place was to see how dumb America was. How dumb the world is."

Hydrick sought *power*—albeit counterfeit *powers* that were not real—in order to have *power* over those he perceived to be a threat. He first aroused the curiosity of those around him with his martial arts demonstrations, and then he insured his ability to keep others at bay with his intimidating demonstrations of trickery, passed off as real powers. Paradoxically, first Hydrick snared his following with his demonstrations of "power," then the group enslaved him with their expectations. Many in his enclave refused to believe that he didn't have powers even after he confessed. They wanted him to be something that he wasn't and perform to their expectations even though all was an illusion. Shortly after Hydrick's confession, he was arrested and convicted on a stolen guns charge. Presently, he is serving seventeen years on six counts of child molestation in California.

CHAPTER 16.

"Are You A Dragon?"
Will's Story

Chicago summer nights are hot and steamy, unless Lake Michigan favors the Windy City with a cool breeze. It was hot the night Will, nicknamed "Woody," boldly cocked his fist like the .22 caliber revolver he often carried under his belt to intimidate visually. Forefinger extended and thumb poised like his gun's hammer, he took aim and fired an imaginary round at Chico, rival gang member of the Latin Kings. Terrified, Chico flinched, but glared back. His stomach sickened, remembering the slug he took in the thigh three months ago during a fire-fight with the Insane Dragons. He could still hear his own screams. He didn't remember the face of his assailant until Woody taunted him. *Then* he remembered. He remembered it was *Woody's* .22 that ripped through his thigh.

Not a cop lover, Chico darted off his concrete porch inside his brownstone and called the neighborhood Chicago blue, implicating Woody as the assailant who got away. Chico's terrified call to the Chicago PD in August of 1987 probably saved Woody from an early death on the streets. Woody was sixteen years old.

Woody knew one thing: There had to be more to the world than Shadow, Kong, Tank, Turtle, and Tarzan. These were his cousins who, in the early seventies, started the Insane Dragons, "a turf and babes" gang. Their gang, which spurned drug trafficking, had grown to over 200 in the working-class section in northwest Chicago at Sacramento and Walton Streets. Woody, a gang nickname, wanted more than attending "meetings," where weekly dues of $5 were collected for guns and ammunition, and "hanging on corners" waiting for trouble.

Woody went to "juvy"—juvenile detention—for two weeks when he was fifteen. The "fall" was on a UUW (Unlawful Use of Weapon) for carrying a sawed-off shotgun. In "juvy" he lived with rival gangs, all controlled by two power groups that ruled most of Chicago's gangs: the Folks (who tilted their hats to the right) and the People (who tilted their hats to the left). The Dragons bowed under the Folks.

Even in juvy, attendance at gang meetings was mandatory. It provided a twisted sort of order, complemented by rules of detention: walk the halls with your hands behind your back with your head pointed straight ahead.

Gang interest for Woody outside the walls was nil—not one Dragon wrote a letter. Woody wanted to go somewhere, do something, and *be somebody*.

"At Christmas, I looked at the neat commercials on TV with families opening gifts around the tree near the fireplace and I wished I had that."

Newspapers and news broadcasts were his window to the outside world. Other gang members laughed at Woody when he talked of life "beyond the streets." One day he boasted, "I'm gonna be a cop some day." Right. Woody, the crazy Puerto Rican. The kid who, a year later, would pull a "hit" on Chico to prove himself. The kid who started to "hang" with gang members when he was eleven; who was a "peewee" gang member at thirteen—the first step towards full gang status; who zealously gave "head-to-toe"—a two-to-five-minute beating by your peers when you want out.

"I've seen guys with blown-up ears who nearly died. All you could cover up was your face. And the blows came hard . . . seven and eight per second. Or it could be worse. Before I joined, you had to walk the line."

Walk the line: the quitter, who wants out of the gang, runs a gauntlet between two lines of gang members while being pummeled. At the end, the bloodied soon-to-be ex-gang member is bludgeoned over the head with a pepaso—a taped lead pipe.

"Once in a gang, that's it. I only know a few guys who ever got out of a gang, and they left town. But most guys don't have the money to leave. I didn't. My Mom's divorced, and my stepfather didn't make much. He drove a forklift for Sears. And I didn't get along with him." (Kong was one of the few who managed to get out without head-to-toe. He was thirty. Some joked that he asked for his pension and the guys said forget it. It was cheaper to let him quit.)

When talking about home, few gang members talk about "Dad." When talking about divorce, they say, "Mom's divorced." The effect of derelict fathers is devastating, evident by the absence of the word "Dad" or "Father" when they describe their roots. (On the back of Woody's left hand, between the thumb and forefinger, is the small tattoo "MOM," which he was told stood for Mind Over Matter.)

"And getting a job . . . You've got no job experience, lack education, can't get a job in another neighborhood because of rival gangs . . . and you never change your looks."

Former gang members are also easy to spot. Their appearance is the most immediately damning wall to change. It invites harassment from other gangs while instantly labeling them as a pariah to those outside gang life.

"They have a look about them: the bouncing shoulders as they talk; the sway-

ing swagger as they walk; the cock of the head, with the chin down and angled to the side as they look at you out of the corners of their eyes. You just can't shake the look."

Another option open to gang members looking for an "early out" of the gang is *death*. Death was everywhere. You might mumble: "Death happens!" For Woody, it was a common part of street life.

"From the time I joined my first gang until the time I finally left the hood, I had been to about 20 or more funerals."

In August of 1987, just three months after being released from juvy, Woody shot Chico. The night before, around midnight, Woody was talking to Lucy who lived on the third floor in the corner building on his block. Everything was familiar and comfortable. It was Woody's turf. The only thing out of place was another teenager pedaling around the block on his bike.

The bike-rider stopped and asked Woody, "Watcha be about?" prompting Woody's gang identification.

"Insane Dragon," Woody replied and with his hands, displayed his gang signs.

"Are you sure? Are you sure?"

The bike-rider kept pressing, back stiffening, his voice hostile. Woody sighted the cross tattooed between the thumb and forefinger, the sign of a Latin King. In the same instant, Woody's eyes darted to the wooden bulge in the waist of the bike-rider. It was the handle of a pistol, and he saw the tattooed hand grab the chrome-plated gun.

"I am going to kill you, muther_____!"

Woody lunged at the gun to avoid being shot, but as they wrestled, his assailant's free hand slammed him to the ground. As Woody fell, he heard the pistol hit the sidewalk. Jumping off his bike, the Latin King retrieved his pistol and fired. But by this time, Woody was already twenty feet away, zigzagging as he was taught. It saved his life.

The next night the Dragons engaged the Kings in a fire-fight to avenge the attack. This was the turning point. After Woody shot Chico, he knew that he had to exit the Dragons. He had to get out, once and for all.

In October of 1987, Woody entered Valley View, an Illinois minimum-security youth center. He was sixteen and here he got a break. He was sent to Valley View because his evaluation showed that he was bright and not an imminent threat. This would be his home, his sanctuary, until April 1989. It was like juvy, so gang tentacles remained strong. Attendance at Folks and People meetings were mandatory. Then, something happened. A prison ministry group from Wheaton College began working with youths at Valley View. Woody, who wasn't looking for spiritual answers, decided to attend a meeting. One of the detainees told him there were some good-looking college girls there. Woody wasn't hostile towards spiritual matters, but he didn't see its relevance to his life.

"When I was ten, a church from Hammond, Indiana used to come around with a bus and ask us if we would like to go to Sunday school. I asked my mother, and she thought it was a good idea. So I went every now and then with my friends for about two years. It was kind of exciting taking a bus out of the city."

About the time he became a peewee Dragon, his church attendance dropped to three or four times a year. On the streets in the early part of 1987, Gordon McClean, a gang expert, worked with some of the older gang members. He took them to summer camps and gang-prevention meetings. He was the one who talked to Woody about making a change. Woody liked McClean and his spiritual emphasis on life, but "it didn't click." Extended time in Valley View ripened his desire to change and was strengthened by the meetings led by the local college students.

"At first I was just interested in the girls, but that changed fast. I started asking questions. I had prayed to become a Christian when I was ten, but I didn't make a decision to actually live the life until those meetings."

Word got around that Woody was changing. He wasn't showing up at the Folks meetings: he was going to Christian meetings. Woody bought time by explaining that he was buried in his advanced studies, earning his GED (which he earned before being released).

Skeptical, some of the guys pressed him, "Are you a Christian now?"

"Yeah," Woody would say.

"Are you also a Dragon?"

Woody hedged. "Yeah, I'm still a Dragon!" His answer was empty. Woody knew he was changing, even though the transition was ragged.

Woody left Valley View in April of 1989 after sixteen months of detention. He returned to the Insane Dragons. Everything seemed great the first few days back on the block, but he felt something was amiss. He was uncomfortable, out of sync.

"Oftentimes I felt God speaking to my heart, letting me know that what I was doing was not very pleasing to him. Sometimes I'd listen, most of the time I didn't."

Woody wanted out of the Dragons, but he didn't want to endure a head-to-toe. The more time Woody spent with his fellow Dragons the easier it was to ignore those softly insistent, inner voices.

One night, while cruising in a friend's car, they were unknowingly followed by a car full of Latin Kings. When they stopped at a traffic light, the Kings opened fire. One bullet penetrated through the side of the car door and armrest. Incredibly, the bullet didn't penetrate Woody's arm. Its force simply knocked his arm across his chest, causing a massive bruise and swelling.

"It swelled up like I had a can opener under my skin."
Because of grudgeful relationships with some of the Dragons and the risk of being killed as a Dragon, Woody started to hang with the Imperial Gangsters (I-Gs), whose turf was across town, near the home of a girlfriend. He was "blessed" into the I-Gs, and didn't have to undergo the usual initiation (beating). While with the I-Gs, Woody opted to keep as low profile as possible until he was eighteen, and could be recruited into the National Guard in January of 1990.

Then, in April of 1990, Woody was almost killed again.

[The Dragons pulled a drive-by hit on me, shooting at me several times while I was hanging with the Imperial Gangsters. They shot the guy two feet to my left in the knee and shattered every window of the car I hid behind for cover.

"In August, I was told to pull a hit for the I-Gs. They said that I had been around for awhile and my turn had come up. When they asked me to make the hit, I was evasive. I didn't want to get into any serious trouble. If I did, with a tarnished record and a felony record, it would ruin my chance to get into the army— my goal—and get a good job. So I prayed. I prayed hard: God help me . . . don't let them ask me again. They never did."

In November of 1990, Woody joined the army and left gang life. He never went back to "the hood," and never had to undergo a "head-to-toe." He is now Specialist Will Babilonia. He served in Desert Storm and is a criminal justice major at Central Texas College through an educational extension at his base in Europe. In 1992 he married Sabrina, a California native, and in 1994 they had their first child. Uncommonly articulate, Will and Sabrina work as chapel volunteers two and three nights a week with the youth on their base. His life is testimony to the fact that there is always a redeeming escape from clutches of a gang.

16.1. Will Babilonia and his wife.

CHAPTER 17.

Why Youths Disengage
From Gangs

Will Babilonia disengaged from his gang for a number of reasons. First, he was concerned about his safety. Second, he wanted to keep his record "clean" so he could pursue a career. He didn't want to be arrested. Third, he made a renewed spiritual commitment that directed his *moral thinking*. Fourth, he was able to remove himself permanently from the "hood" when he enlisted in the army, eliminating the day-to-day gang influence in his life. Although Will's gang was an inner-city type, the reasons why he disengaged are also common for youths in *affluent* gangs.

There are *eleven* reasons why youths disengage from affluent and inner-city gang activity. This information can be an valuable tool when attempting to disengage a youth from a gang and when taking preemptive action to prevent gangs from forming in a specific neighborhood. Some of the reasons why youths disengage are obvious; others will be a surprise. The reasons are not presented in a hierarchical order so that the reader isn't coaxed into picking one over another. Every young person and his situation is unique and should be given individualized attention. As in Will's case, more than one reason will often come into play.

The degree of interest a youth has in gang activity and his/her commitment to the gang can influence the most likely reason why a youth will disengage. As you will recall, law enforcement officers currently use *four different terms* to specify the intensity or commitment to gang activity: Full-fledged, Associate, Wanna-be, and Hanging Out. A Wanna-be is more likely to disengage because he fears being harmed, whereas a full-fledged gang member has already experienced "harm" and wears it like a badge. Will Babilonia is an example of a full-fledged gang member who was motivated to leave his gang because he was afraid of being shot. So, while there may be certain reasons that will more likely fit one youth than another, helping a youth disengage from a gang is always an *individualized* effort. Here are the eleven reasons.

1) Get Older, Lose Interest—When surveyed, the most common reason the Budapest skinheads (chapter 6) left their gang was because they got older or became married. In inner-city gangs, youths lack mobility to move to another neighborhood away from their local turf. That's why inner-city gang members who are able to get stable jobs *out of their neighborhood* usually disengage when they reach their middle to late twenties.

Affluent gang youths have more mobility and aren't forced to live in the same neighborhood. They simply disengage at younger ages because they start college, get a job, and move on. In some cases, a gang loses its steam if a few members move because parents change jobs and the core-hub is no longer present. In many situations, older teens simply tire of what they did when younger, such as their taste in music. The harsh, discordant sounds of heavy metal, punk, thrash, and grunge are the fare of youths 12-17. An older youth's energy level and impulsiveness is not as erratic as those who are younger. As aging affects these aspects, their desire to affiliate with kids that like this sort of thing also wanes. This is the typical pattern, but the key word here is *typical*. There are always exceptions.

In Europe, for example, where soccer gangs—football hooligans—are common, it is not unusual to find adults with professional vocations in the middle of a fray (or foray). A parallel in America, though not as common as the adult football hooligan phenomenon in Europe, are skinheads who later become adult members of neo-Nazi or hate groups.

2) Replacement Activity or Pursuit—Will Babilonia was motivated, in part, to leave his gang because of his desire to join the army and later to become a police officer. Ivan Rock stopped running with the Arsenal Gooners when he was recruited by Stevenage, a local soccer club. Fort Worth Justice of the Peace, Manuel Valdez, who frequently has gang members in his courtroom, says that football helped him resist gang activity when growing up in the sixties. He said that it gave him something to devote wholeheartedly his attention. Jobs, hobbies, the arts, and sports are options for kids to direct their creative energies to sever gang ties. For affluent gang members, local neighborhoods have more resources and facilities to provide such alternatives for youths who want to disengage.

3) Gang Fails to Fulfill Expectations—As detailed in chapter 9, at the most primal level youths seek from gangs *a mask, distraction*, or *empowering device* to deal with pain experienced from troubled homes. Although typically unspoken by a youth, if a gang does not provide relief, some will disengage. A minority, who are consciously aware of the pain/gang connection, disengage when they realize that the gang is a lying illusion and isn't a permanent solution to their pain/problem. Other youths, who don't experience relief, will express agitation and sometimes outright hostility, feeling out of sorts with those in the gang. Over a period of time, these youths disengage out of discontent, although many never really identify why they feel the gang let them down.

In some gangs, the level of severely erratic behavior by others in the gang eventually drives everyone apart. In other instances, youths disengage if they don't receive a desired level of acceptance from others in the gang, which can occur in any type of organization. Naturally there are other lesser important payoffs sought from gang activity, such as monetary gain and the "rush" or "thrill" of gang fights, but youths don't quit because they aren't making enough money or don't get their fill of fights. They quit because their primal needs aren't met, albeit illicitly.

4) Become Frightened by Gang Activity—Fear of a gang's activities is a common reason for disengagement. It is often a factor when a gang member isn't as committed as a full-fledged member, but prefers instead to remain at the periphery of extreme gang behavior. Ivan Rock, the former English football hooligan, made it clear that he wanted out of his gang when he became terrified at the random violence he witnessed on the streets after matches. For other youths, fear might originate from the threat of being arrested, from rival gang retaliation, or when they see a gang member lose control and become dangerously violent.

5) Become Frightened by Associated Activity—This is more subtle than fear of a gang's activity. Here a youth is frightened by associative activity with which a gang comes in contact. For example, when Kuba Belok, the former Warsaw skinhead (chapter 10), saw violent skinheads from Łodz hanging out with gangs in Warsaw, he wanted out. He wasn't afraid of his gang and what they might do. There was some self-control to their mischievous acts directed at authorities as a form of protest. Their activity did not pose a threat to life or limb. But the skins from Łodz terrified him with their random acts of violence, absence of self-control, and "hooligan acts without a [true] political agenda."[1]

In 1991 the son of a friend of mine was contemplating joining an occultic gang. I spent two afternoons with the youth, whom we'll call Rick. He spoke enthusiastically of his newly formed occultic gang and how they met in various wooded spots within a few miles of his million dollar home. I asked him about the buying and selling of drugs when they met and mentioned that he might be robbed by a drug dealer. He was incredulous and thought my suggestion was only meant to scare him.

"No one is going to rob us."

"Why not?" I responded. "You come from a wealthy home and drive an expensive Mercedes."

This suggestion apparently planted a seed, but he still wasn't convinced. He didn't think he was at-risk. I further suggested that we go to one of the wooded parks where he and his friends met for their "rituals."

It was about two o'clock on a hot, summer's afternoon. We parked in an out-of-the-way location known to be a drug-dealing site. Rick didn't know this.

"Look, over there," I said, pointing out three grisly looking men. "Those are drug dealers. They aren't teens like those from whom your friends buy drugs. Do you think you would like to meet those guys at three o'clock in the morning? How do you know that one of your friends you buy drugs from isn't buying from those men?"

For the first time, Rick looked uneasy.

"I don't think those men would have any problem pulling out a gun or knife and robbing or killing you. Would you like to stay here a little longer?"

"No, that's okay," he replied.

He was plainly frightened. It was the first time he realized that he could be harmed by peripheral activity that wasn't *directly related* to his gang's activity. Showing him that he could be harmed by something he wasn't looking for was a key reason he chose to stop his involvement with the gang. Pointing out to a youth, who is *not* a full-fledged gang member, the danger of associated activity *not* directly related to the gang's activity is a very common reason for disengagement.

6) Realization That the Gang Is Exploiting Them—As noted throughout this book, youths typically join gangs as a *control mechanism* over their internal pain. Simultaneously, many youths in gangs don't like people controlling or telling them what to do or think. They prefer to believe that being affiliated with a gang will give them more independence, make them mentally stronger, and provide them with more control. In some gangs, however, leader(s) exert extreme manipulative control over members. Some full-fledged gang members will disengage from a gang if it is exposed and they acknowledge that they are being exploited. For example, Terry, the leader of the drug-selling gang detailed in chapter 3, exploited his members to turn a profit and sexually exploit *female* members. Some members of the gang eventually disengaged because they realized, in part, that he only cared about his own agenda.

Finally, demonstrating to strong-willed youths that they are being exploited and don't have control can quickly make them develop a deep revulsion for gang activity.

7) Realization That They Fit a Predictable Profile—The secretive initiations, hand signals, passwords, activities, and so on are very appealing to gang members, adding an additional thrill. It is racy for youths when those outside the gang can't understand how they think or know what makes them tick. They like to believe that their actions and motivations are completely unpredictable. The exception is when a gang's activities are designed to inspire fear or terror in others. Then gangs want to be perceived as predictable. The tacit signal is—"If you encroach on our territory, you will have to reckon with us." But youths don't like it when they are perceived as being predictable.

Capitalizing on this factor, I helped one youth disengage from his gang. The dialogue went something like this:

"John, my research shows that there is often a common profile of a youth who gets involved in a gang. There is usually divorce, separation, or abuse of some kind. Or one of the parents is severely dysfunctional. Does this apply to you?"

"How did you know?"

"What do you mean?" I answered.

He then detailed that one of his parents had a specific and severe dysfunction that caused him much heartache. He added that he was unnerved by my observation of the background profile of a gang member. It was discomforting that a contributing factor for his gang involvement was *predictable*. For him, the secretive factor was an enticement for joining the gang, and he didn't like being "found out" and understood. He also realized that he really didn't have control to keep others "out of his head." Realizing that he was predictable was a key factor that caused him to disengage. He acknowledged that he really didn't have *ultimate control* over others *outside* the gang who understood the profile of a gang member.

8) Family Relationship Restored—If a troubled home is a catalyst for increasing a youth's vulnerablity to gang recruitment, it's also reasonable that *repairing relationships* will reduce a youth's vulnerability. For youths already involved in gang activity, regardless of the level of commitment, restoring family relationships is one of the most powerful catalytic forces to encourage disengagement. This is an obvious reason, but is sometimes overlooked by parents and youth workers. For example, when I asked a fifteen-year-old girl why she left her gang, she replied, "My Mom started to be a mom again. Two years ago my parents were divorced. I was hurting and no one seemed to care."

Now a single parent, her mother, teary-eyed as she listened to her daughter during our interview, admitted that she never understood the toll the divorce took on her daughter.

"The healing didn't start to take place," she said, "until I was honest with myself. I had to face my denial that the divorce had really devastated her. When I did that and gave her the love and time she needed, Ginny came back."

The impact a parent can have on an at-risk youth should never be underestimated. When youths feel loved and secure—not financially secure, but emotionally secure—the needs that drive them into gangs often vanish. Andy Kriz of Minneapolis, who formed a delinquent gang (chapter 3), said that a key factor that inspired him to forgo a life of crime was when his father reentered his life and said he would help.

Of all the factors that might encourage a youth to disengage from a gang or resist gang activity, the *restoration of the family* is the singularly most powerful reason I have encountered.

9) New or Renewed Spiritual Commitment—Although Will in the previous chapter was a member of a lower-income gang, his story is typical of youths who disengage from a gang because of a first-time or renewed spiritual commitment. It seems that a faith in God coupled with an accepting and following a moral code has a dual effect. First, a youth obviously rejects criminal and immoral conduct. Second, seeking and placing one's faith in God acts to diminish the Missing Protector Factor in their lives.

When I encountered the spiritual commitment factor in the mid-1980s, I thought that the connection was being exaggerated by these youths. It seemed more likely that replacing gang friends with those from a church was a more important factor. Over time, however, I observed that for these youths, their spiritual beliefs, which undergirded their moral convictions, were truly a dominant reason for disengagement. What follows is from an interview with one such youth who had joined an occultic gang.

I had interviewed Terry several times over the course of a year, beginning with his initial emergence. I watched during the ensuing months as his emotional state stabilized and his grades returned to their former high level. What made this particular interview unique was that Terry shifted the subject to why Christianity was so important for his disengagement.

"Did you become a Christian first to get away from the your [occultic] gang, or did you go to the hospital first?"
"Went to the hospital."
"Who was it that talked to you about Christianity at the hospital?"
"Nobody did."
"How did you figure it out?"
"They told you in AA to find a higher power, and so I picked Jesus as my higher power."
"Now did you think of him just as a religious figure?"
"No, as a friend."
"Why do you think that was significant instead of just going through AA? You were with a support group that was there to help you."
"Because you have to realize that there is a higher power greater than yourself and that you are not the most important thing in the world."
"Do you remember Jesus ever coming to your aid?"
"Well, there were some weird times when I was somewhere I shouldn't have been, and I wasn't hurt. Like one night we were supposed to leave a nightclub at 12:30, but we decided to leave at 11:00, and someone was

shot at 12:30. But there was no burning bush or anything. It was more a trusting thing than making me believe in him."

"Now you have seen a lot of others in treatment centers and have known a lot of kids who were into the same kind of trouble. Did you ever see somebody out and just stop it without becoming a Christian?"

"No. No, I have not."

"Now are you just saying that?"

"No. Phillip has tried many times, and he has not beaten his addiction. Rick has been into treatment. Sheila has been into treatment. Ashley has been into treatment. Jack has been into treatment, and he's the only one who's okay, but he also became a Christian."

In addition to these types of anecdotal accounts, the University of Michigan's Institute for Social Research came to a similar conclusion regarding deterrents to drug abuse. In its definitive 1991 study that sought to identify the most effective deterrent to drug abuse, the five-year survey of 70,000 students from 135 schools during 1985 to 1989 concluded that: *Youths with strong spiritual beliefs were less likely to abuse drugs than those who didn't have any.* Coauthor of the study and sociologist, John Wallace, also noted that the study identified that both Black and White youths who attended churches that embraced the basic tenets of the Christian faith were "least likely to use drugs."[2]

10) **Find Assistance to Address Root of Internal Pain**—Youths may or may not be able to influence the restoration of family relationships, but learning other ways to address the damage inflicted by family turmoil will cause some to cease and desist. Because each circumstance is different, there isn't one particular means of assistance that seems to work better than others. The core-idea here is that with some measure of creativity and compassion, a youth learns to cope with and redirect how they feel in a *constructive* rather than destructive manner. This may mean counseling or simply quality time spent with a concerned adult who will give the youth attention. For others, integrating replacement activities or pursuits will work.

11) **Incarceration and the Law Enforcement Deterrent**—For some youths incarceration is the only deterrent that will cause them to disengage. When youths have had deficient and inappropriate discipline and restraint at home, the law enforcement deterrent becomes the restraining and disciplining mechanism missing for many of these youths, corraling their angry and antisocial acts. Arrest, juvenile court, incarceration, etc. can be prescriptive to influence them to restrain and redirect their behavior. For other youths who resist discipline and disregard parental restraint, the law enforcement deterrent protects the citizenry and can provide the final wake-up call for a youth.

Many youths told me that their incarceration and the threat of being arrested was a factor for their disengagement. Ivan Rock (chapter 8) said that the threat of arrest caused him to think twice about continuing to run with the Arsenal Gooners. Andy Kriz (chapter 3) confided that prison was probably the only deterrent to his continued gang activity. Will Babilonia (chapter 16) repeatedly stated in interviews that incarceration *over a period of time* was crucial to his disengagement. He said that incarceration for *a short period* often backfires as a deterrent because youths, like himself, simply wear their short-term imprisonment as a badge—a sign of how committed they are to their gang.

"When you are in prison for a year or more, you have more time to think about the consequences of your actions." He stated that sustained incarceration that is longer than one or two months should be limited to correction facilities specifically designed for youths. He said that youths imprisoned with older, craftier criminals, often become a better, more accomplished criminal and a greater threat because they learn from older *experts*.

When applying the law enforcement deterrent to gang activity and violent juvenile crime, the approach must be tempered and regularly evaluated.

Currently, there is much public debate over the "three strikes and you're out" policy being adopted by many states. Simply stated: commit three class-A felonies and you get a life sentence *without parole*. In Alabama, a finely tuned application of this principle has proven to be a positive deterrent to violent crime. From 1975 to 1980 violent crime rose 37%. Their "Habitual Offender Law," which focuses on "selected incarceration of selected individuals,"[3] was passed in 1980. In the following years, 1980–94, violent crime dropped 22%. Regarding sentencing, it's creative and measured for each case. For first- and second-time offenders—particularly for those in their late teens and early twenties—an effort is made *through the courts* to educate and find jobs for these people as well as teaching those in prison real job skills. So, the emphasis isn't simply on a method of incarceration, but also on how to give a person the knowledge and tools they need to be productive citizens.

Regarding incarceration: Crimes are classified as A, B, or C class crimes. Class A includes most murders, robberies, and rapes, and convicted felons can be sentenced to life imprisonment. Class B crimes include most burglaries and various types of violent assaults. Those convicted can receive sentences of 2-20 years. Class C which includes thefts under $1,000 can receive sentences of 1-10 years. Once a person commits a second offense, such as a Class C felony, he/she receives a sentence as if they committed a Class B felony. If a third offense is committed, they are then sentenced as if they committed a Class A felony. If a felon commits three offenses and then commits a Class A felony, he/she is locked up without parole.

Another juvenile justice response to the increasing number of gangs are "boot camps." Here the convicted youth forgoes jail or prison time for time in a military-style work camp. "The idea of shock incarceration is to 'shock' young, nonviolent, often drug-addicted offenders to change their ways through intensive exercise, military drills and hard labor during a relatively brief sentence."[4] But according to experts, these programs have just as high a recidivism rate as youths incarcerated in other facilities. They are, however, a significantly less expensive alternative than housing youths in jails and prisons. In New York the estimated savings for 1,800 beds at four facilities over a seven year period of time (1987–94) was over $300 million.[5]

As noted in chapter 4, juvenile crime is expected to climb as the number of youths in the US rises to 70 million. This means that the juvenile justice system at all levels will be stretched to its already over-extended limits. While it is tempting to say, "just lock them all up," the reality is that we can't afford it. The best overall philosophy is to maintain a feared and respected deterrent, use the system to direct youths who are willing to change, while individuals in communities work preemptively with at-risk youths beginning in elementary schools. Although the affluent gang trend isn't as severe as the numbers of inner-city gangs, affluent communities must work sacrificially, committed to the long-haul with these youths to help turn those neighborhoods around. If they don't, more cases of suburban youths like Andy Kriz, who formed his own gang after hanging around inner-city gangs, will become more common.

CHAPTER 18.

Helping Youths
Disengage from Gangs

The evidence from several years of research in many countries is that a gang *disengagement* program has never been developed that has proven itself to be effective long-term and broad-based. There are hundreds of individualized programs that *do* help some youths and they shouldn't be abandoned. I personally worked with some of them, and from a moral standpoint, they must be continued even if only a few youths are helped. Youth camps, gang prevention talks by juvenile officers, YMCAs, church ministries, and programs established by local communities must continue their efforts and receive our support.

Most professionals who interact with *inner-city* gangs acknowledge that once a youth is in a gang, there isn't much hope that he/she will disengage. The ingrained social conditions are simply overwhelming: broken homes, absentee fathers, poor education, lack of jobs for youths, few resources to provide creative activities that will help develop a youth, and so on. The best hope for reversing the rising number of affluent and inner-city gangs lies not in helping current youths exit from a gang, but by concentrating on gang-prevention strategies and programs. It's the old an-ounce-of-prevention-is-worth-a-pound-of-cure tactic. Target youths *before* they are old enough to join a gang. I believe that effective preventative strategies that target youths before they join gangs can reverse the current rising gang trend. This means thinking about the long term—ten to fifteen years—which isn't conducive for the political arena. Elected officials must show *immediate results* or face opponents who are eager to show their ineffectiveness. This means the responsibility reverts to the *neighborhood and community level* and must be led by individuals, *then* supported by state and local governments.

But there are youths involved in gangs now who need help *now*. Some can be convinced to quit and follow a better path. Fortunately, most *affluent* gangs aren't institutionalized and networked with other gangs. Therefore, direct one-on-one intervention is more likely to succeed. Al-

215

though still arduous, *one is three or four times* more likely to succeed in helping a youth disengage from an affluent gang than an inner-city gang. In affluent gangs, easily one-third are likely to respond to the kinds of strategies suggested in this chapter.

The focus in this chapter is on *one-on-one intervention* because this has been historically the most effective tack, as opposed to dealing with a group and trying out generic dialogues. The individual(s) who intervenes can be a suitable parent, relative, teacher, law enforcement officer, neighbor, coach, instructor in the arts—anyone with the knowledge, motivation, and ability to communicate. There isn't any "magic bullet." Success isn't guaranteed, but the ideas presented here have proved effective when applied to youths willing to respond.

SUGGESTED STRATEGY: A MATCHING PROCESS

The reasons why youths engage in gangs are *predictable*. What they seek from gang activity, and why they disengage are also *predictable*. The fact that these two key motivational elements are predictable makes it easier to establish a starting point.

To disengage a youth from a gang, it is suggested that one match the contributing familial problems and the pay-off sought (mask, distraction, or empowering device) with the most likely reason(s) for disengagement (presented in the last chapter) that would apply to that specific youth. The idea here is to identify which reason(s) for disengagement is likely to work with a youth given the catalyst for his gang involvement and the pay-off he thinks that gang activity provides.

Youths are individuals. Stereotypical solutions won't work across the board with all youths. Identifying the following, however, will help develop a youth-specific disengagement strategy.

- As already noted, identify the specific familial conditions as well as the specific pay-off (mask, distraction, or empowering device).
- Specific behaviors that are present: depression, aggression, insecurity, obsessive desire for power and/or control, etc.
- The type of gang a youth is involved in and its specific activities.
- The level of commitment to a gang—i.e., full-fledged, associate, "wanna-be," or a youth who is just "hanging out."
- Given the above factors, the probable reason(s) for disengagement (chapter 17) that might apply to that youth.

What follows are *three* examples of implementing this matching process from actual cases. The common reasons for disengagement (chapter 17) are listed below as a helpful reference.

1. Gets Older and Loses Interest
2. Replacement Activity or Pursuit
3. Gang Fails to Fulfill Expectations
4. Frightened by Gang's Activities
5. Frightened by Associated Activity
6. Realization That Gang Is Exploiting Them
7. Realization That They Fit a Predictable Profile
8. Family Relationship Is Restored
9. Spiritual Commitment
10. Finding Assistance to Address Root of Internal Pain
11. Incarceration and the Law Enforcement Deterrent

John: His mother is severely bulimic. She unknowingly and regularly takes out her anger on him, and he has joined a gang as a *distraction* from what is going on at home. Likely reasons for disengagement that might apply here are 2, 8, and 10. His mother received counseling that helped her realize the impact of her behavior, which led to restoration of their relationship (8). John received short-term counseling (10), disengaged from his gang, and turned his energies back to his personal and constructive hobbies (2).

Bob: His parents are recently divorced and neither show him any attention. He joined a gang as a *mask* for his pain, and his gang gives him a false sense of worth that he doesn't receive at home. Gang attire and secret meetings fuel his façade. His gang is also dealing drugs. Likely reasons for disengagement that might work in Bob's case are 5, 7, and 10. By pointing out to Bob that he fits a predictable profile (7), deflated and devalued the raciness and secrecy that enshrouds many gangs. By demonstrating that he could easily be harmed by rival drug dealers (5), enough reasonable fear was instilled in him so that he chose to disengage. Finally, since there was no parental support, assistance from an adult (10) was vital to address the MPF.

Sarah: Her father regularly physically abuses her. She joins a gang to have power over her father—an *empowering* device over the source of her pain. Here, compassionately directing Sarah towards reason number 3, that the gang won't ultimately deal with her physical and emotional trauma, was the first tack attempted. Additionally, number 10, getting her immediate aid and assistance, was imperative for both her long- and short-term welfare.

The reasons why a youth might disengage may seem obvious in some situations and not so obvious in others. For example, in the case of Sarah, developing a disengagement strategy that focused on number 10—neutralizing her father's ability to abuse her further and getting her counseling, if necessary—was an obvious tack. However, drawing Bob's attention to the fact that he fits a predictable profile, number 7, wasn't a reason that was as readily apparent. Those with an on-the-street understanding of youths, coupled with proven experience of interacting with youths, will often be able to select the most likely reasons for disengagement. To execute this process, it is also helpful to have a *framework* in which to put this information to work in a one-on-one environment.

A BASIC FRAMEWORK

The framework that follows has been successfully used in real-life circumstances and is the result of interviews and dialogue with scores of mental health care experts, juvenile officers, teachers, and other authorities. The framework is broken down into *eight* components which may be prioritized according to the needs of the situation.

1. Appoint a strategist
2. Establish effective communication
3. Investigate the facts
4. Develop a preliminary strategy for resolving the problem
5. Implement and refine a long-term strategy
6. Employ a system of checks and balances
7. Seek professional help when appropriate
8. Employ necessary follow-up

1) Appoint a Strategist—In many situations, parents are not equipped to formulate a strategy because of emotional involvement, lack of knowledge about the specific issue, or other impediments. In such situations, Margaret Singer, a foremost expert on aberrant groups and adjunct professor of psychology at the University of California, Berkeley, recommends that someone be appointed who can act as a *strategist*—someone who can identify the "who, what, why, where, and when" questions, followed by some ideas of how to approach the troubled youth. Then a tentative course of action can be mapped out. The option of using a strategist can be applied to any of the trends discussed in this book. The strategist role may also be filled by two or more people working together whose combined strengths can acheive the desired objectives.

The key characteristics of an effective strategist should include:

- Common sense and an ability to develop a short-term plan of action
- Calm under pressure and not given to hysteria
- Equipped with some understanding of the particular issue(s) affecting the youth
- An ability to relate to youths and establish trust if the strategist is going to interact directly with the affected youth

Possibilities for a strategist are: a neighbor, relative, teacher, juvenile officer, experienced psychologist, minister, or a person who is acutally experienced at working with gangs. The strategist must be able to survey the situation calmly, which is why emotionally involved parents are often not suited for the task. The strategist, or someone the strategist selects, must be able to forge a dialogue with both youth and parent(s), and then suggest a likely course of action.

When a youth is affected by a trend that is spreading in a school, neighborhood, or community, getting help may involve consultation or coordination with institutions or authorities that work with youths. Therefore, it is important that a strategist maintain a balanced perspective and communicate a sense of urgency without hysteria. Otherwise, he/she could be dismissed as an extremist, which might prevent valuable information and assistance from being made available to help the youth involved. A reasonable and calm manner can prevent needless hysteria. If a strategist is qualified to give good advice but isn't suitable for interacting with community organizations, another person should be selected for making that contact.

2) Establish Effective Communication—The strategist or a suitably appointed person should work to establish communication with affected youth. What is important here is that whoever establishes communication can:

- Speak the language of the youth
- Develop trust and/or respect
- Possess a style of communication that is appropriate for the affected youth

3) Investigate the Facts—The first charge here is to verify that a youth is actually in a gang and that the group is indeed a gang—that is, a group of youths that have commited a crime(s). If one is a school principal, for example, direct dialogue with affected youths in tandem with a juvenile officer is often a logical first step to ascertain: (a) The nature of the alleged activity (b) data that will assist with the current or a future situation (c) what action should be taken to neutralize an actual threat, get help to affected persons, calm fears, and educate those who need to know, such as parents, about the actual facts and what is being done to address the situation.

Once it has been determined that a youth is actually in a gang, some helpful questions to develop a disengagement strategy are:

- Are one or more of the parents willing to help? If not, who is close to the youth who can be provide support or act as a protector?

- What are the known facts?
- Is the youth currently approachable? Who should talk to him or her? Where is the best location to talk to the youth?
- Is there a current threat to the youth so that law enforcement must be contacted or precautions taken?
- Have any crimes been committed, requiring contact with law enforcement or the retention of an attorney? (Law enforcement should *always* be contacted if gang activity is suspected in order to reduce a potential threat. Whatever is learned should be communicated to juvenile officers so that gang data can remain current.)
- Is the situation so complex that a professional with experience should establish the opening dialogue with the youth? (This might be necessary, for example, in the case of rape or extreme forms of terror.)
- Is addiction, rape, or physical or sexual abuse a factor, thus requiring the involvement of a mental health care expert?

What is crucial is that the actual facts are gathered as quickly as possible so that effective action can be taken and unwanted hysteria can be avoided, especially if the situation has been exaggerated. Consider the following example.

At a Dallas suburban elementary school in late 1994, a female janitor in her thirties approached a group of sixth graders (ages 11 and 12) and stated that she was a "Crip," which is a gang network comprised of tens of thousands of members that has branched out across the US. On a Thursday she told them that if anyone ever gave them trouble that all they had to do was make the hand sign of a Crip and she would protect them. That everything would be okay. But, if they ever told anyone about her, they'd be "dead." Fortunately, the children who were confronted immediately told their parents because they knew and believed that their parents could be trusted and that they would be protected. Additionally, with swift action grounded in the facts, a panic was not set off at the school.

The prinicipal, who consulted me on Friday, immediately contacted the local police department who ran a check on the woman's name in their gang database. Nothing turned up. Since it is very unusual to find an older adult female in a gang, with further probing it was determined that she was simply vying for the kids' attention. The janitor, who denied she told the children anything, was fired. The testimony of the youths who reported her comments was believed due to the nature of their character. and the MPF was not applicable in the lives of any of the children. The principal immediately called all the affected parents, apprised them of the situation, and sent a letter home to the parents telling them of the situation to dispel any rumors that may have started. By Monday, the whole affair was virtually forgotten. Careful fact gathering combined with swift action resolved the situation.

4) Develop a Preliminary Strategy for Resolving the Problem—After the known facts have been evaluated, a *preliminary* strategy should be developed that will:
1. Reduce the danger to a youth, or other affected youths, if a threat factor is present
2. Establish communication with a youth
3. Identify reasons why a youth might disengage

5) Implement and Refine a Long-term Strategy—A long-term strategy for helping youths in trouble should ideally seek to achieve the following universal goals:
1. Permanent removal of the threat of harm to the youth and/or the threat a youth might pose to others.
2. Identification of the underlying causes for the youth's vulnerability, and addressing those root problems.
3. Strengthening of healthy family relationships and/or addressing the Missing Protector Factor.
4. Positive alternatives to gang activity.
5. Effective discipline when necessary. There is often a temptation to focus solely on discipline or punishment when a youth has committed a crime. Discipline may be appropriate, but parental examples and clear communication of expectations can be even more powerful forces over the long term.
6. Direction that will help a youth in the long-term future. It is important to recognize that disengaging youths from harmful activity doesn't mean that their susceptibility to being deceived or harmed again has been erased. Only when youths understand *why* they choose gang activity can they take measures to protect themselves and reduce their vulnerability to other harmful activities, such as drug abuse and destructive relationships. Youths should understand *why* they were deceived, *what* in their life set them up for buying into a lie, and finally *what good things* they can claim as their own that will not only reduce their vulnerability, but actually turn the liability into an asset—a personal strength.

6) Employ a System of Checks and Balances—The strategist and other participants in the disengagement process will find it helpful to have other, unaffected persons/experts to use as a sounding board as the strategy takes shape and is implemented. This averts unwanted biases and provides a broader base for finding solutions.

7) Seek Professional Help When Appropriate—Sometimes circumstances warrant recruiting the assistance of an individual with a proven track record of interacting with youths in gangs, such as a law enforcement officer, trained gang counselor, or even a mental health care professional.

Regarding the assistance of a mental health professional: Today, counseling doesn't carry the stigma it once did. Most alienated youths already know a friend who is in counseling, which allays their reticence. There are no absolute methods for finding the right qualified professional counselor or therapist for a given situation. Referrals from a family doctor or a school counselor can be good places to start. Sometimes law enforcement officers will decline requests for recommendations because of restrictions against making recommendations for medical or legal assistance.

Care must be taken when selecting a mental health care professional as some states don't require licensing or accreditation to go into business. Checking with state licensing boards is recommended if a particular professional's background is uncertain. Also, one should resist making a selection based solely on the reputation of a clinic, hospital, or treatment center. One should inquire into who *specifically* will be interacting with the youth. It's not uncommon for affluent families, who have the finanical means, to end up with a bad match—or even worse, a therapist with severe emotional problems.

When funds aren't available for counseling, treatment or financial assistance is often available from local, county, state, or federal agencies. Since these agencies experience frequent fluctuations in their funding, one will need to inquire about each specifically.

Finally, professionals, along with teachers and school counselors, are often the first ones to spot negative youth trends because of the many kids they see on an *individual* basis. They can provide insight into what youths are doing and be a valuable source of information. Sometimes kids will speak more openly with a therapist than with a police officer, especially when there is associated criminal activity. Youths perceive that the counselor/therapist is there to *heal the internal problems*, whereas the officer's job is to charge suspected offenders and uphold the law. While many police departments focus on crime prevention, this is not what resentful, suspicious youths believe is an officer's intent.

8) Employ Necessary Follow-up—Ideally, a parent should assume this role. When a parent won't participate, those who are willing to fulfill the role of a protector and/or mentor should be identified to monitor and help acheive the long-term objectives.

PARENTAL INVOLVEMENT

When possible and appropriate, parental involvement should be encouraged when helping a youth disengage from a gang and when implementing a long-term strategy to assist a youth. Parental responses to these needs can vary.

For some parents, the realization that their child is in a gang is accompanied by a natural feeling of anger and even jealousy directed towards the gang. They feel that their child has been invaded and taken over. In short, the gang has adopted their own child and now has emotional custody. Faced with this realization, some parents will make every effort to assist their child and restore the torn family fabric. This effort to assist their child and the family, by giving the situation first priority, is healthy and good.

Other parents unconsciously take on the project to "rescue" their child in order to occupy their thoughts and minimize and deflect their own angst or accountabililty. By focusing on their child's condition, some parents delay dealing with their own agony or possible contribution to the troubled situation. In the short term, this rescue orientation can have a positive benefit. As the child receives their support, parents have time to accept the reality of the situation gradually without triggering an emotional overload. For some parents, this eschews complete denial and shirking their responsibility. For parents who have harmed a child, their efforts can represent to the affected youth and to themselves a small, bridging act of atonement.

Some parents who realize how they have contributed to their child's situation, unfortunately, have more negative responses. For these parents, acceptance is unbearable. In this case, common responses include: denial that the child is in trouble; denial of responsibility for the child's lack of emotional well-being; or acceptance of the reality of the situation and yet an unwilliness to help the child. At the extreme end are those parents who just don't care, and spurn the opportunity to be a part of the solution.

Other parents fall in the middle and adopt what might be called a "crusader complex." For them, the project to save their child becomes obsessive, often resulting in an all-out effort to save other youths as well. Although there is the outward, positive benefit of attempting to help their child and others, the underlying problems are left unaddressed. Parents on an obsessive crusade tend to hide root problems behind the front of saving their child and other youths. These neglected problems typically fester, and neither the child nor the family ever experiences complete healing.

Each parent has a different capacity for acknowledging, absorbing, and addressing contributing familial factors. Some can help their child while *simultaneously* addressing the root problem; others can't. Whatever the parents' capacity, it is critical that a strategy is implemented for addressing *root problems* in whatever time frame is possible. For only by successfully addressing root causes can a long-term cure result.

———————◆———————

One-on-one or individual engagement with a youth in an affluent gang has been found to be the best tack to disengage a youth from gang activity. To this end, it is helpful to have a strategy for disengagement and a framework within which to implement the strategy. The ideas presented in this chapter should be used only as guidelines because each youth is unique and must be approached as an individual.

In the long term, eradicating the affluent or inner-city gang trend requires intervention in an at-risk youth's life *before* he/she is a candidate for a gang—the focus of the next two chapters.

CHAPTER 19.

Prevention Part I: Obstacles, Pitfalls, and Some Success

G ang prevention is willful, prescriptive action. But it's not a program per se. It's an attitude and philosophy about caring for and reducing *at-risk* youths. Moreover, it's an *individual* response that engenders communal responses—like the proverbial pebble dropped into a still lake. The ripple effect can be far-reaching. Mechanical public offerings without individualized caring for individual youths always fails in the long run. Given the continued, rapid decline and breakup of the American family, preemptive strategies must exist and be at work *before* a youth is old enough to join a gang.

This chapter reviews some of the complexities and inherent pitfalls of eradicating gangs when the response is focused on centralizing solutions, when the programs are devised and administered by local, state, and federal governments. We also present an example whereby individualized concern and a civic response successfully merged to help many youths in an affluent community where gang activity was growing. It is an isolated case, but it illustrates that government and the private sector can work together for the betterment of youths.

The following chapter presents what currently seems to be the only viable solution to prevent gangs from forming in a community, considering today's social climate. It is the only solution I've come across that is broad-based and will work in the long run.

MISSING THE MARK

How does a community prevent gangs from forming? Logically, you seek root causes and solutions. Next you find a core of responsible doers who will take action-steps to address the problem. To date, most gang programs focus on the inner-city gang crisis because of the highly publicized carnage and visible crime on the streets. In reality, very few programs of any type, whether addressing inner-city or affluent gangs, have been successful over a sustained period of time. The city of Ft. Worth, Texas, for example, has years of experience testing *every type* of inner-city gang-prevention program. The police department's gang intervention task force has been touted as "state-of-the-art." Other police departments regularly call Ft. Worth to find out what does and doesn't work because most programs in America fail to attain a high level of success.

In May 1994, out of desperation, the police department actually suggested putting six gang leaders on the police payroll at $10,000 each. The public screamed and many asked: How can we reward criminal activity with financial aid? The police department's aim was to recruit gang leaders as "dispute mediators" and "antiviolence counselors," hoping to reduce violence. Departmental officials conceded that the plan was unconventional, but one officer said, "What do we have to lose? Sometimes innovative ideas that are at first scoffed at, actually work." Shortly after it was proposed, the plan was jettisoned in favor of a more comprehensive and more costly gang-intervention program to be administered by the local

19.1, 2. Neighborhood convenience stores in affluent communities now routinely post gang prevention posters.
Photo—Dan Korem.

Boys and Girls Club of America.

Most American cities are facing the same inability to respond to the rising gang problem. From time to time some programs work for a short time, but like the rest, they ultimately fizzle. Ft. Worth launched a "zero-tolerance" crackdown on street gangs in 1993, arresting curfew breakers, illegal loitering, and so on. This successfully halted the rise of crime temporarily, but as exemplified by its 1994 action, police roundups were not a long-term solution. Other private programs, such as youth homes, make an invaluable contribution, but they typically only help a small percentage of youths due to sparse funding, the frustrating impedimenta of governmental and regulatory red tape, and local indifference. It's like the citizen's mumbling reply to the question, "Do you think that gang crime is due to ignorance or indifference?" He merely shrugged his shoulders and said, "I don't know and I don't care!" Indifference and inertia are major obstacles.

Most government programs aren't effective in the long run because they don't address the central problem of troubled/broken homes. Without specifically attacking the root cause, gangs will continue to exist and grow in numbers. But city and state governments are reluctant to identify concretely troubled/broken homes as the primary culprit. This is exemplified by the state of California, which has one of the worst gang problems in America.

The Attorney General from California released a comprehensive report in 1993: *Gangs 2000: A Call to Action*. The report primarily addressed the issue of urban, inner-city gangs. It also noted that there would be an estimated 600 skinheads by the year 2000—current trends indicating that most of them will come from middle-income families. Ten pages out of eighty specifically addressed the issue of gang prevention. The goals outlined were:

• To develop strategies that prevent young people from joining gangs.
• To provide a reason and means for young people to get out of gangs.
• To empower individuals, families, schools, and communities so that they can take action to solve problems associated with gangs; to assist them in working with law enforcement; and, ultimately, make them less dependent on the police.[1]

The same report stated that to "develop a sound prevention strategy," it is important to identify the *profile* of the youths most likely to enter gang activity. The "high-risk" factors detailed in the report were:

Low neighborhood and community attachment; low expectations of success; lack of student involvement; academic failure; little commitment to school; early antisocial behavior; favorable attitudes towards drug use and gangs; greater influence or reliance on peers than parents; friends who use drugs, alcohol, and tobacco; and association with gangs.[2]

None of the five predictable family factors identified in chapter 6— *divorce, separation, physical abuse, sexual abuse, one or more parents is severely dysfunctional*—were mentioned. The commission's report reflects the common public omission that troubled families is the most important factor to be addressed if gang activity is to be stopped. Privately, this is often admitted, but not publicly. It's deemed "political suicide" to do so. To identify publicly the family factor often invites the denial of an angry electorate, many of whom have troubled homes. It's not politically astute for an official to state succinctly: *If parents learned to get along and nurture and discipline their kids, our community's gang problem would begin to disappear.* Such a statement provides easy ammunition for political opponents to shift blame and say: "He is putting the blame on deteriorating families because he doesn't have the knowledge and resolve to provide leadership and develop viable programs that address the real problems." Others say, "Dictating to family members how to behave in their *private* lives (apart from criminal activity) is opening the door for Big Brother."

Al Brantley, a gang expert for the FBI, echoed the same opinion: "Government dictating the private lives of families would open a constitutional Pandora's box and should be avoided."[3]

Occasionally, officials lucidly identify the root cause of the problem. This happened when an aspirant for the governor's office of one of the largest states in America called a closed-door session with representatives of law enforcement, state and local prison officials, a justice of the peace, and others to discuss the issue of rising juvenile crime. He acknowledged that troubled homes provide the trigger for gang activity. He also added that government can't force parents to love one another and raise their children properly. It isn't government's responsibility. Government can help fund productive programs and enforce the law, but beyond that, government is virtually powerless to stop the *formation* of gangs.

So, the first question to answer regarding affluent gang prevention is: Can government do *anything* that will help? The answer is yes, but only in a limited context. A governor, for example, can use his bully pulpit to set a moral tone for individuals to get involved in the lives of youths. But as soon as government begins to interact *directly* with families, the land mines just waiting to explode can easily sabotage well-intended initiatives. Consider the dilemma of trying to enforce laws designed to reduce and punish domestic violence. A police officer recently observed: "We have a Catch-22. The state family violence statutes prohibit members of a household from beating up each other. This was originally designed to prevent a father from beating his wife, but it's now extended to protect the *kids*. But the family code says that a parent can discipline a child, using force up to but not including *deadly* force. In many cases we have to make a judgment call and hope we are right."[4]

Imagine what happens when city or state employees try to find ways to help parents get along and give much needed attention to their children. Now it gets murky. Yes, some communities establish classes and mentor programs to teach parenting skills, but these programs are typically ineffective in the long run and help only a very small percentage of the at-risk families. The result of this no-win situation forces most public officials to retreat. The prevailing attitude is: we will attack those areas where we have the ability to do something. This means beefing up law enforcement efforts, educational programs in schools, and when funds permit, increasing job opportunities and summer programs for affected youths. This is how most communities deal with the rising inner-city gang problem. Fortunately, the affluent gang trend is another issue. If acted upon *now*, before it becomes institutionalized like in inner-city communities, the problem can be resolved.

A TEST OF INDIVIDUAL RESOLVE

For most community programs and approaches, unless the will of the grass-roots community is resolute to change and attack the heart of a problem, the best intentioned programs usually fail. This is especially true for an issue that deals with youths and families, because government cannot fix the majority of internal marital and child-rearing affairs. This is an individual, *private* responsibility; and when parents won't respond, the responsibility is diverted to other caring adults. *These adults must individually teach the next generation of youths that troubled/broken homes don't have to be the norm;* that there are other ways of dealing with one's problems besides gangs. Still, various institutions can become significantly involved in bolstering grass-roots efforts.

The following checklist indicates which local government agencies, civic, and moral institutions might be called upon to assist a prevention effort. These suggestions are intended to be a primer for initiating a response to affluent gang activity. Keep in mind that affluent gangs are a relatively new phenomenon. The same strategies that these institutions have used to combat inner-city gangs might not always apply to affluent gangs.

WHERE TO LOOK FOR HELP

Schools—This is one of the first stops in coordinating a gang prevention effort. In addition to antigang prevention assemblies, schools are a natural place for youths who want to address the Missing Protector Factor to ask for help. PTA meetings can be a catalyst to inform and recruit families to pitch in and assist. Regarding teachers and administrators, they can help guide youths, but they can't be a surrogate parent to every child. They can't be expected to teach and also instruct on the moral good to all students individually. They might want to, but it simply isn't possible. Schools are best used as a common meeting ground to tackle youth problems, rather than trying to shuffle off all the responsibility to teachers.

Moral Institutions and Agencies—YMCAs, churches, and synagogues are other natural places to start. They are usually committed to teaching and promoting the "moral good of the commonwealth." They work at strengthening families, and often offer help when families fail and youths are put at-risk. The issue of youths committing crimes is a social and *moral* issue. Many of these institutions *already* have youth programs in place and there are workers who may already be dealing with a problematic affluent gang trend, even before city officials know it is present. These youth workers typically have to be on top of what is happening in the youth culture simply to carry on an effective youth program. These institutions can be an effective rallying point for a neighborhood awareness and prevention drive, and they provide a natural venue for identifying willing adults, desirous of getting involved. They can also provide nongang prevention youth programs that provide positive alternatives and a place to grow and be nurtured.

The specific beliefs of each institution will vary, but there is little to prevent different groups from sponsoring an antigang effort in a community when there is a sincere effort to help youths.

Juvenile Officers—Many communities today, by necessity, have juvenile officers directly working in local schools. Initially these officers were put on the beat because of rising drug trafficking in schools, but now they have to deal with weapons being brought to school and the formation of gangs. This is true in many affluent communities. These officers can provide an excellent resource, if properly trained and equipped, for presentations in schools to both youths and parents. They are also some of the best informed about gang trends and many attend special training on gang activity. They can teach a youth about being street-smart and let kids know where they can turn if there is trouble.

Other Elements of Law Enforcement—As discussed in chapter 17, law enforcement and the juvenile justice system can be a factor in deterring some youths from joining or continuing on in their gangs. Together they impose restraint on the individual that the individual himself refuses to impose on himself. It is by no means the primary solution, but it is a part of the solution, particularly for youths who fear incarceration.

Dr. Richard Guilianotti, a sociologist at Aberdeen University in Scotland and a leading expert on football hooliganism, said that police arrests were a significant element that contributed to the recent decline in acts of violence by football hooligans in Great Britain.[5] In addition to arrests, police developed strategies for crowd control before, during, and after a game. In the early 1980s, the area behind the goal was an area where people stood, rather than sit in a seat. For hooligans of an opposing team, it was a challenge to sneak into an opponent's goal area and cause havoc—what is called "taking the end," referenced in chapter 8. Police helped reduce violence by suggesting that seating be assigned and ticket owners be seated in physical seats. Police also studied the hooligan tactics of engaging hooligans of opposing teams just outside stadiums and developed strategies to keep the two groups apart.

In Ft. Worth, the "zero tolerance" roundup of gang members who broke even minor laws was exemplary of a *short-term* strategy that drove down specific acts of violence. This might be particularly effective in affluent communities where there are fewer youths in gangs and where even a short period of incarceration might have the desired effect. Primary reliance on this type of strategy, however, will not be effective in the long term.

One final note. Accompanying the increasing recognition and acceptance that family deterioration is typically the most significant factor in youth gang formation—and often juvenile crime as a whole, there is also increasing discussion in the private and public sector for inflicting at least monetary punishment on parents for crimes their children commit. In some communities, for example, antigraffiti laws have been passed that demand that business owners remove graffiti on their establishments or be fined, even though they were not responsible for the graffiti itself. This naturally prompts a response: If they're going to punish me for something I didn't do, what about the parents of the kid? Aren't they supposed to keep them in line? Additionally, when those in the juvenile justice system repeatedly hear juvenile delinquency cases in which the parents of a juvenile are grossly neglectful and abusive, there is the natural tendency to want to initiate some kind of punishment to inspire these parents to change their ways and provide the nurturing and restraint their kids need so the system doesn't have to intercede. This is a simplification of a very complex issue, but an issue that is likely to grow in public debate as gangs and juvenile crime proliferate. There are so many potential liabilities and potential failures for such a tack that *any* such discussion and/or action must be tempered, and approached slowly with the utmost care.

Justice of the Peace—In many states, these officers of the court are often the first stop for at-risk youths who either break the law or are caught for truancy or dropping out of school. They often have incisive perspective when a new gang trend surfaces because they see the *patterns* of what is breaking down. They know where and for what reason. Texas juvenile expert, Judge Deborah B. Hollifield, whose area of jurisdiction is Colleyville, a new Dallas suburb, put it this way:

We see what the shared value is or isn't in a community and we get a feel for the rhythm of how a community operates. We are elected and are a part of the local government, but we also see what is happening in private homes and in many neighborhoods in ways that most people don't.

Where I serve, you have two-income families where parents leave at 7:00 A.M. to commute thirty miles. They drop the kids off at day care and return twelve hours later. And when the kids get older, in order to save on day care, the kids are left to fend for themselves or for each other. On the weekends, parents are tired and they don't plug into the community. In our town of about 25,000, you won't find more than about 300 cars in the church parking lots. Multiply that by three and you have less than 5%. So the churches are struggling.

These kids are being raised exclusively by TV, schools, and baby sitters. I call it the *Lord of the Flies Syndrome*. These are kids who have raised themselves, created their own society, their own economy, and their own value system. They don't want what we want. They want to be king of their own turf.[6]

Although they don't receive much press, justices of the peace and other types of juvenile judges can be some of the most valuable people to know when setting up a gang-prevention program. They can often provide valuable information about what public and private agencies and institutions can and are willing to assist. This is because the justice of the peace often seeks outs and delivers various kinds of creative assistance to aid youths and families who are seeking help. They are squarely in the middle of troubled homes, schools, the juvenile justice system, and both government and private agencies and organizations who help troubled families and youths. For those areas in which a justice of the peace does not have this kind of jurisdiction, consult your local city hall, juvenile authorities, or child protective services for the equivalent.

Independent Organizations—Many communities already have different organizations that are working hard to deal with troubled youths: youth homes, mentoring programs, and summer camps are examples that provide input into an at-risk youth's life. What isn't needed here is for those in the business community to solely make financial contributions and donate only a couple of hours a month to help a youth. Kids need someone who will give them quantity and quality time.

There are organizations that are well run and those that aren't. Careful selection should be based upon more than political pressure and expediency. If the affluent gang problem in a community is minimal, perhaps one or two of these organizations combined with some local governmental support will be sufficient to neutralize a rising gang problem.

Social Agencies—State and local social agencies can be of *limited* assistance, and except in the cases of extreme abuse, are not often the best places to help launch a preventative program. They are better suited for intervention when trying to put the pieces of the puzzle together when disengaging a youth from a gang. For example, in cases of severe domestic violence and abuse, some agencies have the legal authority to place a youth in the home of an out-of-state relative or in some cases, a willing neighbor. Drug rehabilitation programs and counseling are some of the other services appropriate social agencies can provide.

City Hall—"City hall" is used loosely here to specify the *local* city government. Sometimes it can be an asset; other times it will work to quash even the recognition that there is a local problem for fear of driving away current and prospective businesses. Local governments work hard to protect their tax base, and for some, the logical, or rather illogical, view expressed is that serious public discussion about a problem is to be perceived as a loser and an undesirable community. One exemplary response to the increase of gang activity in an affluent community can be found in Farmers Branch, Texas, a North Dallas suburb.

ONE CITY'S RESPONSE

Richard Escalante became the city manager of Farmers Branch in 1987. A tall, robust, and feisty Chicago native of Hispanic descent, Escalante comes from a family of steelworkers. He cares about kids and has two teenagers of his own. With a population of over 25,000 and about 3,000 youths, in 1990 Farmers Branch police intelligence had identified approximately 15 gangs involving about 500 youths. About 250 youths lived outside of Farmers Branch but came there to "hang." Investigator and gang point officer, Terry Adams, said, "Being in a gang was in vogue like wearing a pair of Nike shoes."[7]

In 1991 a state-wide law enforcement survey asked local communities to quantify their gang activity. Carrollton, a similar suburb next to Farmers Branch, indicated that they didn't have a gang problem. In fact, from just the calls I had received and off-the-record discussions with police officers, Carrollton had a worse gang problem. It was two years later, in 1992, that acknowledgement finally occurred, in part because most neighboring suburbs were being affected by gangs and admission wasn't preceived to be unique. Farmers Branch, however, acknowledged the increased trend and took action.

In 1988 Farmers Branch followed the national trends of youth problems: increased crime, acts of violence, drug abuse, teen pregnancy, and so on. Because it wasn't an inner-city environment, these problems were addressed primarily by a cadre of private agencies and churches. Escalante and others noted that a number of specific problems were becoming common in urban areas:

- The beginning of gang activity centered among troubled youths from middle-class and upper-income families, as well as from areas in which apartment dwellings were deteriorating.
- Lack of summer programs for all youths.
- Increased number of "latchkey" kids who came home from school without at least one parent consistently present.
- Insufficient after-school child care for working, single parents.
- A denial factor at work by affected institutions. Many school officials, for example, resisted acknowledging their inability to address the growing gang problem. To do so would be an admission of defeat by city professionals. The exception was the new school superintendent whom Escalante believed was freed up to attack the problem because he was new to the district and had not yet developed close allegiances.
- One directly affected city department, the parks board, didn't identify the growing problems because it didn't perceive itself as having the responsibility to respond. The board considered this the job of the police, schools, and social agencies. Therefore, it was not initiating any studies to determine if all segments of the community were participating in available youth programs. Escalante believed that this kind of myopic approach needed to change because of the complexity of the problems, and so he organized a task force.

The task force Escalante spearheaded didn't form in response to community pressure; rather, it was preemptively initiated by government officials who saw a number of growing problems that would only become worse in the future. To foresee the outcome, if not addressed, all they had to do was look at Dallas with its seemingly out-of-control gang problems and violent juvenile crime.

Farmers Branch had traditionally assumed such issues as gangs in schools, drug abuse, and latchkey kids to be the responsibility of schools or social services, not the city. But this view changed when latchkey kids started committing crimes; it became apparent that in order to solve this problem the city had to consider implementing after-school programs for kids whose single parents worked.

To take effective action, city hall had to change its problem-solving philosophy from *problem-oriented policing* to *community-oriented policing*. *Problem-oriented policing* centers around assigning a particular problem to a specific department or agency. Gang activity, for example, would only be handled by law enforcement. In contrast, *community-oriented policing* views a problem with all its complexities and asks that *any* department or agency that can contribute to a solution to do so. This avoids the typical turf wars that render competing city government and private agencies ineffective.

The community-oriented approach might sound naive, but many communities have made it work, and the idea is catching on at city manager regional and national conferences. Simply put, the realization is taking hold that to make things better, everyone must contribute unselfishly to get the job done.

With this change of philosophy, the task force was composed of Escalante, the chief of police, the chief librarian, the parks and recreation department head, and the head of community services—which included everything from building inspection to housing to city codes. Although many communities form such blue-ribbon panels from the private sector, Escalante felt that he would have a better chance of implementing programs that actually worked if those who were compiling the recommendations were the *same people* who would later implement them.

The questions that Escalante wanted the task force to answer were:

- What are the needs of today's youth?
- Who, if anyone, is attempting to meet those needs?
- What should be the city's future role in meeting those needs?

"A key component," Escalante said, "was that the evaluations were *not* to be department based, which can cause people to become *defensive*. We weren't interested in blaming anyone. We simply wanted to identify the problems and then ask who in the public and private sector was meeting or could meet those needs. By approaching the issue in this way, we avoided turf battles and placing blame.

"The most important factor that we found driving the problems we identified was the disintegration of the nuclear family: a family in which there is a breadwinner, two parents, someone home raising the children, and a family dinner at home on most nights."

After two-and-a-half months, the task force made its presentation for recommendations to the city council. One hundred percent of the recommendations were accepted. Follow-up community and civic group forums helped ensure community participation and backing. The recommendations implemented included:

- Work with existing inventory of facilities, both public and private, instead of rushing into a building program.
- Expand from half-day to all-day the ten-week Summer Sunshine Program for two hundred students. Scholarship funds were to be provided for about one-third of the families who

couldn't afford the program. No segment of the city was to be excluded.

- Increase the number of workers in all departments where needed.
- Employ additional youth officers, whose sole responsibility was to walk the halls, eat lunch with the kids, work with the teachers, and pay visits to families with youths who were at risk for becoming involved in a gang. These officers were not to work cases, so that they could befriend kids and be seen regularly, like the cop on the beat in former generations. The idea was to build a one-on-one trust between officers and students.
- Establish an after-school program for four hundred kids whose parents worked. This would serve as an academic growth and activities-oriented program, not as a day care program.
- Waive some fees for kids at swimming pools and other public recreational areas, and encourage city baseball and football programs to provide scholarships when needed.
- Initiate parenting classes for up to three hundred families. In addition to parenting skills, other practical skills would also be taught: study skills, purchasing insurance, managing a budget, etc. During classes, they offered child care, and youth officers met regularly with the kids to build trust.
- Conduct weekly ride-throughs by maintenance and building code inspectors to upgrade safety in lower-income apartment complexes.

It is important to note that this community chose to head off an encroaching gang problem by developing programs centered around helping kids find *positive outlets*, and to assist families in counteracting the effects of deteriorating family conditions. Escalante hammered home the point that *kids need help all year long* on a multitude of levels.

While Escalante concedes that government cannot "fix" all the ills wrought by family decline, his city made some marginal gains related to its gang problem:

- Within a year, wearing gang colors was no longer "cool" or fashionable.
- Unlike similar communities, Farmers Branch experienced only one gang-related shooting from 1989 through the spring of 1992, and there were no acts of gang violence in the schools. Additionally, the number of other acts of gang violence, such as assaults and intimidation, was dramatically down. (Crimes against property committed by gang and nongang

members, however, rose. Police believed that gang members, many of whom were criminally active before they joined a gang, acted without the direction of the gang hierarchy.)
- Scout troops were formed for the first time in lower-income apartment dwellings.
- Churches increased their outreach efforts to affected youths.
- A local psychiatric hospital offered free first-offender counseling for sixty-two kids the first year.

The cost for the total package of programs for the first year was $200,000. "No new taxes were required the first year," said Escalante, "just a refocusing of priorities." The second year, additional tax funds were sought because of declining property values due to over-speculation in the eighties. "But," Escalante added, "when we had to ask for additional revenue to fund the youth programs because of the drop in overall revenues, no one said, 'Kill the youth programs.'"

In 1992, the strategy was refined to include:
- Juvenile officers had face-to-face meetings in the homes of youths who had been identified as either being a member of a gang or likely to join a gang. These meetings with parents took place before a youth was ever arrested or had been observed to commit a crime. Not one parent objected to this preemptive effort by the police.
- Intelligence officers maintained careful records of the specific activities of each gang and individual gang members. Gang activities were also regularly videotaped.
- First Offender Program was initiated which included three counselors who met every week with offenders.
- Adopt a School Program—Police officers, and later other city employees, volunteered to take on a school as their own. Officers, at their discretion, could expend time and resources to help the school they chose to adopt. Twenty-one officers of seventy volunteered and "adopted" seven schools.
- Gang prevention efforts were initiated in elementary schools. They found that kids are more receptive than older youths and will carry what they accept when they are young into junior high and high school. Each school's officer was introduced to the youths and the picture of the officer was hung at the entrance to the school with the telephone number if they ever needed help.
- Internally, city hall clearly communicated that the city would rather see a reduction in the number of traffic tickets written if officers were spending more time with youths.

• Gang policy in the police department was established from the "bottom up," not dictated down from city hall, common in many suburbs.

In spite of the genuine effort, an unpredicted obstacle ensued for one of the key components initiated earlier. The state threatened to stop the after-school program because it claimed that the schools, which housed kids all day long, didn't meet the state's requirements for day care after school. It claimed the city was operating the program illegally because it should be licensed by the state. "It was crazy," Escalante complained. "Even though the kids spent eight hours a day there, it was the last two that the state objected to," Escalante shrugged. "I have probably spent more time with this issue than any other, except putting a budget together."[8] (The issue was not yet resolved as of the writing of this text.)

By the end of 1994, the city's collective efforts diminished identifiable gang members from 500 in 1990 to about 150, which includes those who actually live in Farmers Branch and those who spend significant time there. Additionally, in 1993 and 1994, only one drive-by shooting occurred—for a total of two between 1990 and 1994. Police chief, Jim Fawcett, said, "It's not popular to brag anymore about your gang or to wear colors."[9]

Escalante believes that there were four basic reasons why they were successful in reducing an expanding gang problem. They:

1. Avoided turf battles and pointing blame.
2. Adopted a community-oriented policing philosophy.
3. Took a businesslike approach. "We presented the facts, the solution, and the resources to do it. It had to make financial sense to the business community. We also keyed off timely news accounts."
4. Realized that the mechanisms for solving social problems were not the same as those for solving city problems, such as street repair. They realized they needed a broader approach.

He recommends three foundational goals for cities that want to develop the perspective necessary for tackling specific youth problems:

1. Develop an understanding of the overall community itself: diversity of neighborhoods, types of businesses, source of tax revenues, etc.
2. Without the expectation of a quick fix, inquire about the specifics of the problems, and investigate which structures, combined with what resources, can respond.
3. Recruit department heads who will adopt a comprehensive view in order to avoid political infighting.

"There is nothing that we have done that is different from other communities except a total commitment with a nondepartmental approach. City government can't do everything, nor should it try," says Escalante. "Churches, scout troops, private business, and agencies can all do a better job in specific areas than we can."

One final note. One might assume that the unusual esprit de corps at this city hall was in part inspired by the fact that key city employees, such as the chief of police, lived in Farmers Branch and had a personal stake in the city's future. Surprisingly, only about half of pivotal employees resided in Farmers Branch. The rest lived in Dallas and the surrounding suburbs. The Chief of Police, Jim Fawcett, for example, said that when he was hired, he didn't want to uproot his kids from their schools.

PERSONAL REFLECTIONS

Although Farmers Branch is a good example of a community trying to arrest gang activity, no city without the one-on-one cooperation of its adult citizens can prevent the *formation* of gangs. Perhaps in a police state, as was common in the formerly Communist European countries, youths might be too intimidated to join a gang and wear their colors openly. But not in an open, democratic society, where there is a freedom to choose and a Constitution to protect private rights.

In one suburb, about twenty minutes from my home, officers had to arrest a youth whose parents immigrated from Iran. When told that their son was arrested and why, their question was, "When do we have to move from town?" This is how youthful lawlessness is commonly punished in other parts of the world. A youth's crime not only punishes the youth, but the family as well.

The kinds of preemptive action as discussed in this chapter and the next can halt the proliferation of gangs, but personal involvement and accountability are required. When chaos is present and left to continue for sustained periods of time, it is human nature for people to cry out that any measures—no matter how drastic—be taken to restore order. We can't accept this as the cure, because it is certainly worse than the disease.

CHAPTER 20.

Prevention Part II: A Strategy That Will Work

In this chapter is presented a three-point approach to gang prevention. It is based upon my firsthand experience of working as one of a number of lay volunteers over a period of six years with over 400 youths from an inner-city type area in Dallas. During that period of time, not one of these youths to my knowledge ever joined a gang. I have since made numerous presentations of these ideas to youths in America and Europe with a similarly universal response. More than a program, what is presented here is a strategic approach that can be incorporated into an organized effort mounted by almost any private, civic, or governmental group. This strategy is comprised of three key ideas:

1. Addressing and resolving the Missing Protector Factor (MPF) for at-risk youths. As suggested in chapter 7, the MPF is the one factor that puts most at-risk youths at the greatest risk of gang involvement.

   By attacking the MPF, one can neutralize the most important *external* factor over which a youth typically has no control. A youth can't control whether or not his parents, a close relative, or a caring adult won't or are unable to come to his/her aid in a crisis. The MPF is recognized as an *external* factor because it is something that occurs outside a youth's own mind and personal control.

2. Establish the link in a youth's mind that gangs are a *deception*. Why and how gangs are a deception that won't solve personal problems is the focus here. Experience demonstrates that youths at a *conscious* level don't like to think that

241

they can be easily deceived. *This implies that one is weak.* Establishing the gang-deception link creates a negative and unfavorable association in a youth's mind.

By powerfully pointing out the gang-deception link in a youth's mind, one is addressing an *internal*, in-the-mind factor over which a youth does have control. A youth can choose whether or not to accept the lie that a gang is the solution to his/her problems.

3. Begin implementing and teaching the above *before* a youth reaches the age of ten, and preferably when a youth is in the first or second grade in affected communities.

The reason for addressing the above two issues before a youth is ten is that most youths haven't yet begun to go through puberty. Any school teacher will tell you that it is far more difficult to reach youths after puberty, when hormones can wildly fluctuate and youths begin to assert their independence. There is also typically less resistance when youths are asked to put their trust in a "protector," and it is also easier for them to accept the gang-deception link.

This three-point strategy can be communicated in stand-alone presentations, both through individual contact and group presentations, or it can be integrated into existing programs. This strategy can be implemented in most amenable communities and without depending upon expensive and ineffective government action. Most importantly, this strategy directly addresses the damage inflicted by troubled homes and does not hinge upon parental involvement which, although desirable, is often absent for youths in gangs.

ADDRESSING THE MISSING PROTECTOR FACTOR

As noted by Kopp's studies in Hungary, the MPF becomes operative when *youths can't count on a close family relative for assistance when there is a crisis in their life* (chapter 7). She states that the MPF is also the most likely candidate for the premiere factor that will put a youth at risk of gang activity. The MPF could also become operative if in addition to a youth's family, a youth also couldn't find *any* willing adult to come to his/her assistance.

I have observed that when an at-risk youth acknowledges this concept and takes action to find someone whom they can trust to help them if a crisis arises—regardless of whether the "protector" is a family member or not—then the MPF often becomes inoperative for that youth. The result:

his/her vulnerability to gang activity plummets. Prevention efforts that first target the MPF will obtain the most significant long-term prevention of gang activity.

I suspected that this might be true after working as a lay volunteer with the 400 Dallas youths. In their neighborhoods gang activity was plentiful. Approximately one-third of the youths had actually seen an act of violence such as a stabbing or a shooting.[1] The initial desire of the volunteer group wasn't to implement an antigang program, but that is what happened. We simply saw an opportunity, working under the auspices of a local community church, to help give these youths direction and personal assistance to break out of the trappings of their neighborhood. Two of the most effective ideas that these youths responded to that resulted in zero gang participation was addressing the MPF issue and second, the gang-deception trap, which is explained shortly.

At the time, we didn't think of our efforts as addressing the MPF, but that is what we did. We made sure that each youth knew that they could count on us to be there for them whenever, wherever, and for whatever crisis came up in their individual lives. And if we didn't feel equipped to help, we did our best to find someone who could. Additionally, we focused our efforts on those youths who were twelve years or younger, the reasons for which will be expanded later in this chapter.

During the time period that I worked with these exceptionally at-risk youths (1985–92), I also investigated numerous cases of affluent gangs across the US, with a significant focus beginning after 1988. As I learned from direct contact with present and former gang members, these youths nearly always stated that they believed that a stable home would deter gang activity. Additionally, I received occasional requests to speak to youths from affluent communities, both in schools and in camp settings (over 50,000 students across America and Canada) on the current destructive youth-culture trends. Here again, I observed that youths from broken/troubled homes were more likely to engage in harmful activities. I also observed that youths who found someone to turn to when there was a crisis in their life more readily resisted harmful activities, such as drugs and gangs. (It should be noted that this perspective is not really a new one, although its presentation in this format has been received as such. The Boys and Girls Club of America and the Big Brother program are organizations that have long recognized the concept behind the MPF.)

PROTECTORS AND MENTORS

What must be understood is that addressing the MPF is *not* the same as a mentoring program. Mentoring implies more than just providing assistance and protection when there is a crisis in a young person's life. Mentoring involves teaching morals, imparting discipline, teaching discernment regarding who one's friends are, communicating love and affection, investing significant amounts of quality time, etc. In short, one becomes an almost surrogate or adoptive parent. No doubt, a mentor in a youth's life is more desirable than someone who is solely a protector.

Unfortunately, it's terribly difficult, as I discovered working with the Dallas youths, to recruit people who are willing to give significantly of their time in order to be a true *mentor*. I found that it wasn't nearly as difficult, however, to recruit *protectors* because there is a smaller time commitment required. We found more people willing to take on the task of protector—an ennobling concept—than those who might qualify as a mentor. For an individual to qualify as a mentor is also more difficult because of the interaction requirements. To qualify as a protector, however, one only has to be able to communicate and gain the trust of the youth, have some common sense, maintain regular contact, and be willing to help if called upon. Mentoring, while preferable, requires more skill and depth of understanding. My experience, though, is that often when an adult volunteers to be a protector he or she can be encouraged to become a mentor and then channeled into a local community mentoring program or church outreach.

One of the reasons that we probably had an extraordinary success rate working with the Dallas youths is that the volunteers worked in conjunction with a regular church Sunday school program. Here, the kids not only had the offer of protectors, but they also heard moral and spiritual teachings which acted as a form of mentoring. Unfortunately a lot of one-on-one time wasn't possible because of the large number of youths and the small number of workers. The ratio often was 1 worker to 50 kids. But the reinforcement of right and wrong, the establishment of limits, etc. added to the "protector" factor. In most situations, it is common that volunteer protectors will offer this kind of guidance as it is an instinctive part of being a *protector*.

THE MISSING PROTECTOR FACTOR: GUIDELINES FOR INSTRUCTION

To begin to attack an encroaching gang trend, most any youth with some assistance can find a protector. It *is* something over which they can have control and take action.

What follows are guidelines for direct presentations to youths so that they can take action to resolve the MPF. The same ideas can be communicated to concerned adults, but of course modified.

1) Clearly articulate that youths who fit the predictable profile for gang involvement have a greater risk factor of gang activity than youths who come from stable, loving homes. Have youths think of and recall for themselves gang members they know and their family profile. When youths realize this is typically true, two things happen: a) They realize that the person talking to them has done their homework and has some understanding of the youth culture. b) Youths personalize this perception with their own examples.

2) *Explain the MPF concept with examples.* Point out that gangs often prey on people who are in pain and who have no one to turn to. It should be acknowledged that a youth usually doesn't have control over destructive familial factors. Neither can a youth control the fact that a willing relative, such as an aunt or uncle, can't help due to obstacles of distance, responsibilities, etc. What youths can have some control over, however, is searching out an adult protector. (A sample explanation of how to describe the MPF to most youths is presented later in this chapter.)

3) *Provide explicit examples of what constitutes a crisis, especially for younger youths.* One must never assume that a youth understands what is meant by a *crisis*. This should be taught explicitly. Some examples might include: parents in the throes of marital problems; a sibling found to be using drugs or who is pregnant; failing in school; severe ridicule or intimidation from youths at school; sudden illness; etc. Additionally, one should communicate that it is not a sign of weakness to ask for help when there is trouble because no one is smart enough or equipped to tackle all situations by themselves.

4) *Youths from at-risk home environments,* who don't have an adult protector, *should be encouraged to seek help from a relative, teacher, neighbor, juvenile officer, minister, etc.* Their goal should be to seek assistance from someone who can help them find an adult that they can call upon—day or night—if there is a crisis. Sadly, there are always those cases when a parent might object to such intervention, but in many cases neglectful parents aren't even aware of the details of their child's life and won't voice disapproval. For tactical purposes, the closer the protector lives to a youth the better, providing a youth greater immediate access. In some cases, however, when an angry parent might resist a child seeking help from someone who lives close by, a school counselor, teacher, or local juvenile officer working in a school might be a better selection. As with each of the suggestions in this chapter, individual attention must be given to individual youths and their needs.

5) *Youths from* stable homes *should be encouraged to help their at-risk friends, who don't have an adult protector, find one.* In many cases, I have observed youths from stable homes taking the initiative to bring a friend home so that their parents can either be that protector or help find a suitable person. This action creates a neighborhood sentiment of watching out and caring for those who are in a disadvantaged situation; and among youths, this can create a positive peer pressure that can establish an attitude in a school towards service and unselfish acts of kindness.

AN ADAPTABLE STRATEGY

One of the reasons that directly tackling the MPF in a grass-roots type approach can be effective is that it is easily adaptable to almost any environment or context. A local neighborhood, for example, can implement this among neighbors. Schools can set up a program that teaches and implements this concept through assemblies and the local PTA. Churches and synagogues can implement this in their own congregations. Juvenile officers working in schools can attach this concept to drug prevention programs and presentations in schools. Most importantly, though, is that the MPF risk-factor wrought by troubled homes can be neutralized in a personal one-on-one relationship—the type of relationship absent for many at-risk youths. As previously noted, it is preferable that parents participate and recognize their natural role as their child's protector. However, in many cases, parents don't. This means that one must take the case against gangs directly to the youths themselves, and parents of at-risk youths brought into the process as they are willing to participate. Youths have a right to grow up without the threat of gangs harming or recruiting them. In most cases, it simply requires youths saying "yes" to those who offer their help.

What is especially appealing about addressing the MPF is that it gets people in local neighborhoods involved, helping just one youth. It doesn't require big budgets, votes by city councils, or elaborate bureaucracies. Our family, for example, has personally used this strategy with great effectiveness to help youths in our own neighborhood. Also, Kopp's research suggests that addressing the MPF might also result in a major reduction of other youth social ills such as drug abuse and suicide.

One reason that this approach can work remarkably well in affluent communities is that community organizations typically are already in place that can implement such an initiative. Additionally, financial resources are often available, if needed, to print materials and provide additional support efforts such as jobs programs and summer activities and programs when gang activity is typically at its peak.

Some of the potential obstacles and pitfalls for addressing the MPF are:

1) Inconsistent follow-up—Once a person commits to be the person that will help a youth in a crisis, regular contact must be maintained. Because not all volunteers will follow through, a simple monitoring process should be a part of the process so that suitable adult replacements can be found for those who drop out of the program. In addition, monitoring can be used to prompt someone who hasn't consistently visited a youth to do so.

2) Possibility of an Adult Inflicting Harm—When volunteers are involved, there is always the risk of giving inappropriate advice or direction to a youth that might be harmful. Additionally, one must be prepared to screen out child molesters offering assistance in order to take advantage of a youth. Unfortunately there is no sure-fire method to eliminate this risk. Prudent discussions with youths about this possibility and how to defend oneself should be a part of the process. Local counseling clinics, school counselors, and local police departments can suggest materials and strategies for implementing this as a part of the process.

3) *Threat of Lawsuits*—In our tort-hungry culture, the possibility of legal exposure always exists. Candid discussions with local counsel to reduce this risk and appropriate insurance should be a part of the process. This shouldn't deter people who care about kids to get involved. Social agencies, private organizations, and local churches all reach out to youths through thousands of programs, and most without incurring paralyzing lawsuits.

THE GANG-DECEPTION FACTOR: GUIDELINES FOR INSTRUCTION

Deception is a powerful word. It affects every part of our lives, but most people don't want to admit that they can be deceived. This is especially true for youths. Just demonstrate to a youth in a compelling manner that, "You are easy to deceive," and you will get reactions ranging from embarrassment to denial to a bravado that says, "Oh yeah? Prove it!"

For this reason, it is desirable to disarm a youth's resistance to acknowledging that he/she can be deceived by a gang's lying promises. In live presentations, I prefer to draw on my expertise as a professional magician (my professional avocation prior to 1981). Sleight-of-hand and what I like to call sleight-of-mind (tricks that look like they are mind powers) demonstrations are a fun, nonthreatening way to establish that, "yes, we can all be deceived." It quickly reduces resistance to accepting that perhaps we can be deceived by things other than a magician's tricks, such as gangs.

Most people never think about the gang-deception connection: that what gangs offer is a lying illusion. A deception. Gangs don't really take away or heal one's pain. Neither do they offer valid long-term solutions. But at-risk youths banded together in a gang claim that they do. Pointing out the lie/deception behind gang activity can be a powerful motivating device for youths internally—in their own minds—to resist gang involvement.

The effect of addressing this factor is different than dealing with the MPF. The MPF is an *external factor* that affects youths externally *beyond their control*. The gang-deception factor, though, is an *internal in-the-mind* factor that doesn't affect youths until they *choose* to join a gang . . . until they choose to *buy* the lie. Then they become deception's *victim*. Yet, youths don't like to believe that they are weak, easy pushovers, easily deceived. By connecting the idea that gangs exercise deception, youths make the connection that to buy into a gang is to be weak—to become a person who is easily deceived and manipulated; a pushover.

To provide a context of how the gang-deception link might be presented, what follows is a condensation from a presentation I have used with junior high and high school youths. When presented for elementary school youths, the language should be simplified.

Demonstration: I begin by presenting two cards tricks, which can be seen by up to 2,500 students. In the first trick, a youth *thinks* of a card in the deck and I tell them the name of the card. (Audience reaction is quiet, subdued, reflective. They are stunned.) For the second trick, the youth thinks of another card in the deck. I then announce: "If I could cause your card to leap out of the center of the deck, do four somersaults, and land in my left hand, would you say, 'That's incredible!'?" They of course laugh, and nod their head. Then that is exactly what happens. The card leaps out of the deck and lands in my hand! (Audience reaction is spontaneous laughter).

Conversational dialogue that follows: I have found that there is a profile of a person who is often the easiest to deceive. There are actually two factors that make people easy to deceive. And if I am a deceiver, I want to find a person who has these two factors operative in their life. What are these two factors?

First, I want to find a person who typically likes to be entertained or informed *visually*. Why? Because what we see *visually* often causes us to react *emotionally*. I'm not talking about fighter pilots who are trained to trust their visual read of their instruments. I'm talking about people who are addicted to the visual. For example, if I'm a deceiver I want to find people who watch hours and hours of television, because I know that they have been conditioned to react emotionally to what they see. I *don't* want to find a student who reads a lot and thinks through issues.

Now did you know that you just experienced this first factor when I performed one of my tricks? That's right. By using a *visual*, I *caused* you to react *emotionally*. And you didn't even know it. Think about it. When did I do this?

Remember the second card trick? What was your *first* reaction when the card leaped out of the deck? (Audience responds: "wow" or "how did you do it?") Incorrect. What was your *first* reaction *before* "wow"? Think. What was your *first* reaction? (Pause) It was *laughter*. You laughed. Now why did you laugh? You didn't laugh at the first card trick. You were more silent, thinking about what I did. The reason you were silent was that the first trick was a cerebral trick. I had someone *think* of a card and I *told* them the name of their card. The trick essentially involved *words*.

In the next trick, though, you *saw* the card leap out of the deck. You *visually* saw it leap out, and you reacted *emotionally*. You *laughed*.

You see, I have found that when you do a trick that is *visual*, people will almost always react *emotionally*. But if you do a trick in which people have to rely upon listening to words—like the first trick, you don't get the same emotional response.

Now if you want to figure out one of my tricks, do you want to use your mind or emotions? (Response: "mind.")

And if I am a deceiver who wants to harm you, do I want you to operate out of the visual or from what you read and what you think through. (Response: "visual.") That's right. Because what you see *visually* typically tells you to react *emotionally*. [NOTE: The idea here is expanded that visuals *can* be instructive and helpful and people can be trained to use visuals unemotionally, such as fighter pilots who are trained to trust the visual readings of their instrument panels. Other examples of visuals used to manipulate emotions are also provided, such as dictators who plaster monolithic pictures of themselves on buildings.]

Did you know that gangs use the same kind of idea? They want you to operate out of your *emotions* by using *visuals* to deceive you?

Think about it. What's the first thing you think of when you think of gangs? (Response: "colors, bandannas, jackets, caps, hand signals, etc.") Right! These are things that you see! They don't usually pass out eloquently written letters on fine stationery. They like you to key off the visuals, like what they wear.

Why? Because they know that what you see *visually* will cause you to react *emotionally*. And what is one of the emotions that they want to inspire? (Response: "fear.")

Gangs are a rip-off. They want to deceive you.

Now do you wake up in the morning and say, "Yes, today is the day I get to be deceived! Today is the day I get to be ripped off! I can't wait until someone lies to me again!"?

Obviously not. But gangs want to deceive you.

Now what is the second factor that makes a person one of the easiest people to deceive? Here it is.

If I am a deceiver, I want to find someone in pain who is not honestly confronting or dealing with their pain. And I want to find someone who has *internal* pain, like from a troubled home. I'm not looking for someone who simply has sprained an ankle.

If I am a deceiver, I would rather find someone who is in pain than a greedy person. Why? Because greed is something that you want to *get*. Pain is something that you want to get *rid of*. Think about it. Who would probably have a higher motivational level? Someone who wants something for nothing or a burn patient with third-degree burns over their entire body? (Response: "the burn victim.")

Now gangs know this. They know that if they can find people in pain, it is easier to rope them in. Think about it. Why is it that almost every gang member comes from a home where there is divorce or separation, physical or sexual abuse, or one their parents is severely dysfunctional [expand here]? Especially if there is no one there to protect them when there is a crisis in their life. Why?

Because they are in pain and they think that the gang can take away their pain. [This idea is expanded with examples.] But does the gang solve their pain? (Response: "no.") That's right. The gang only exploits that pain—takes advantage of that pain. So who's being ripped off? Are gangs a rip-off?

Now imagine if you use a visual on someone who is in pain. Remember, what you see visually typically tells you to react how? (Response: "emotionally.") And imagine if you use a visual to emotionally tell a person: "We can take away your pain." Do you think that person will be easy to deceive and manipulate? [Expanded here with illustrations.] Do you think that gangs will just give somebody something for nothing? No. Gangs always want something back, and *on their own terms*.

Now how many of you can't wait until you can be deceived by a gang? Anyone?

Finally, how many of you would like to know exactly what it takes to stop gangs from forming and growing? (Response: raised hands.) Well here it is.

First, those of you that come from a home that is like the kind I described *and* don't have an adult that you know you can count on for help when there is a crisis in your life, your are the ones most at risk of getting into a gang. [Expand on what is meant by a crisis and the role of a protector.]

If you know that you fit that description, make up your mind today that you will talk to a teacher, coach, youth pastor, friend . . . someone who can help you find that person whom you can call . . . anytime, day or night, if there is a crisis in your life. When you find that person whom you know you can trust to help you, follow his or her advice if and when you have a crisis. Then you will become the person who is the toughest to recruit by a gang. Then they can't come around and tell you that they will be there for you and that they understand you, that they can help you because no one else will.

Now if you come from a stable home that *isn't* like what I described, here's your job. Your responsibility is to think of at least one friend that you know who *does* fit the profile and help them find someone to be their protector. You can take them home to your folks and they can help. Or maybe you can take them to a teacher they like who will get involved. The key is to be persistent. Don't give up until the two of you find someone who will be there for them if they have a crisis in their life.

If you each will do just this one thing, then with time, you will see gangs start to disappear from your neighborhood. It's worked for others. And it can work right here in Sherwood Heights (name of area).

As already suggested, the above presentation of ideas must of course be modified for each presenter and for the context in which the ideas are presented. What is presented here is in condensed form and should be expanded and personalized. It is important to recognize that at a primal level youths like to believe, as do adults, that they are difficult to deceive, or at least that they are the kind of person who doesn't want to be deceived. In the mind of a youth, to be deceived—except by something like a sleight-of-hand trick or a trick play in an athletic event, etc.—is a sign of mental weakness. And what gangs promise is a deception. They promise power over pain that in reality is only a mask, distraction, or illusive power device. Gangs don't really heal people's problems. They only compound them. Linking in a student's mind that gangs represent deception and that people who join gangs are only asking to be deceived is a powerful deterrent to gang activity. When carefully nurtured, most youths will accept this idea and begin to view gangs as a rip-off for the weak. This in turn can initiate peer pressure on those who view gangs as something racy, exciting, and an answer to their problems.

I am not suggesting that all youths will immediately turn away from the lure of gang activity because they are exposed to the gang-deception concept. There are always those youths that will think: I can't be deceived. Gangs aren't a rip-off for those *in* a gang . . . who are the leaders. But my experience is that most will resist and turn away from gang involvement. As already stated, this is particularly true when this message is communicated in a timely manner, and with regularity (at least once a year), beginning with kids in elementary school.

It seems that even more than adults and older youths, younger youths are more wide-eyed to ask "what is the truth?" and act upon it. This is not to suggest that older youths won't respond and should be neglected. Each year I speak at a number of universities on the issue of deception and students eagerly respond. One student from the University of Gdansk in Poland, in a letter he sent me, penned: Truth is so desirable. I wish it would be that—If someone says a lie, that the thunder would roar and the sun would go dim so no one is misled.

However, when trying to encourage youths to resist gang activity, the earlier one begins instilling the crucial ideas in a youth's mind, the more likely he or she will resist.

One young girl, thirteen, after a presentation asked, "So the reason Annie [who was an older girl from a broken home in a gang] sometimes swears at me and threatens to hit me is that she's just taking her anger out on me because of her home?"

"What do you think?" I asked.

"I think that's it. I'm going to try and get to know her better. Maybe I can help her. Maybe my mom can help me too."

This young girl's response is about all we can ask of any young person.

THE AGE FACTOR

In retrospect, it appears that one of the reasons that we had such extraordinary success with the Dallas inner-city youths was that we concentrated our efforts working with youths who were ten years or younger—the age before puberty. Why before puberty?

Common sense hands-on experience dictates that the earlier you teach a child the right path, the more likely he/she will stay on it. After a youth reaches puberty it is typically more difficult to teach and instruct even the finest of youths. Just observe a group of elementary school youths and how they will typically lap up almost any good idea presented, juxtaposed to junior high students—7th through 8th grade students—who are often considered by caring teachers as the most difficult age to instruct. Elementary school students pay particularly close attention to ideas that will protect them. For these young youths, the issue of gangs is perceived as far more threatening than something like drug abuse. Why?

Most elementary school kids don't have the desire to do drugs. So they don't perceive drugs to be an immediate personal threat. And more importantly, drugs are something that you have to *take* to hurt you. Gangs don't operate that way. You don't have to go looking for trouble to be roughed up or even shot by a gang. In a young person's mind, gangs are something you need to know about because *gangs can find you even if you try to avoid them.*

During the last two years, 1992–94, when giving talks to elementary school kids in affluent communities on the subject of gangs, I made an interesting observation. In most presentations, I employed professional sleight of hand tricks as a visual device to help youngsters understand the deceptive nature of harmful youth trends. When speaking on drug prevention, the kids would typically pay closer attention to the tricks than to even the most compelling story of drug addiction. Yet, when I spoke on the subject of gangs, it was a different story. The kids were always more intense and attentive to the *content* of a gang prevention talk than even the most amazing trick I would perform.

As already suggested, the reason for this is that gangs can hurt kids even when they don't go looking for them. Also, kids in gangs are typically older, and thus can bully younger kids. And no child wants to live in fear and be picked on. So when they hear how to *prevent* gangs from forming in their neighborhood, they listen with great intensity.

Unfortunately, as kids get older, their caution diminishes, unless there is a catastrophic event in their neighborhood. We saw this occur when a young man was gunned down in our local high school parking lot. Prior to the shooting, high school students were almost typically indifferent to hearing about a gang message. After the shooting, most were eager to listen, setting aside their natural desire for more independence and an attitude that says, "I have heard all this before." Sometimes they are right. But often if an important idea doesn't take hold *before* a youth reaches puberty, there is a slimmer chance that they will act upon that good idea when in trouble.

To repeat, this doesn't mean that a community should neglect instructing older youths about the MPF and how to take action. But *long-term* prevention must start with younger youths so that as they grow older the necessary mindset to resolve the MPF will already be in place. Also, this message must be reinforced each year with *increasing intensity* and with examples that are *more explicit* so that a child continues to accept the guidance offered at their subsequent levels of maturity and development.

As I watched many of the Dallas youths grow older with whom I had worked, they had already made up their mind what they would do for themselves or their friends before they reached that crisis point. So when they entered junior high and high school they carried the antigang attitude with them *even though their personal family and neighborhood conditions remained unchanged.*

PERSONAL REFLECTIONS

To keep kids out of gangs, my every instinct as a father and having worked directly with at-risk kids is to get parents positively involved in their children's lives. No doubt, this would have a far greater impact in the lives of most youths than even the best intentioned efforts of neighborhood volunteers. If my personal wish could be answered, I'd:

- Encourage parents to love and cherish one another.
- Encourage parents to love and cherish their children and teach their kids to do the same for each other.

It is a wish list, and wishes and dreams sometimes do come true when people care enough. . . .

And for those kids who won't grow up in such a home—I'd want everyone of them to know that if and when they get married, that marriage vows and raising kids are sacred. And that if two people desire and commit in their hearts to love one another selflessly, they *can* experience great joy. It doesn't have to fail.

Today, there are enough adults who can be the protector for a child who doesn't have one. But what if the current generation of youths and young adults don't cherish their wedding vows and their children? Then, in the near future, there won't be enough caring adults left to be the protectors for the next generation.

The current reality endorsed in the popular media is that broken/troubled homes are acceptable. This can't be acceptable. For those who live in urban communities and have been perpetual victims of out-of-control juvenile crime, there is a raw anger that is increasingly being directed at this mindless philosophy. Black Dallas resident Charlotte Jennings exhibited her outrage when her twenty-five-year-old son, Sebastian—a Persian Gulf War veteran, was pistol-whipped by "Black punks" stealing his car. Mrs. Jennings stated: "I'm sick of every time you look around, someone's whupped up on a woman or whupped up on a college student. We have to strive to be somebody." Turning her frustration towards absent parents, she asked: "Where is your mama, where is your daddy? That is all I want to know. . . . What did they teach you?" Her son, who attends night school at a local community college, added: "Without my father, I probably would have been dead. I would have hit the streets. [My mother] couldn't show me how to be a man if she's not one herself."[2]

Reaffirming the need for neighborhood volunteers to be protectors and the need for cherishing the home and parental responsibility, let us conclude with another story I encountered while working on this project. . . .

———————◆———————

Jack was exhausted. His boss hammered him all day and traffic was murder. Entering the door, he unloaded his briefcase and plopped himself down on the couch. He just wanted to be left alone.

"Hey, Dad. I'm ready to throw the football like you promised." Ricky, a lively seven-year-old, remembered his Dad's promise when he tucked him into bed the night before: "When I get home from work, I promise we'll throw the ball around. I just can't do it tonight."

Kids never forget a dad's promise. It's the measure of a father's character and the barometer of his love.

"Ricky, you go clean up your room and as soon as you are done, we'll play ball. Okay, tiger?"

"You bet, Dad." Like a whirling tornado, Ricky tore into his room and was back in ten minutes. Jack was almost ready to doze off.

"Hey, Dad. I'm done. I cleaned up a little bit before you got home. I knew you wanted me to get my room clean. Can we throw the ball now?"

Fidgeting and annoyed, Jack said, "First go see if you can help Mom get dinner ready."

"All right!" But Ricky was back in a flash.

"Mom said she doesn't need any help and that we should go play ball. Can we go now?"

Frustrated, Jack, out of the corner of his eye, saw a picture of the world on the front of Time.

"Hey, I got one more little project for you. This is going to be fun!"

Methodically, Jack tore off the cover and then proceeded to shred it into many small pieces.

"I know that you love puzzles. Hold out your hands." Dumping the pieces into Ricky's hands he said, *"When you finish putting the pieces of this puzzle together, then we'll play ball. How does that sound?"*

"Hey, that sounds great, Dad!" Relieved, Jack watched Ricky run back to his bedroom, thinking: *Finally, he's out of my hair. It'll take him a good hour to piece that thing back together.*

But Jack misjudged Ricky. Ten minutes later, just as Jack was about to doze off, in came Ricky beaming, holding the cover perfectly pieced together on a sheet of construction paper he used that day at school.

Grumbling, Jack opened his eyes and couldn't believe what he saw.

"How did you know where to put all the pieces? Last week, you had trouble finding Florida on the map when we showed you where we were going for spring break."

Proudly, Ricky said . . .

"Dad, you're right. But when you were tearing up the world, I saw that on the back was a big picture of a boy. And so I just put all the pieces of the boy together first, and then the whole world came together too!"

EPILOGUE

September 7, 1994

It's fall now. My kids are back in school. This year, kids across America are returning to new strategies that will protect them. . . . Metal detectors installed in many high school football stadiums for the first time. Kids being forced to buy clear book bags so school officials can make sure weapons aren't in tow. Lockers permanently sealed off so they can't store mini-arsenals. More kids than ever in affluent neighborhoods hope that when their name is called out in a hallway that it's just a friend. And not someone who means them harm.

During the 1992 Los Angeles riots, some police officers discovered that if they recognized a youth and called out his name—distinguishing him from the mob—that the potential looter was more likely to put down whatever was in his hands and leave.

For kids from troubled homes cruising streets lined with manicured lawns, who will call out their name before the gang calls it out first?

It doesn't matter that the *overall* crime stats are down. When kids aren't safe, no one feels safe. That's just the way it is.

During the middle of this project, in February of 1993, I accepted an invitation from students at the University of Belgrade. Their friends' families were at war. A real war. Less than two hundred miles away, Serbs, Bosnians, and Croats were killing each other. I agreed to accept the invitation only after getting clearance from a representative of the State Department.

I was apprehensive. An American giving a lecture at the University was a logical place for a terrorist to attack. I felt ashamed of my apprehension after one Belgrade reporter finished interviewing me after my lecture.

"Why do you want to interview me?" I asked. "I am not someone important."

"*I just wanted to know why you were willing to come in here.*" Two weeks before, the twenty-one-year-old reporter watched her boyfriend go mad— it's the only way to describe it.

"*His best friend had his brains blown all over him. And he went crazy. He became just like an animal and no one can talk to him. . . .*" I'll never forget her probing and haunting questions. My personal concerns about safety became insignificant.

My lecture topic that night was *Lies, Cons, and the Truth.* Six hundred students filled the concert hall, even extending out into the foyer. I didn't talk about war, I just talked about who is the easiest person to deceive and how not to become that person—kind of like talks I had given to inner-city kids in Dallas, fighting another war. And if you could only see their eyes . . . I could have been in front of those Dallas youths. The starved look for the truth was the same. The look is unmistakable. It is the look of those from ruptured homes.

Curious, after the lecture I asked many students about their home life. For a disproportionate number, parents lived together (the church is still powerful and divorce forcefully rejected), but the father had affairs and the family wasn't close. A number of students had even fallen into American-bred cults that had migrated in the eighties to Serbia.

Their consistent answers forced me to ask many of them, "Is it possible that perhaps much of this war is just an unleashing of that pent-up anger? That it really isn't about Turkish invasions centuries ago or even the Croatian Ustashe slaughtering your great-grandparents?"

And their answer was almost always the same, *"Perhaps . . ."*

I know how people react and can be culled out with seductive lures when they are in pain. I still wonder if the war in the former Yugoslavia wasn't just a warring of *national gangs*. People in inexorable pain, corporately, together adopting a giant mask, complete with signals and regalia, pretending they were something they were not.

Perhaps . . .

Notes

Chapter 2
1. Anna Macias, "FW Clerk Slain in Robbery," *Dallas Morning News*, 31 May 1994.
2. Seth Mydan, "Not Just the Inner City: Well-to-Do Join Gangs," *New York Times*, 10 April 1990.

Chapter 3
1. The Cure, "Lullaby," *Disintegration*, Elektra/Asylum Records, a division of Warner Communications, Inc., copyright 1989.

Chapter 4
1. Clifford Krauss, "No Crystal Ball Needed on Crime," *New York Times*, 13 November 1994.
2. 1994 FBI Uniform Crime Reports (compiled from information reported by police departments).
3. Ibid.
4. Ibid.
5. Ibid.
6. Ibid.
7. Ibid.
8. Krauss.
9. Kraus's quoting from FBI Uniform Crime Reports.
10. Adrian Nicole LeBlanc, "While Manny's Locked Up," *New York Times Magazine*, 14 August 1994.
11. Melinda Henneberger, "Gang Membership Grows in Middle-Class Suburbs," *New York Times*, 24 July 1993.
12. Douglas Kreutz and Joe Salkowski, "Slow Rise in Gangs Charted in Tucson," *Arizona Daily Star*, 10 June 1990.
13. Ibid.
14. Ibid.
15. 23 February 1994 and 23 May 1994 telephone interviews with Malcolm Klein.
16. 23 February 1994 telephone interview with Irving Spergel.

17. Edward Burns and Thomas J. Deacon, Ph.D., "A New Investigative Approach to Youth Gangs," *FBI Law Enforcement Bulletin*, October 1989, Vol. 58 #10, p. 20-24.
18. Dan Korem, *Streetwise Parents—Foolproof Kids* (Dallas: International Focus Press, 1993) p. 232.
19. Herbert C. Covey, Ph.D., Scott Menard, Ph.D., Robert J. Franzese, Ph.D., *Juvenile Gangs*, (Springfield, IL: Charles C. Thomas, 1992) p. 16.
20. February 1992 interview in Budapest, Hungary with Laszlo Czendes.

Chapter 5

1. Jaquielynn Floyd, "2 Cite Race As Motive In Slaying," *Dallas Morning News*, 10 March 1993.
2. Tracy Everbach, "Ex-Skinhead Describes Threat Against Synagogue," *Dallas Morning News*, 22 February 1990.
3. Lee Hancock, "Skinheads Indicted On Civil Rights Charges," *Dallas Morning News*, 30 September 1989.

Chapter 6

1. 23 February 1994 telephone interview with Malcolm Klein.
2. 1994 US Census Bureau Report.
3. As reported on *Los Angeles Times* wire service, "Traditional Families on Wane, Study Finds," 30 August 1994.
4. US Census Bureau.
5. Department of Health and Human Services, Public Health Services, Centers for Disease Control, National Center for Health Statistics.
6. US Census Bureau.
7. Department of Health and Human Services.
8. Donald Hernandez, *America's Children*, US Census Bureau report, 1994.
9. Ibid.
10. Judith Wallerstein and Sandra Blakeslee, *Second Chances: Men, Women & Children a Decade After Divorce* (New York: Ticknor and Fields, Affiliates of Houghton Mifflin Co., 1989).
11. Barbara S. Cain, "Older Children and Divorce," *New York Times Magazine*, 18 February 1990, p. 26.
12. September 1990 interview with Margaret Singer, psychologist, University of California, Berkeley.
13. Maria Kopp, Ph.D. and Arpad Skrabski, *The Hungarian Mind* (Budapest: Végeken Alapitvany, 1992), p. 208.

14. 1990 Youth Risk Behavior Survey conducted by the Centers for Disease Control.
15. 11 February 1992 interview with Laszlo Czendes.
16. 12 February 1992 interview with Maria Kopp.
17. 20 March 1994 interview with Barbara Fatyga.
18. 21 January 1994 interview with Richard Giulianotti, University of Aberdeen, Scotland.

Chapter 7
1. Maria Kopp, Ph.D. and Arpad Skrabski, *The Hungarian Mind* (Budapest: Végeken Alapitvany, 1992) p. 167.
2. Ibid. p. 123.
3. Ibid. pp. 123-4.
4. 2 February 1993 interview with Maria Kopp, Ph.D.
5. Ibid. p. 211.
6. Ibid. p. 125.
7. Ibid. p. 211.
8. Ibid. p. 124.
9. 1994 *New York Times/CBS News Poll.*
10. Maria Kopp, Ph.D., "Anxiety, Freedom and Democracy," *Behavioral Psychotherapy*, British Association for Behavioural Psychotherapy, #18, 1990, pp. 189-192.
11. 26 September 1994 telephone interview with Det. Ebenezer Palkai.

Chapter 8
1. Bill Buford, *Among the Thugs* (London: Mandarin, 1991), p. 15.
2. Peter Marsh, Elizabeth Rosser and Rom Harré, *The Rules of Disorder* (London: Routledge and Kegan Paul, 1978), p. 71.
3. Nick Hornby, *Fever Pitch*, (London: Victor Gollancz, 1992), p. 231.
4. 20 January 1993 interview with Ivan Rock, University of Greenwich.

Chapter 9
1. Bill Kellar, "Russia's Restless Youth," *New York Times Magazine*, 26 July 1987, p. 14.
2. Barri Flowers, *The Adolescent Criminal—An Examination of Today's Juvenile Offender* (Jefferson, NC: McFarland & Co., 1990), p.108.
3. Flowers, p.108.

Chapter 10
1. 27 February 1994 interview with Kuba Belok in Warsaw, Poland.

Chapter 11

1. 16 May 1990 telephone interview with Kenneth Lanning.
2. Judas Priest, "Eat Me Alive," *Defenders of the Faith*, Columbia Records, FC39219. Written by Glenn Tipton, Rob Halford, K. K. Downing. Copyright 1984, April Music Inc.; Crewglen Ltd.; Ebonytree Ltd.; Geargate Ltd. Administered by April Music, Inc.
3. Carnivore, "Predator," *Carnivore*, Roadracer Records GWD90534. Written by Peter Steele. Published by Roadster Music.
4. Suicidal Tendencies, "Suicidal Failure," *Suicidal Tendencies*, Frontier FLP1011. You'll Be Sorry Music. Copyright 1983, American Lesion Music.
5. Slayer, "Necrophiliac," *Hell Awaits*, Combat/Metal Blade MX 8020. Lyrics and music by Hanneman and King. Published by Bloody Skull Music. Administered by Bug Music.
6. Venom, "Sacrifice," *Here Lies Venom*, Combat Records MX8062. Written by Dunn, Bray, Lant. Published by Neat Music. Licensed from Neat Records by Combat Records.
7. As submitted by Stephen Silver (staff writer, *Searchlight Magazine, London*), "Music of Hate," Op-Ed for *New York Times*, 8 February 1994.
8. Ibid.
9. Ibid.
10. Ibid.
11. Irwin Sual, "Home Grown Variety", Op-Ed in *New York Times*, 22 February 1984.
12. Interview with Kuba Belok in Warsaw, Poland, 26 February 1993.
13. Ibid.
14. 18 March 1994 interview with Sgt. Sue Hanley.
15. Ibid.
16. Ibid.
17. 26 February 1993 interview with Kuba Belok.
18. Quoted in *New York Times*, 31 December 1989.

Chapter 12

1. Herbert C. Covey, et al., p. 127.
2. W. B. Miller, "Gangs, Groups, and Serious Youth Crime." In D. Shichor and D. Kelly (eds.), *Critial Issues in Juvenile Delinquency*, (Lexington, MA: Lexington Books, 1980).
3. 1991 survey by the British Department of Health.
4. 1992 survey by the Swiss Federal Bureau of Statistics.
5. J. Bushnell, 1990. "Introduction: The History and Study of Soviet Youth Subculture." *Soviet Sociology* 29:3-10.

6. 21 January 1994 interview with Richard Giulianotti, University of Aberdeen, Scotland

Chapter 13
1. Covey et al., p. 32.
2. 1994 Estimate by Chicago Police Department.
3. *ABC Nightly News*, 28 September 1994.
4. Ibid.
5. Ibid.
6. From an unpublished manuscript, *The Art of Profiling*, Dan Korem and Bruce Saari, Ph.D.
7. "Young and Violent—The Growing Menace of America's Neo-Nazi Skinheads," Anti-Defamation League, 1988, p. 1.
8. "Young Nazi Killers—The Rising Skinhead Danger," Anti-Defamation League, 1993, p. 5.
9. Clifford J. Levy, "Crusading for Harmony as a Skinhead Spy," *New York Times*, 4 April 1994.
10. Young Nazi Killers—The Rising Skinhead Danger, p. 23.
11. Mark S. Hamm, *American Skinheads*, (Westport, Connecticut: Praeger, 1993), p. 12.
12. 1994 FBI report on hate crime, as reported by the *Chicago Tribune Wire Service*, 28 June 1994.
13. FBI director, Louis Freeh as reported by the *Chicago Tribune* wire service, 28 June 1994.
14. "Young Nazi Killers—The Rising Skinhead Danger," 1993. p. 3.
15. As quoted in *New York Times*, 12 December 1993.
16. Ibid.
17. 1994 FBI report on hate crime.
18. Ibid.
19. 6 June 1994 interview with Mark Hamm.
20. William A. Marovitz, "Hate or Bias Crime Legislation," In Nancy Taylor, ed., *Bias Crime: The Law Enforcement Response*, (Chicago: Office of International Criminal Justice, 1991).
21. Jason DeParle, "1989 Surge in Anti-Semitic Acts Is Reported by B'nai B'rith," *New York Times*, 20 January 1990.
22. Ibid.
23. June 1994 estimate by Buck Revell, FBI chief of Dallas bureau.
24. 1 May 1994 interview in Lettenbruck, Germany.
25. Stephen Silver.
26. Stephen Kinzer, "Germany Outlaws a Neo-Nazi Group," *New York Times*, 28 November 1992.
27. Hamm, p. 204.

28. Hamm, p. 52.
29. Hamm, p. 34.
30. "The German Neo-Nazis: An ADL Investigative Report," Anti-Defamation League, 1993, p. 4.
31. November 1993 interview in Solihull, England with Nick Johnson.
32. Hamm, p. 49.
33. Selwyn Crawford, "Brosky Arguments May End," *Dallas Morning News*, 11 November 1993.
34. "Skinheads Target the Schools," Anti-Defamation League, 1989, p. 8.

Chapter 14
1. From sources noted in *American Skinheads*, p. 36.
2. John Tagliabue, "New Hitler Youth Trouble Germany," *New York Times*, 14 May 1991.
3. George Rodrigue, "Anthems of Violence," *Dallas Morning News*, 29 November 1992.
4. "Neo-Nazis Again Attack Refugee Homes," Reported by Reuters in the *Dallas Morning News*, 14 September 1992.
5. Craig Whitney, "Germans Begin to Recognize Danger in Neo-Nazi Upsurge," *New York Times* 21 October 1993.
6. "Germany Can't Solve Most Crimes Tied to Neo-Nazis," *Associated Press*, 7 September 1994.
7. Stephen Kinzer, "German Mayor, Blamed for Inaction in Violence Against Foreigners, Resigns," *New York Times*, 11 November 1993.
8. Rodrigue.
9. *Associated Press*, 12 November 1994.
10. Ibid.
11. *Associated Press*, 8 November 1994.
12. Barbara Fatyga, et al., "Report on Polish Youth" (Warsaw: Wydawnictwo Interpress, 1992), p. 365.
13. Ibid, p. 369.
14. Peter Applebome, "Skinhead Violence Grows, Experts Say," *New York Times*, 18 July 1993.
15. 20 June 1994 telephone interview with Mike Hamm.
16. "How-To for Neo-Nazis," *Time Magazine*, European edition, 22 August 1994.
17. Ibid.

Chapter 15
1. 1989 telephone interview with Officer Lee Reed.
2. Letter from Officer William Manning, 26 April 1990.
3. 3 July 1990 telephone interview with Janet Maitlen.

4. Anton Szandor LaVey, *The Satanic Bible* (New York: Avon Books, 1969), p. 30.
5. Ibid., p. 31.
6. Ibid., p. 34.
7. Ibid., p. 25.
8. Ibid., p. 88.
9. Covey, et al., p. 142.
10. 16 May 1990 telephone interview with Robert Hicks.
11. May 1990 telephone interview with Kenneth Lanning.
12. Kenneth V. Lanning, "Satanic, Occult, Ritualistic Crime: A Law Enforcement Perspective," *The Police Chief*, October 1989.
13. Jerry Johnston, *The Edge of Evil: The Rise of Satanism in North America* (Dallas: Word, 1989), p. 4.
14. 30 August 1990 telephone interview with Dr. Al Carlisle.
15. From Jerry Johnston's 1989 press kit for his book, *The Edge of Evil*.
16. Charlie Brennan, "Killer Blames Satan for Turn to Crime," *Rocky Mountain News*, 16 March 1987.
17. Ibid.
18. Ibid.

Chapter 17
1. Interview with Kuba Belok, 27 February 1993.
2. Telephone interview with John Wallace, 23 September 1991.
3. 19 July 1994 *ABC News* interview with State Attorney General Jimmy Evans.
4. Ian Fisher, "Prison Boot Camps Offer No Quick Fix," *New York Times*, 10 April 1994.
5. Ibid.

Chapter 18
1. California Department of Justice, Division of Law Enforcement, Bureau of Investigation. March 1993. *Gangs 2000: A Call to Action—The Attorney General's Report on the Impact of Criminal Street Gangs on Crime and Violence in California by the year 2000*.
2. Ibid.
3. Interview with Al Brantley, 20 October 1993.
4. Interview with Sgt. Sue Hanley, Grapevine, Texas Police, 18 February 1994.
5. Interview with Dr. Richard Guilianotti, 21 January 1994.
6. Interview with Judge Deborah B. Hollifield, 8 February 1994.
7. Interview with Officer Terry Adams, 2 September 1994.

8. Interview with Richard Escalante, 19 August 1994.
9. Interview with Farmers Branch Chief of Police, Jim Fawcett, 19 August 1994.

Chapter 20
1. Based upon informal survey of the youths when they weregathered together.
2. Alexei Barrionuevo, "Mother Voices Outrage Over Attack on Son," *Dallas Morning News*, 28 November 1994.

Index

Other Materials

By Dan Korem

YOUTH GANG REVIEW

The international affluent youth gang trend is constantly mutating and changing. For those who need the most current information, a semi-annual update will be sent out in 1995 and 1996. The cost for the four updates is $7.50.

STREETWISE PARENTS, FOOLPROOF KIDS (Revised Edition)

Written for parents, educators, and professionals who interact with youths, this revised edition (320 pages—$13.00 postage paid) includes the following:

- Profile of the youth who is the easiest to deceive and how to instruct a youth to resist becoming that person.
- A simple method for helping a youth discern whether someone is lying or telling the truth.
- How to distinguish between illusion and reality.
- When it is and isn't appropriate to use deception—i.e., trick play in football versus cheating.
- Guidelines for distinguishing when fantasy and imagination can turn harmful.
- Good versus bad secrets—when it is and isn't appropriate to keep a secret and what to do with harmful secrets.
- Guidelines for healthy decision making and the parent's role.
- Additional chapters that affect the youth culture, including: entertainment and news media, drugs, gangs, and cults.

PSYCHIC CONFESSION

Forty-eight-minute videotape presentation in which the psychic demonstrations of cult-like leader James Hydrick are exposed as trickery, and he provides history's first recorded confession of a noted psychic. This excellent program, critically acclaimed by the *Los Angeles Times*, is suitable for both adults and youths. ($20.00 postage paid)

To obtain any of these materials, write:

Korem Productions
P.O. Box 1587
Richardson, TX 75083

Author

Dan Korem is an independent investigative journalist, author, documentary producer, speaker and a world-class magician (his profession prior to 1981). He is the president of Korem Productions, a Dallas-based communications company that researches issues relevant to the international community and communicates through electronic and print media. Korem is a frequent keynote speaker and lecturer for corporate, professional, and university groups in the US and Europe. Issues addressed include: deception as it affects business, ethical and social trends; profiling in corporate as well as confrontational environments; formation of aberrant groups; methods of paranormal power fakers; international youth trends; and youth gangs.

He produced the documentary, *Psychic Confession*, the first exposé and confession of a cult-like figure who claimed to have paranormal powers, and the educational four-part children's video series, *Kid Tricks*, that instructs youths through the vehicle of simple sleight of hand tricks how to resist deception. He is also the author of several books, including *Streetwise Parents, Foolproof Kids, Powers: Testing the Psychic and Supernatural* and *Korem Without Limits* (a text of original secrets sold only to magicians.)